CHALLENGERS TO
CAPITALISM

Collective Farm Women Workers Going To Work by Tarras Gaponenko

CHALLENGERS TO CAPITALISM

MARX, LENIN, STALIN, AND MAO

Second Edition

by
John G. Gurley

W · W · NORTON & COMPANY

NEW YORK · LONDON

W. W. Norton & Company, Inc., 500 Fifth Avenue, New York, N.Y. 10110
W. W. Norton & Company Ltd., 37 Great Russell Street, London WC1B 3NU

This book was published originally as a part of THE PORTABLE STANFORD,
a series of books published by the Stanford Alumni Association, Stanford,
California. This edition first published by W. W. Norton & Company, Inc.
in 1980 by arrangement with the Stanford Alumni Association.

Library of Congress Cataloging in Publication Data

Gurley, John G
    Challengers to capitalism. (Second Edition)

    Bibliography: p.
    Includes index.
    1. Communism.   2. Capitalism.   I.   Title.
HX56.G87   1979   335.4   79-20664
ISBN 0-393-95005-0 paper edition

4   5   6   7   8   9   0

FOREWORD

This book grew directly out of a mini-course on Marx, Lenin, and Mao that I gave on two occasions for the Stanford Alumni Association, once at Stanford and once in Los Angeles. Those lectures, in turn, were fashioned from more extensive material that I have presented over the past several years in Economics 120, The Marxian and Radical Tradition. The course itself is the progeny of one taught by Paul Baran, who was a professor of economics at Stanford from 1949 until his death in 1964, and who greatly influenced my own thinking.

Paul Baran, as a Marxist, but, more relevantly, as an active supporter of Fidel Castro, incurred the wrath of not a few Stanford alumni, trustees, and administrators. He died at a transition—a Marxist is tempted to say, at a dialectical point—when increasing pressure was being exerted by some alumni and others to hush him up, but when, owing to changing objective conditions in the world, Stanford students were just starting to wake up and to ask for a better understanding of the world they were living in. It is a terrible shame that his death came on the very eve of what turned out to be a radical resurgence.

This book, then, has not only Stanford's but Baran's imprint on it. I confess that I delight in the irony of this relationship. I know that many others' imprints are here, too, but I can acknowledge only a few: that of Paul Sweezy, Baran's closest friend, who has made outstanding contributions to Marxism for four decades and who has helped me greatly in many ways; that of my former student, Geoffrey Stevens (Class of 1969), a victim of cancer in 1972, who, by sharp and persistent questioning and discussion, helped to open my eyes to an important part of reality; and that of my wife, Yvette, who has been my best friend and sharpest critic for almost as long as I can remember. In addition, I wish also to dedicate this book to the memory of Ruth Lilienthal, who, in the all-too-brief time I knew her, taught me what the Marxian notion of being "fully human" really means.

I have dispensed with footnotes throughout. The Reader's Guide at the end gives all of my sources for the quotations and other references in the book. It did not seem necessary or wise to document each with page numbers.

John G. Gurley

Stanford, California

CREDITS

FRONTIS-   Gaponenko, Tarras. *Collective Farm Women Workers Going to Work*. 1933. Painting. Tretyakov State
PIECE   Gallery.

FACING   Shadr, Ivan. *Cobblestones, The Weapons of the Proletariat*. 1928. Sculpture. Museum of the Revolution
PAGE 1   Moscow.

PAGE 4   Wu Shih. *And the United Nations Join Hands*. From *Contemporary Chinese Woodcuts* (London: Fore
Publications & Collet's Holdings Ltd., 1950).

PAGE 6   Gillray, James. *A March to the Bank*. 1787. Hand–colored etching. British Museum, London.

PAGE 9   Cheremnikh. *Before*. 1933. Cartoon. From the album *Towards the Prosperous Life*, U.S.S.R., 1933.

PAGE 11   Cheremnikh. *October 1917*. 1933. Cartoon. From the album *Towards the Prosperous Life*, U.S.S.R.,
1933.

PAGE 22   Gillray, James. *The Liberty of the Subject*. 1779. Hand–colored etching. British Museum, London.

PAGE 30   Anonymous redrawing of Cruikshank's version. *A Free Born Englishman!* Hand–colored etching. British
Museum, London.

PAGE 38   Gillray, James. *Temperance Enjoying a Frugal Meal*. 1792. Hand–colored etching. British Museum,
London.

PAGE 44   Daumier, Honoré. *Diplomacy*. 1866. Lithograph. Rogers Fund 1922, Metropolitan Museum of Art,
New York.

PAGE 62   Kalensky, V.D. *Hail the Socialist Revolution*. 1967. Poster. U.S.S.R. Union of Artists, Moscow.

PAGE 73   Anonymous. *Long Live the Third Communist International!* Poster. U.S.S.R.

PAGE 88   Deineka, Alexandr. *The Defense of Petrograd*. 1927. Tretyakov State Gallery.

PAGE 90   Brodsky, Isaac. *Lenin at the Smolny Institute*. Tretyakov State Gallery.

PAGE 96   Stalin. Photo courtesy of the National Archives.

PAGE 115   Soviet posters from the 1930s.

PAGE 132   "Sailing the seas depends on the helmsman, making revolution depends on Mao Tse-tung thought."
Sculpture. From *The Rent Collection Courtyard: Sculptures of Oppression and Revolt* (Peking: Foreign
Languages Press, 1970).

PAGE 139   Li Hua. *Harvest*. From *Contemporary Chinese Woodcuts* (London: Fore Publications & Collet's Hold–
ings Ltd., 1950).

PAGE 146   *Smash Economism*. 1967. Chinese Communist poster.

PAGE 151   "If the army and the people are united. . . ." Sculpture. From *The Rent Collection Courtyard: Sculptures of Oppression and Revolt* (Peking: Foreign Languages Press, 1970).

PAGE 155   "The crushing load of rent. . . ." Sculpture. From *The Rent Collection Courtyard: Sculptures of Oppression and Revolt* (Peking: Foreign Languages Press, 1970).

PAGE 160   Wan Shih-ssu. *Cooperation*. From *Contemporary Chinese Woodcuts* (London: Fore Publications &
Collet's Holdings Ltd., 1950).

PAGE 165   Ku Yuzn. *Reconstruction of the Steel Mill at Aushan*. From *Woodcuts from the Liberated Areas* (Peking: People's Art Press, 1962).

PAGE 184   Daumier, Honoré. *European Equilibrium*. 1866. Lithograph. W.R.G. Allen Estate, Museum of Fine Arts,
Boston.

PAGE 197   Daumier, Honoré. "Je vous dis que vous avez dérangé la limite. . . ." 1845. (Cat. H.D. 2237).

PAGE 202   Daumier, Honoré. "Messieurs Cobden . . . n'ayant plus . . . à faire en Europe. . . ." 1856. (Cat. H.D.
3096).

Special thanks to Michael Sullivan, professor of art at Stanford, and to the Stanford Art Library for their cooperation
and assistance in researching illustrations.

TABLE OF CONTENTS

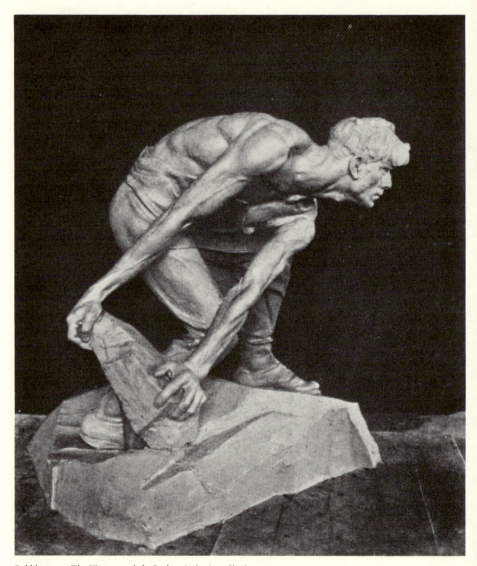

Cobblestones, The Weapons of the Proletariat by Ivan Shadr

CHAPTER ONE

MARXISM AND CAPITALISM

MARXISM AND CAPITALISM are now engaged in an intense, worldwide struggle. When Americans look beyond their borders, many are dismayed, even frightened, by what they see. Societies organized according to Marxian principles seem to be cropping up everywhere; in fact, in the last 65 years, they have spread from zero to a third of the globe, and there is every indication that the expansion is still going on. The Russian revolution of 1917 shifted a fifth of the world's land area from capitalism to Marxism. The 1949 Chinese revolution captured another huge piece for the Marxian cause, and at about the same time most of Eastern Europe came under Soviet suzerainty. Since then, Marxist states have been established in several key areas of the world, and Marxist parties continue to have strength in Italy, France, Japan, India, and elsewhere. With less fanfare, Marxist guerrilla units hide in many of the mountains and jungles of the world. The student protests and uprisings of the 1960s in the United States, France, Mexico, and other countries had Marxian coloration. The ideals of Marxism continue to inspire, as capitalism does not, millions of people around the world, mostly the poor, but many intellectuals, and not a few priests and other clergy; even Pope Paul has lauded some features of "the Mao way."

Moreover, American tourists to China in the last few years have had the opportunity to contrast the optimism of the Chinese with the pessimism here at home. No visitor to China can help but be impressed by the confidence of the Chinese in their future, by their buoyant spirits, their sense of purpose. It is the purposefulness—the dedication to the attainment of common goals—that leaves the deepest imprint. The Chinese one meets are on the go, planning far into the future, and mobilized for action.

When the traveler returns home from China, he is at once aware, more acutely than ever before, of the apprehension and loss of assurance that pervades his own society. Things no longer work the way they used to, problems multiply much faster than solutions to them can be found, the future appears terribly uncertain, even fearsome. The human spirit in America seems depressed. Throughout much of the capitalist world, the same doubts about the future can be heard.

Does that mean that Marxism is the wave of the future and that capitalism is on its way out? Perhaps, but that is far from certain. Still, it is true that, if centuries can be characterized in a few words, the present one is certainly marked by a series of violent revolutions on a worldwide scale against capitalism—and by capitalism's own internecine wars. This has been the century in which world capitalism's expansion reached a maximum and was then rolled back. It has been the century in which the outward rush of European and Japanese capitalism and the subsequent global explosion of U.S. capitalism were finally contained. That, of course, does not mean the end of capitalism, nor does it mean that capitalism's expansionist urges have been quelled— far from it. There is assuredly much strength left in the private enterprise system. The United States is still the most powerful nation on earth, and weaknesses are being revealed almost daily in communism's progress. Nevertheless, the Marxist check to capitalist expansion would seem to signify at least the temporary end of its profit making and consumption on an easy-come-easy-go basis, the close of its most exuberant period.

When cracks appear and the forward momentum loses steam, deterioration can set in very rapidly: problems begin to mount and each becomes more stubborn to a solution. Furthermore, allies, coalitions, and markets that were once secure begin to fade away as the erosion becomes apparent to others. Thus, the *New York Times* recently asked a prominent sociologist about Brazil's new attitude toward the United States. "With the decline of the United States' economic and political influence in the world," he answered, "there has been a change in the correlation of international forces, with new poles of power such as

Japan and the Arab world, which gives Brazil room for maneuver and a more independent policy." In the same issue, it was also reported that Thailand and China had established formal diplomatic relations, which "means that Thailand, once one of the firmest allies of the United States, has drastically shifted although continuing to profess friendship with the West. China, in a little more than a year, has established relations with the Philippines and Malaysia—which like Thailand are members of the Association of Southeast Asian Nations, once considered a potential bulwark against communism." And so it goes around the world when the U.S.S. America springs a leak. Thus, our recent awareness that we are not able to deal as effectively with ourselves and the world as we once did is probably an accurate perception. When one is no longer so clearly in the ascendant, the world does seem to break apart and to become more difficult to manipulate.

Capitalism's current troubles do not arise entirely from the successes of Marxism; it is perfectly capable of generating its own contradictions, as we shall see later on. Furthermore, unemployment, inflation, rampant crime and violence, urban decay, the breakdown of authority patterns, as well as the many other ills of capitalist society today, have complex and manifold causes. Marx is not the only *bête noire* lurking in the shadows. However, the gains of Marxism and its continuing challenge to capitalist societies have made profit making around the world more difficult, more expensive, and riskier; they have diverted U.S. resources and energies from urgent domestic problems to the fighting of revolutionary fires in every byway of the world; and they have encouraged anti-capitalist movements and attitudes throughout the world. The sweep of Marxism in this century, therefore, has to a considerable extent shaken the foundations of capitalism, thereby multiplying and intensifying its problems.

And, yet, while all of this has been going on, Americans generally have remained ignorant of the theoretical underpinnings of a worldwide advance that so importantly affects their very way of life. What were Marx's principal criticisms of capitalism? Do they still apply? What about his prediction of the ultimate demise of this economic system? What was Lenin's theory of imperialism and how does it relate to the national liberation movements now going on? What is Maoism, and why is it gaining so much popularity among the poor? Many Americans are hardly able to begin to answer these questions. Moreover, they are unaware of Marxism as a philosophical world-outlook, a useful framework for understanding much of what is going on in the world. In a way, this is strange, inasmuch as hundreds of millions of people around the world know and use Marxism, at least to some degree; it is probably

And the United Nations Join Hands by Wu Shih

the most prevalent set of ideas in the world today. A study of Marxism is not only useful for understanding the robustness of the continuing attacks on capitalism and the Western way of life, but it is also helpful, almost indispensable, for understanding capitalism itself. Marxism offers new and surprising insights into this subject.

This book explains the elements of Marxism by examining four revolutionaries who, over the course of more than a century, have fashioned a most potent theory and movement. Karl Marx (1818-83), on the basis of the rise of the European industrial proletariat in the first half of the 19th century, analyzed the contradictions of capitalism, subjected the system to scathing criticism, and predicted its downfall. V. I. Lenin (1870-1924), influenced by the development of monopoly capitalism and imperialism toward the end of the 19th century, studied the strengths and weaknesses of this later phase of capitalism and showed how to carry out a successful revolution against it. Joseph Stalin (1879-1953), starting from the isolation of the Soviet Union in a hostile world, laid the socialist foundations for the development of Soviet power. Mao Tse-tung (1893-1976), basing himself on Lenin's and Stalin's theory and practice and the further development of capitalist imperialism, succeeded in carrying out a revolution against the old order in a way that has led to a highly attractive socialist society in the eyes of many of the world's disadvantaged. Marx supplied the critique of the "old" society, Lenin the revolutionary means to overthrow it, Stalin the socialist foundations of Soviet power, and Mao the newer, "higher" socialist society. Together, the four of them have shaped and defined contemporary Marxism, in theory and in revolutionary practice.

This book is principally about Marxism and not about the problems of U.S. society or of other capitalist nations, although the latter topic will be discussed in the final chapter. But it is also clear that this short study cannot cover all of Marxism. In particular, it says almost nothing about the present Soviet leaders, and it does not include the many valuable theoretical contributions of present-day European and Japanese Marxists. There are other serious omissions, too. Still, Marx, Lenin, Stalin, and Mao are the giants, and one must understand them before much sense can be made of the rest. Finally, Marxian theory cannot be divorced from social history, for it springs from that history and in turn greatly influences it. Therefore, the reader will find in these chapters a fair amount of historical references mixed in with the theoretical discussion, a combination of theory and practice that is in keeping with Marxism.

March to the Bank by James Gillray

CHAPTER TWO

THE TRIUMPH OF CAPITALISM

THE ECONOMIES OF ANCIENT GREECE AND ROME, and to a lesser extent Egypt, were built largely on slave labor. Roman society was succeeded in Europe by feudalism, a cellular rural society, the labor of which was performed by serfs and others tied to the land and dependent on their lords, and the production of which was mainly for personal use and local markets. During the 16th century, merchant capitalism began to make serious inroads on feudalism, which had already been under internal strain for at least two centuries. This impending replacement of one society by another was heralded by the growth of internal trade and the consequent rise of towns, the gradual breakdown of feudal obligations and the flight of serfs from the manor, and the overseas explorations to the East and to the New World. Trade, markets, money transactions, and towns all undermined the insular manorial system and the serfdom on which it was based. However, the rising class of commercial (and, later, industrial) capitalists required not only time but also revolutions to overturn the old order. While this sometimes bloody transformation was in process, the triumphal procession of the ascending bourgeoisie, with its trumpets blaring and cannons roaring, spread out from Western Europe to begin the transformation of virtually every corner of the world.

Paeans to Capitalism

Karl Marx and his lifetime collaborator, Friedrich Engels, in their *Manifesto of the Communist Party* (1848), acclaimed the dynamism of this new society, which by their time was in full bloom, with such abandon as to baffle those later generations of readers who grew up imagining these authors to be bearded revolutionaries spewing forth nothing but vituperation. The bourgeoisie, Marx and Engels enthused, "during its rule of scarce one hundred years, has created more massive and more colossal productive forces than have all preceding generations together. . . . It has accomplished wonders far surpassing Egyptian pyramids, Roman aqueducts, and Gothic cathedrals; it has conducted expeditions that put in the shade all former Exoduses of nations and crusades." Marx and Engels were dazzled by the energy with which the bourgeoisie, over and over again, revolutionized production, applied science to industry, communications, and agriculture, built railroads, canals, electric telegraphs, and constructed machinery to produce even more machinery. The result was an enormous increase in all kinds of products, which required continually expanding markets to absorb them. This need, the *Manifesto* declared, "chases the bourgeoisie over the whole surface of the globe. It must nestle everywhere, settle everywhere, establish connections everywhere." It must batter down "all Chinese walls" and attempt to turn the entire world into its own image.

Marx and Engels could deliver these paeans because they viewed capitalism as the latest historical stage of social development, a stage that clearly surpassed earlier ones in its productive powers. However, they also believed that capitalism itself would be transcended by a still higher form of society—socialism—in which the workers would be the ruling class, the means of production would be collectively owned, and economic planning would guide production and distribution. Thus, they could be both admirers and critics of capitalism, commending the bourgeoisie for its conquest of the old aristocracy and the consequent release of new energy for economic activity, but at the same time recognizing exploitative, alienating, and oppressive features of the new society, all of which, they thought, would be overcome when the proletariat, the working class, successfully rose against the system. But, while Marx and Engels could praise and damn capitalism in the same breath, in truth they were predominantly critics, and very severe ones.

The Materialist Conception of History

Marx and Engels developed a theory about the movement of history that purports to explain why feudalism gave way to capitalism and

Before by Cheremnikh

why the latter will be succeeded by socialism. It is essential to understand this view of social development, which they called "the materialist conception of history," if one is to have any grasp of Marxism, for it lies at the heart of almost all Marxian reasoning today.

According to this theory, which is principally Marx's, people in a society, at any given time, have a certain level of productive ability. This depends on their own knowledge and skills, on the technology (machines, tools, draft animals, and so on) available to them, and on the bountifulness of the natural environment in which they live. These together are called "the material forces of production" or, in short, the productive forces. Marx alleged that the productive forces determine the way people make their living (for example, in hunting and gathering, agriculture, or industry) and, at the same time, the way they relate to one another in producing and exchanging the means of life (for example, as lord and serf, master and slave, or capitalist and worker). These production and exchange relationships are what Marx called "the [social] relations of production." The productive forces plus the relations of production, which Marx referred to as "the economic structure of society," shape the "superstructure" of people's religious, political, and legal systems and their modes of thought and views of life. That is, people's material lives determine their ideas and their supporting institutions.

In a famous passage, which deserves careful attention, Marx summarized the theory that "became the guiding principle of my studies":

> In the social production of their existence, men inevitably enter into definite relations, which are independent of their will, namely relations of production appropriate to a given stage in the development of their material forces of production. The totality of these relations of production constitutes the economic structure of society, the real foundation, on which arises a legal and political superstructure and to which correspond definite forms of social consciousness. The mode of production of material life conditions the general process of social, political and intellectual life. It is not the consciousness of men that determines their existence, but their social existence that determines their consciousness.

The key relationships are depicted below, with the main causal connections shown running upward but with downward reciprocal relations also present. These components are separated purely for expository purposes; in fact, each is by no means independent of the others.

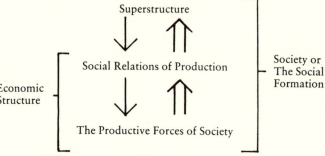

That is essentially the materialist conception of history. Each of its major components will now be discussed more fully to give readers an opportunity to get their bearings. After that, the theory will be illustrated in several ways.

The Productive Forces

The productive forces are the material means of production that people fashion and use to gain a livelihood from nature. Productive forces include machines, instruments and tools, raw materials, and natural resources; they also include human beings themselves—their knowledge, talents, aspirations, and needs. Productive forces develop through the labor and activity that people expend in extracting a living from their natural environment. Part of their development includes the

October 1917 by Cheremnikh

growth of human abilities and needs. As people change their world, they develop their own capabilities as well as their desires to change the world still further. People thus make their living and themselves simultaneously. Human activity is, therefore, an integral part of the productive forces; an interpretation of the Marxian theory as being a form of "technological determinism" emasculates it by excising the human factor.

Human beings differ from animals in that they engage in purposeful productive activity—they *produce* their means of subsistence, consciously and not instinctively. At any one time, this purposive labor is performed with a certain technology, in a given environment, and within a particular class society—that is, it is performed within a certain mode of production. Human nature, according to Marx and Engels, is determined by the mode of production that people work in to maintain human life, and since the mode of production changes, so does human nature.

Feudal man, for example, within his own mode of production, had different values, aspirations, abilities, and needs than has capitalist man within his higher mode of production. The change from the feudal to the capitalist mode of production, however, was made by human beings themselves, as they fashioned better tools, altered and controlled their environment, and, in this very process, changed themselves. Thus, capitalism could succeed feudalism not only because people designed superior technology, but also because, in the process of doing this, they changed their values and skills, their outlook on what is important, and so on.

This Marxian view of social development is important because it stresses that such development is not imposed on us from the "outside," nor do we simply adapt, in passive ways, to social changes. We, in fact, initiate those changes and, by so doing, make ourselves worthy of the new conditions. Thus, human nature, as seen by Marx and Engels, is essentially subject to change: man makes himself through productive activity.

The scheme below traces out these relationships which underlie the productive forces of the previous diagram.

DYNAMIC CHANGES IN THE
PRODUCTIVE FORCES OF SOCIETY

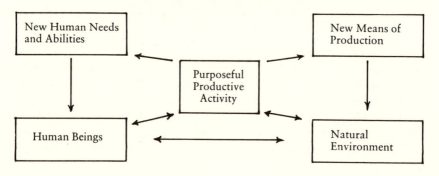

Social Relations of Production

According to Marx's formulation, the stage of development of society's material means of production—its productive forces—determines the social relations of production and exchange. The latter are the institutions and practices most closely associated with the way goods are produced, exchanged, and distributed. This includes property relations; the way labor is recruited, organized, and compensated; the markets or other means for exchanging the products of labor; and the methods used by the ruling classes to capture and dispose of the surplus product. The social relations of production are, in effect, the class structure of a society that is revealed in the work process. The mode of production of a society is seen principally through its class structure. A mode of production could be of the slave type, feudalist, capitalist, or anything else which describes the dominant manner in which people organize to make their living. Although societies may contain more than one mode of production, one mode is usually dominant.

As people change the world, they develop their own abilities and needs to change it further. Thus, productive forces grow over time. Sooner or later, the developing productive forces come into conflict with the prevailing class structure—the social relations of production. The newly developed ways that people extract a living from their natural environment become incompatible with the older ways they relate to one another in the work process. For instance, the rise of trade and commercial activity in the 16th century became incompatible with feudal relations in the countryside and with guilds in the towns.

This growing contradiction takes the form of a class struggle between the rising class associated with the new means of production and the old ruling class whose dominance was based on its control of the older, waning forces. This class struggle, under appropriate conditions, intensifies the contradiction between the means of production and the class structure until, as a result of revolution, new relations of production which are compatible with the superior productive forces are established. Thus, the bourgeoisie after 1500 gradually gained strength on the basis of new productive forces, such as sailing ships, improved weaponry, new energy sources, machinery, factory processes, accumulation of technical knowledge, and so on. These productive forces under their control enabled them to challenge successfully the older feudal ruling classes, whose privileged positions had depended on land rights and control of rural work processes as well as the judicial and military systems. The mode of production was changed, in a series of revolutions, sometimes spreading over a century or more, from feudalism to capitalism, from a class structure of lords and vassals, guildmasters and apprentices, to one of capitalists and wage-laborers. As Marx once put it, "The handmill gives you a society with the feudal lord; the steammill, society with the industrial capitalist." Even though coming from Marx, this is a grossly simplified aphorism that overemphasizes the technological to the neglect of the dialectical.

Marx has expressed these transformations in the following passage known by heart to many people around the world:

> At a certain stage of development, the material productive forces of society come into conflict with the existing relations of production or—this merely expresses the same thing in legal terms—with the property relations within the framework of which they have operated hitherto. From forms of development of the productive forces these relations turn into their fetters. Then begins an era of social revolution. The changes

in the economic foundation lead sooner or later to the transformation of the whole immense superstructure.

The Superstructure

Marx postulated that the economic structure of society molds its
superstructure of social, political, and intellectual life, including senti-
ments, morality, illusions, modes of thought, principles, and views of
life. The superstructure contains the ideas and systems of authority (political, legal, military, etc.) which support the class structure of that society—that is, the dominant position of the ruling class. In brief, how
people make their living shapes their mental conceptions and supporting institutions. It follows that the transformation of the economic
structure of society eventually causes the character of the superstructure
to change—after ideological struggles, the overthrow of older systems
of authority, and attrition have taken their toll. The defeat of the feudal
ruling classes by the bourgeoisie, for example, not only opened the way
for the further development of society's productive forces but in addition spelled the doom of feudal values, ideas, and institutions—all of
which supported the feudal ruling classes but fettered the rising capitalists. The values associated with vows of homage and fealty, for instance, were vital to manorial life but simply got in the way of—and
were incongruent with—commerce and market transactions.

Inasmuch as human beings change themselves by labor, it is clear that
they alter, at the same time, at least some of their mental conceptions.
They produce both material goods and their ideas. Thus, productive
activity and the attending class struggles change not only the economic
structure of society but the superstructure as well. Since this is so, interactions between the two are inevitable and are, in fact, both numerous
and intricate. That is, the way people make a living determines their
ideas, but these ideas in turn affect the way they make their living.
However, modes of thought are shaped and limited, in the first place,
by the mode of production. Accordingly, the ideas that become influential in a society cover only the narrow range reflecting the material activities and interests of the dominant class. Many ideas do not gain
prestige because they conflict with real positions of class domination
which themselves rest on a certain attained level of the productive
forces. For example, the current idea of "no growth" is incompatible
with the fortunes of a capitalist class that are generated by industrial
growth.

History is not the development of ideas, Marx and Engels tell us, but
rather the development of productive forces, and the formation of ideas
is explained by these underlying material changes. "Life is not deter-

mined by consciousness, but consciousness by life." Their theory of history "does not explain practice from the idea but explains the formation of ideas from material practice." This leads Marx and Engels to the conclusion that in every society the ideas of the ruling class are the ruling ideas. This does not mean that, at any given time, there is only a single set of ideas which serves the ruling class. The class structure of a society is often complex and the ideas of each class are likely to be expressed in complex ways in the superstructure. Therefore, revolutionary ideas may exist side by side with conventional ones because of the existence of a revolutionary class. (Marxism thus explains itself by the rise of an industrial proletariat in the first half of the 19th century.) But these revolutionary ideas can at best displace some other ideas; they cannot by themselves overthrow the prevailing class structure, which gave rise to the ruling ideas. So Marx and Engels write that "not criticism but revolution is the driving force of history." From the Marxist view this means, to use our previous example, that the idea of "no growth" can become dominant, not through criticism of the idea of "growth," but only by the revolutionary overthrow of the capitalist class.

The superstructure contains not only ideas but also institutions and activities that support the class structure of society—the state, legal institutions, family structures, art forms, and spiritual processes. The Marxian presupposition is that the superstructure of ideas and supporting institutions, although in some respects and to some degree capable of developing a life of its own, strongly reflects the economic structure of society. Thus, according to some Marxists, the prehistoric cave-wall paintings of animals in southern France and northern Spain reflected the magical need of hunters to depict their prey accurately and naturally. The later geometric pottery designs of settled agriculturalists, it is claimed, were reflections of the more abstract, mysterious forces that determined whether crops would prosper or die. This revolutionary change from hunting and gathering to settled agriculture, which occurred because of radically new productive forces (which in turn transformed the relations of production), also altered other elements of the superstructure, such as family structures, religions, rules and laws, governing bodies, the games played, and military organizations.

Marx regarded the religious world as "the reflex of the real world." Religion is a consolation for man's degraded condition; it is the imaginary realization of human perfection. It will finally vanish "when the practical relations of everyday life offer to man none but perfectly intelligible and reasonable relations with regard to his fellowmen and to Nature." For capitalism, Marx reasoned, "Christianity with its *cultus* of abstract man, more especially in its bourgeois developments, Protestantism, Deism, etc., is the most fitting form of religion." Engels carried the analysis further by linking some changes in religious views to changes in material life over a period of 2,000 years. But Engels was careful to note that once an ideology (such as a set of religious views) arises, it develops in part independently of the economic structure, subject to its own laws.

In Marxian thought, the state, a product of society at a certain stage of development, as a rule is the institution that protects the property and privileges of the ruling classes and preserves order among the oppressed and exploited classes. It is an instrument of class rule, the manifestation of the irreconcilability of class antagonisms. Nevertheless, Engels added: "By way of exception, however, periods occur in which the warring classes balance each other so nearly that the state power, as ostensible mediator, acquires, for the moment, a certain degree of independence of both." Marxists assert that over long periods the form of the state has changed—for example, from decentralized to centralized monarchies, to constitutional governments, bourgeois democracies, fascist dictatorships, and so on—in response to changes in economic structures. The state is the guarantor of a given set of property relations, and in capitalist society its highest function is the protection of private property. Marx believed that the bourgeois state would have to be smashed by the proletariat and a dictatorship of that class established in the new socialist society. As socialism gives way to communism (which will be discussed in Chapter 3), the state will wither away because, in a classless society, no organ of class rule is required. The state, however, as an administrator of things, such as a five-year plan, rather than an oppressor of subordinate classes, remains.

Dialectical Materialism

Marx's view of social development has been called by others "dialectical materialism." The phrase refers to Marx's method of analyzing social change, a method that is strongly present in all of his major works. Marxian materialism reverses the idealist approach of viewing abstract ideas, concepts, and consciousness as divorced from real people and their activities. According to Marx, materialism begins with "real, active men, and on the basis of their real life-process demonstrates the development of the ideological reflexes and echoes of this life-process." The ideas in the human brain (morality, religion, and all the rest of ideology) do not live completely independent lives. A person, in trying to understand social history, should not start with these phantoms—with, say, the concept of "freedom"—for they are all sublimates of the real material life-process. For example, the 16th century is not explainable by "the idea of expansion," as though some people got this idea around 1500 and then proceeded to carry it out. Instead, the idea of expansion came from revolutionary changes in the economic structures of Western European societies, attended by transformations of the relations of production.

To understand the world, a person must begin with what is basic—with real human beings and their activities in the world. Marx and Engels felt that work was the most basic and most important of all human activities. Most of people's lives are spent working and much of the rest is spent in an environment which is shaped by the kind of productive technology available to them. For example, Indians lived in huts or tents near the rivers they fished, while early industrial workers lived in the company towns built around the factories. In both cases, the work process exerted an all-pervading influence on their lives, shaping the conditions of their existence and therefore of their thoughts. Marxian materialism maintains that ideas, philosophies, religions, and so forth all take form within the influence of real material conditions and are therefore determined by them.

Materialism is also at the base of the Marxian concept of social class, for classes are the result of people's lives being formed by the work process within a strict hierarchical work structure. Marx and Engels believed that two major classes, the bourgeoisie and the proletariat (along with several minor ones), emerged with capitalism. The bourgeoisie and the proletariat are distinct classes because the former owns and controls the physical means of production—raw materials, energy, and capital goods—while the latter owns only its labor-power and must sell it to the bourgeoisie to survive.

Although Marx believed, along with other materialists, that objects exist independently of human beings and their consciousness, still his materialism was quite different from that of the 18th century, as anticipated in the writings of John Locke. Bertrand Russell, in his *A History of Western Philosophy*, has best delineated this difference by pointing out that the older materialism regarded sensation of the subject as passive, with activity attributed to the object. Russell explains that in Marx's view, on the other hand, "all sensation or perception is an interaction between subject and object; the bare object, apart from the activity of the percipient, is a mere raw material, which is transformed in the process of becoming known." Consequently, knowledge is not passive contemplation, as Locke and others would have it. Rather, Russell continues, "both subject and object, both the knower and the thing known, are in a continual process of mutual adaptation." Russell then connects Marx's materialism to his economics:

> For Marx, matter, not spirit, is the driving force [of human history]. But it is matter in the peculiar sense that we have been considering, not the wholly dehumanized matter of the atomists. This means that, for Marx, the driving force is really man's relation to matter, of which the most important part is his mode of production. In this way Marx's materialism, in practice, becomes economics.

Marx stated that we can really know an object only by acting on it successfully. "And since we change the object when we act upon it," Russell appends, "truth ceases to be static, and becomes something which is continually changing and developing. That is why Marx calls his materialism 'dialectical.' " When a person gains knowledge through investigation of the material world he not only changes that world— and hence "the truth"—but changes himself at the same time, for in the process of knowing an object he acquires new information, abilities, and needs. This has been phrased very well by Ernst Fischer, the Austrian poet and critic, who wrote in *The Essential Marx*:

> From the very start the species man has not appropriated the world passively but actively, through practice, labor, the setting of goals, the giving of form. As men *changed* the world they expanded and refined their ability to *know* it, and the growing capacity for cognition again enhanced their ability to change it.

What Fischer is describing is the dialectical relation between human beings and their natural environment, an important instance of the dialectical process that Marx and Engels believed pervaded human societies. In its broadest sweep, the dialectic method stresses the following elements:

(1) All things are in constant change;
(2) the ultimate source of the change is within the thing or process itself;
(3) this source is the struggle of opposites, the contradiction, within each thing;
(4) this struggle, at nodal points, brings about qualitative changes, or leaps, so that the thing is transformed into something else; and
(5) practical-critical activity resolves the contradictions.

Formal logic, which has dominated Western thought for some 2,000 years, is based on the simplest and seemingly most commonsense axioms, such as *A* is equal to *A* and *A* is not equal to *non-A*. But by being based on axioms like these, which freeze reality into fixed categories, formal logic loses its ability to explain structural change. Thus, one difference between the bourgeois (traditional) and Marxian approach to economics is that the former postulates only *quantitative* change, with each element maintaining its basic identity as it grows or contracts, whereas Marxian change allows for *qualitative transformation*, with each thing capable of turning into something new by becoming a synthesis of itself and its opposite.

Marxian dialectics is the logic of constant change: *A*, which includes not only itself but its opposite, *non-A*, is in continuous evolution. The fundamental cause of change in all things lies in their internal contradictions, in the struggle of opposites, in their self-movement. Whatever *is* has emerged from something else. Capitalism has evolved out of feudalism; socialism will emerge out of the contradictions of capitalism, not because it is "a better idea." Within capitalism, wealth exists in unity with its opposite, poverty; the very same economic processes have created both wealth and poverty, and one cannot exist or even be defined independently of the other. Similarly, workers in capitalism can only be discussed in relation to their opposite, capitalists. The one is inconceivable without the other, and social change occurs as a result of the struggle between these opposites.

Dialectical thought, which Marx learned from the work of the German philosopher Hegel (1770-1831), has been called the power of negative thinking. This is because, according to the dialectical view, everything includes its opposite (its negative); a thesis has an antithesis. The struggle of these opposites leads to the transformation of the thesis into some other and higher form of being—a synthesis. The development of the thesis which results from the contradiction does not stop at the opposite of what it was, but rather moves to a synthesis of itself and its opposite. Thus, a thing or process is never simply this or that; it is always both. "The simple-minded use of the notion 'right or wrong,' " English philosopher Alfred Whitehead wrote, "is one of the chief obstacles to the progress of understanding." This is because right includes wrong and wrong contains right. Likewise, Engels wrote that one knows "that which is recognized now as true has also its latent false side which will later manifest itself, just as that which is now regarded as false has also its true side by virtue of which it could previously have been regarded as true. One knows that what is maintained to be necessary is composed of sheer accidents and that the so-called accidental is the form behind which necessity hides itself."

Marx can hardly be understood unless his dialectical approach is kept constantly in mind.

Applications of the Marxian Theory

Engels emphasized that, in searching for explanations of historical change, one should not seek them "by deduction from fundamental principles" but instead should discover them "in the stubborn facts of the existing system of production." Further, the materialist conception of history can be successfully applied to a historical example, not by "mere empty talk," but only by "an abundance of critically examined historical material which has been completely mastered . . . . " One must also allow for many interactions among the elements of the historical episode being studied. For example, in some societies religion might inhibit the further development of the productive forces, while in other societies certain work institutions might play such a retarding role. If one does not make historical studies, Engels asserted, "the application of the theory to any period of history would be easier than the solution of a simple equation of the first degree."

Marx once complained, along the same lines, that a critic had tried to use his theory in a "super-historical" way:

> He feels he absolutely must metamorphose my historical sketch of the genesis of capitalism in Western Europe into a historico-philosophic theory of the general path every people is fated to tread, whatever the historical circumstances in which it finds itself, in order that it may ultimately arrive at the form of economy which ensures, together with the greatest expansion of the productive powers of social labor, the most complete development of man. But I beg his pardon. (He is both honoring and shaming me too much.)

Marx then pointed out that, although ancient Roman society had seeds of capitalism within it, it nevertheless developed into slavery:

> Thus events strikingly analogous but taking place in different historical surroundings led to totally different results. By studying each of these forms of evolution separately and then comparing them one can easily find the clue to this phenomenon, but one will never arrive there by using as one's master key a general historico-philosophical theory, the supreme virtue of which consists in being super-historical.

Marx and Engels, then, took pains to warn both friends and critics about the dangers of using the materialist conception of history in a mechanical and undialectical way, in which it is simply superimposed on any and all historical situations without regard to strong individual differences. The materialist conception of history provides a framework for analysis, a method, not ready-made answers.

The Emergence of Capitalism

Despite the fact that Marx's and Engels' analysis led to the conclusion that socialism would succeed capitalism, their sharpest focus was on capitalism itself, not on the future society. Marxism is concerned with the continuing evolution of the material and human world in all of its complexity, but most specifically it seeks to explain the dynamics of capitalism—the historical moment of its birth, its later development, and its future demise. Fundamental to that explanation, and the natural starting point, is an analysis of the forces that brought capitalism into being, a topic that will illustrate the use of the materialist conception of history and that will, at the same time, prepare us for an analysis of capitalism itself.

Capitalism has often been defined as either a commercial system (a money, exchange economy) or as a particular spirit of enterprise and profit rationality. These definitions, however, are historically imprecise, for both imply the existence of "capitalism" throughout most of history. Commercial and money systems reach back to antiquity, and the enterprising profit spirit of the Phoenician traders seems little different from that of the British East India Company or of our own exporters today. The first definition is vague; the second is idealist, in the sense that it assumes that elements of the superstructure lie at the heart of the system.

Marx defined capitalism by its mode of production. It is that mode of production in which the bourgeoisie, as owners of the means of production, directly opposes and exploits, in the production process, its antithesis, the proletariat, who owns only its labor-power and sells it as a commodity. The chief aim of the bourgeoisie is the production of surplus value (profits, rents, interest, executive salaries and bonuses). While capitalism produces its products as commodities, which are exchanged for money in a predominantly monetary economy, these exchanges are not the hallmark of the system. "The historical conditions of [capitalism's] existence are by no means given with the mere circulation of money and commodities," wrote Marx. "It can spring into life only when the owner of the means of production and subsistence meets in the market with the free laborer selling his labor-power."

The Liberty of the Subject by James Gillray

The heart of capitalism is not in the circulation but in the production sphere, where the laborer works under the control of the capitalist (to whom his labor belongs) and the product is the property of the capitalist. This definition clearly establishes capitalism as a special historical phenomenon, distinguishing it from its immediate feudal predecessor. In that earlier society, the bulk of the population, in possession of its own primitive tools, was tied to the land as serfs and vassals or united with their artisan capital in the guilds and in the homes. The definition also distinguishes capitalism from the classical periods of slavery, in which the slaves themselves were legally owned and exploited by others.

When capitalism is seen as a distinctive economic system, one must infer that there have been crucial points in economic development when qualitative changes occurred, when one system changed into another. Such abrupt changes are bound up with classes, the rise of the new class challenging and overcoming its predecessor, usually by force. When one ruling class replaces another, in response to the development of society's productive forces, that society undergoes a change in its mode of production, a qualitative transformation. Thus, development is not entirely gradual and quantitative but is at crucial times subject to "leaps," such as from feudalism to capitalism. The Marxian dialectical view, as we have already observed, is that the principal determinants of feudalism's decline lay within feudalism itself, within its own contradictions. This viewpoint does not rule out the impact of forces external to feudalism. As Mao Tse-tung has written about the dialectical approach: "It holds that external causes are the condition of change and internal causes are the basis of change, and that external causes become operative through internal causes. In a suitable temperature an egg changes into a chicken, but no temperature can change a stone into a chicken, because each has a different basis."

Maurice Dobb, a British Marxist economist who taught at Cambridge University for many decades, surmises that the growth of trade, starting around the 11th century, and the accompanying rise of towns were two forces external to feudalism that played their roles in weakening it. However, in his book *Studies in the Development of Capitalism*, he states that the main force was internal: "It was the inefficiency of feudalism as a system of production, coupled with the growing needs of the ruling class for revenue, that was primarily responsible for its decline." This led to overexploitation of the labor force, to the desertion *en masse* of serfs from their lords' manors, to the adoption by the feudal ruling class of expedients—commutation of labor services, leasing demesne lands to tenant farmers, etc.—and finally to the transformation of production relations in the countryside from feudal forms to commercial capitalist ones. Feudalism's internal contradictions destroyed that society, aided however by the external factors of the growth of trade and of market towns.

Feudalism had fairly well disintegrated by 1350-1400. However, the capitalist period did not begin until 1550-1600, 200 years later. Consequently, Dobb reasons, capitalism did not cause the decay of feudalism but itself developed from the crisis and decline of the old order. In the interval that elapsed between the beginning of feudalism's disintegration and the development of capitalism as a new mode of production, during the 1400s and 1500s, much wealth was accumulated by the rising bourgeoisie.

The merchant bourgeoisie gained its wealth through plunder abroad and through the acquisition of monopoly powers, allowing it to intervene profitably between producers and consumers. Dobb points out that this merchant bourgeoisie "compromised with feudal society once its privileges had been won," so that by the end of the 16th century it "had become a conservative rather than a revolutionary force."

The industrial bourgeoisie, on the heels of the merchants, concentrated capital in its hands through (1) speculative gains from land transactions, (2) usury, (3) profits from widening and freeing markets and from changing the mode of production to raise labor productivity, and (4) forceful acquisition of others' wealth. This rising industrial class came into conflict not only with the remnants of feudalism—urban localism and monopolies of the craft guilds—but also with "the restrictive monopolies in the sphere of trade in which merchant capital" was entrenched. The political struggles of the 17th and 18th centuries reflected the complexities of these several antagonisms.

Thus, the whole period of capital accumulation by the bourgeoisie was an essential stage in the genesis of capitalism, a period that fell between the decay of feudalism and the real beginning of the bourgeois mode of production, a period Marx called "primitive [or original] accumulation." During this period there was both a transfer to and a concentration of wealth in bourgeois hands. This prior accumulation was necessary to enable the new bourgeoisie to break up or subordinate to capital the petty mode of production (independent small-scale agriculture and handicrafts) which was the legacy of feudal society.

However, according to Dobb, the formation of the bourgeoisie was not sufficient to usher in capitalism, because capitalism requires a laboring class dispossessed of its primitive means of production, with nothing left but its own labor-power—otherwise it would not be willing to work for others. Dobb explains: "The essence of this primary accumulation [consists in] the transfer of property from small owners to the ascendant bourgeoisie and the consequent pauperization of the former." That is to say, financial enrichment alone was not enough: it had to be enrichment of the few at the expense of the many. In short, the very same processes both enlarged and concentrated capital and simultaneously created "free" labor, free in the two senses that it could seek employment wherever it liked and that it had been freed of its possessions.

An embryonic English proletariat, for instance, was formed during the 1500s by the disbandment of feudal retainers, the eviction or release of peasants through land enclosures (for the raising of sheep) and changes in methods of tillage, the confiscation of lands of the Catholic Church (which tended to destroy feudal social relations and speed up enclosures), and by natural increases of the population. As a result, during this century a growing army of dispossessed people roamed the countryside as vagrants, whereupon, as Marx said, they were persecuted and harassed with "a bloody legislation against vagabondage." Later, in the 1600s and early 1700s—as land continued to be enclosed, as semi-feudal relations were redefined by landlords to the disadvantage of peasants, and as agricultural depression ruined many small landholders—some of the newly dispossessed sought work in rural domestic industry or as agricultural wage laborers and others drifted into towns and cities to seek employment in manufacturing workshops. By around 1750 the capitalist mode of production was fairly well implanted in agriculture, thus ensuring the existence of a relatively small group of large landowners (three-quarters of the land was owned by landlords) and a mass of dispossessed proletarian wage earners. Subsequently, the English proletariat was swelled by immigration of cheap labor from Ireland and Scotland, the enlistment of women and children into the ranks of wage labor, and rapid increases of population.

In *Capital*, Marx provided much detail on the early formation of the proletariat in England, which he called the classic case. "The expropriation of the agricultural producer, of the peasant, from the soil," Marx declared, "is the basis of the whole process." Marx stressed the role in this process of land enclosures, which took place from the late 1400s into the 19th century, and which replaced communal and semi-communal forms of landholding with private forms. Marx contended that enclosures were a crucial part of the transition from feudalism to capitalism and hence of the birth of the modern proletariat. The expropriation of peasants (accomplished not only by enclosures but in many other ways discussed by Marx) fashioned an "outlawed proletariat" that was then "whipped, branded, tortured by laws grotesquely terrible, into the discipline necessary for the wage system." This "free" labor was thus forced into wage relationships in agriculture, rural industry, and town enterprises.

Marx asserted that this process was repeated in European countries, though, he wrote, it "assumes different aspects, and runs through its various phases in different orders of succession, and at different periods." In Europe generally, the rising commercial capitalist classes acquired much wealth by spanning the globe in search of plunder and profit. In the meantime, European proletariat classes, dispossessed of means of production, were fashioned for the growing factories and manufacturing works. More and more, as time passed, concentrated capital met dispossessed labor on the labor markets.

In the New World, however, the early European capitalists did not find the process of developing profitable enterprises so simple. The seizure of North America with all of its natural resources and the "clearing" of the Indian population that accompanied British, French, and Spanish colonization prepared the way for the rise of American capitalism. Far from being based on the opening up of empty, virgin land, American capitalism was founded on the continual expropriation of a lightly populated but ecologically balanced land. Here the indigenous Indian population either died in great numbers from European diseases or fled into the continental interior. Capital found much potential natural wealth but little labor-power.

Historian Eric Williams, in his book *Capitalism and Slavery*, analyzes how this imbalance between the ready availability of capital in the form of land, raw materials, and liquid funds, on the one hand, and the lack of a sufficiently large labor force, on the other, led to slavery in the early period of capitalist development in the Caribbean. This imbalance, he explains, gave rise to a capitalist-generated slave mode of production and only later to capitalism itself. Throughout the Caribbean, as well as in North America, efforts were made to force Indians into service for production. The failure of these efforts led to heavy reliance, first, on white indentured servants (whose conditions of servitude approached slavery), convicts, and other temporarily unfree labor. But Indian slavery and white servitude were both inferior, from the capitalists' standpoint, to black African slaves, who proved to possess the cheapest and the best labor-power. When the slave trade and later slavery itself were abolished by the British, the sugar planters turned back to white labor and then to East Indians and to a lesser extent to Chinese coolies.

The reason for black slavery, Williams summarizes, "was economic, not racial; it had to do not with the color of the laborer, but the cheapness of the labor. . . . Slavery was not born of racism: rather, racism was the consequence of slavery. Unfree labor in the New World was brown, white, black, and yellow; Catholic, Protestant, and pagan." Capital sought labor-power wherever it could be found, enslaved it if it had to, bought it on markets if it could. Negro slavery, Williams adds, "was only a solution, in certain historical circumstances, of the Caribbean labor problem." When the sugar monopoly of the British West Indies impeded further economic progress by British industrial capitalists, they successfully attacked the slavery on which the monopoly rested. Economics, then, lay at the heart of both slavery and its abolition, though other factors clearly played important roles, especially in slavery's abolition.

Farther north, the American colonies during the 17th and 18th centuries were both pre-capitalist and capitalist in their modes of production. In the southern colonies, some strong elements of capitalism prevailed, for private capital sought profits through the production of commodities for a world market. But, just as in the Caribbean, capital encountered acute shortages of wage-labor that necessitated the employment of black slaves and white indentured servants in large numbers. This unfree labor was, in a sense, grafted onto the capitalist base. Marx wrote that the plantations represented the capitalist mode of production only in the formal sense, "since the slavery of Negroes precludes free wage-labor, which is the basis of capitalist production. But the business in which slaves are used is conducted by *capitalists*."

Such enslaved labor was used in the northern colonies, too, but there the mode of production began largely as pre-capitalist, in which many small freeholders (land owners) produced mostly for their own needs. However, the North very early witnessed the vigorous beginnings of commercial capitalism, too. But, for the most part, Marx wrote, the colonists in the North were not capitalists and did not carry on capitalist production.

In the first half of the 19th century, manufacturing and industry developed robustly in the northeastern states, and small-scale family farming burgeoned with the westward expansion. Indentured servitude vanished behind the opening of the western frontiers and in the face of heavy European immigration. Ultimately, northern capital and the farmers of the West came into armed conflict with the slavery mode of production in the South. Just as the English revolutions of the 17th century were, in large part, capitalist uprisings against absolutism and feudalism, and the French revolution of 1789 broke the obstruction of feudal nobility and clergy to the further development of the French bourgeoisie, so the American Civil War served capital by expunging slavery as a mode of production that prevented the full continental development of the capitalist mode.

With regard to colonization generally, Marx observed that the capitalist mode of production was impossible so long as land was plentiful and cheaply available to labor, for this frustrated the formation of a working class that could be subjected to capitalist exploitation. A solution to the problem of the formation of a proletariat in such circumstances, as the problem appeared in Australia, was suggested by an English author, E.G. Wakefield. He proposed that the government should put a very high price on virgin land in order to compel the immigrants to labor long for wages before they earned enough money to buy land. Thus, the immigrants would have to be wage earners for an extended period before they could become independent peasants. Marx sarcastically commented that the money extorted from the worker by the sale of land at relatively prohibitive prices—violating, Marx noted, the sacred law of supply and demand—would be employed by the government to import more cheap labor from Europe into the colonies "and thus keep the wage-labor market full for the capitalists."

The danger of acute labor scarcity was also present in the United States at various times during the 18th and 19th centuries, largely because virgin land was so easily available to the working force (once the Indians were killed or driven off). The Homestead Act of 1862 exacerbated this tendency toward scarce labor by making land in the West available in lots of 160 acres to workers in the industrializing East, which threatened to raise industrial wages and lower profits. But this threat was mostly averted by the Immigration Act of 1864, which, as Charles and Mary Beard stated in *The Rise of American Civilization*, "gave federal authorization to the importation of working people under terms of contract analogous to the indentured servants of colonial times." By this and other means, the industrial capitalists managed to reproduce cheap labor despite the constant drains that occurred from the "reserve army."

The capitalist mode of production, these examples affirm, depends not only on the concentration of capital in the hands of a capitalist class, but also on the creation and continual reproduction of a working class that is dispossessed of or denied the means of production, and that has only its labor-power to sell. If individual members of this class "escape" to self-sufficiency through the slow accumulation of capital or by being the recipients of land grants, mechanisms are quickly brought into play to replenish the army of workers. This process has repeated itself, Marxists conclude, though with variation in detail, everywhere that capitalism has appeared or has been forced on a population.

Outside of Europe and America, the most notable growth of an indigenous capitalism has taken place in Japan. The rapid early growth of capitalism in the Meiji era (starting in 1868) was accompanied by pressure on the agricultural population similar to that which attended the emergence of capitalism in Europe. William Lockwood, of Princeton University, in his interesting work *The Economic Development of Japan*, has described this process vividly. He relates how masses of peasants were driven into tenantry and debt in the first 25 years of the Meiji period, and how an escape from this condition was made almost impossible by the high price of land, high rents, and usurious interest rates. "The mounting surplus of farm population had to find employment increasingly outside agriculture," he writes. "Those families which remained on the farm also sought supplementary income, either through part-time employment in local industries or through putting their reluctant daughters into the textile factories of the towns and cities." Japan, he says, thus repeated the earlier experience of many European countries, the pressures on the Japanese peasants being especially "reminiscent of those experienced by the English yeoman a century or more before."

Lockwood has also drawn a rough parallel between the ways some of the European and the Japanese proletariat were recruited. In Japan, low-wage female labor was recruited for the textile industries. "Wages were low, even by Japanese standards. . . . There were no factory laws. Any organization of workers to bargain collectively or strike was effectively forbidden under the Police Regulations of 1900." In general, Japanese industrialization along capitalist lines exhibited the same poverty, miserable working conditions, and lack of worker protection as appeared earlier in England.

Even today, in South Korea, Brazil, Iran, Indonesia, and wherever capitalist development is getting started, the same phenomena appear: a separation of the producers from their means of production, a concentration of ownership of the means of production in a capitalist class, and the formation of an urban proletariat, of cheap industrial labor, kept cheap mainly by oppressive means, whose surpluses are appropriated by capitalists, landowners, financiers, and bureaucrats. Lockwood seems a bit surprised that Japan experienced much the same development as Europe, a development that created both wealth and poverty, where the existence of the one depended on the existence of the other. Had he lived to see Japanese capitalism, Marx would not have been the least surprised. This has been the typical pattern of emerging capitalism everywhere.

A Free Born Englishman!, anonymous redrawing of Cruikshank's version

CHAPTER THREE

MARX AND THE CRITIQUE OF CAPITALISM

FEW AMERICANS SEEM to be acquainted with what lies at the very heart of Marx's thought: his economic analysis of the capitalist mode of production. It is not possible to appreciate the Marxian critique of capitalist society without some knowledge of his theories: how this mode of production actually works (which includes the theory of exploitation), how it is consciously or unconsciously distorted by its apologists, and how it will eventually be replaced by socialism. This chapter contains explanations of these theories and with them an understanding of why Marx's ideas continue to live throughout much of the world. The chapter is not always easy going, but it does offer the reader an escape from the superficial.

How Capitalism Works

Marx defined capitalism as a particular, historically-determined mode of production. He analyzed this mode dialectically in terms of a growing contradiction between the productive forces and the social relations of production that would reveal itself in increasingly severe crises and evermore intense struggles between the bourgeoisie and the proletariat. Inasmuch as Marxian theory reflected the rise of the industrial working class, and served that class, it was highly critical of both the capitalist mode and its ideologists. It was also revolutionary in that it was at the same time an analysis, a prediction, and a catalyst of the coming overthrow of the bourgeoisie by the proletariat—and, hence, of bourgeois theory by Marxian theory.

Marx insisted that "capital" is not a thing but a definite social relation which belonged to a specific historical formation of society. "The means of production become capital," Marx wrote, "only insofar as they have become separated from the laborer and confront labor as an independent power." Means of production are capital when they have become monopolized by a certain sector of society and used by that class to produce surplus value—that is, the income of the capitalist class (generally profits, interest, and rent) that comes from the exploitation of another class. Consequently, capital, for Marx, is not only part of the forces of production but it is also a particular employment of those forces, a social relation.

Capital appears in four major forms: (1) industrial, (2) trading, (3) lending, and (4) renting. Industrial capital *produces* and *realizes* surplus value—the former in the production sphere and the latter in the circulation sphere—while the other forms *redistribute* it among the various claimants of capitalists. Capital, in the social forms of instruments of labor, raw materials, and labor-power, produces surplus value in the production sphere. Capital, in the social forms of commodities and money, realizes surplus value for the capitalist class in the sphere of circulation. Capital, in the social forms of merchants' (trading) capital, interest-bearing (lending) capital, and landed (renting) capital, distributes the surplus value among industrial, commercial, financial, and landed capitalists. Surplus value appears mainly as industrial profits, commercial profits, interest, and rent. (Major forms are shown below.)

Forms of Capital	*Surplus Value*
I. Industrial Capital	
A. Productive capital	
1. Constant capital	
a. Instruments of labor	The Production of
b. Raw materials	Surplus Value
2. Variable capital (labor-power)	
3. Surplus value (unpaid labor)	
B. Circulation capital	The Realization of
1. Commodity capital	Surplus Value
2. Money capital	
II. Merchants' (Trading) Capital	The Redistribution of
III. Interest-Bearing (Lending) Capital	Surplus Value
IV. Landed (Renting) Capital	

The Production and Realization of Surplus Value

Marx demonstrated that surplus value is created in the production sphere. However, its realization (the sale of the commodities at their "value"—a term defined below) occurs in the sphere of circulation. Surplus value arises when a capitalist purchases labor-power (the capacity for labor) at its value, employs the labor-power in a work process that he controls, and then appropriates the commodities produced. Surplus value is the difference between the net value of these commodities and the value of labor-power itself.

The *value* of labor-power is the cost of maintaining and reproducing the worker and his family at a socially-accepted standard of living. This level, in some poor countries, may include only the bare necessities, but in others it will also include a "moral element"—what "society," in its real development, has determined to be an average standard of living for a laborer and his family.

A worker sells his labor-power—his mental and physical capabilities —to a capitalist for its value, and the capitalist uses the labor-power to obtain commodities which have a value higher than that of the labor-power purchased. Thus, the secret of surplus value is that labor-power is a source of more value than it has itself. The capitalist is able to capture the surplus value through his ownership of the means of production and his historically-established right to purchase labor-power as a commodity, to control the work process, and to claim the product as his property. This surplus value, according to Marx, is the measure of capital's exploitation of labor.

Marx used a simple model of the firm to illustrate his concept of exploitation. The gross value of a commodity produced by a firm is the socially-necessary labor-time which is embodied in that commodity at all stages of its production. (Socially necessary" means that the commodity is produced under the normal conditions of production with the average degree of skill and intensity prevalent at the time—and that there is a demand for it.) Marx divided the *gross value* of a commodity into three parts.

The first portion of gross value is *constant capital* (c), which is the value—the socially-necessary labor-time—of capital goods and raw materials used up in the production of a commodity. For instance, machinery is used up in the sense that it depreciates when used to produce commodities. Such items are called "constant" because they add no more value to the final product than they themselves lose in the production process. That is, workers may have been exploited when they previously produced the machines and raw materials, but the machines and raw materials themselves cannot be exploited by the capitalist when they are used to produce other commodities, for they do not produce more than their own value; only labor does that.

The second part of a commodity's gross value is *variable capital* (*v*). This is the value of the direct labor which is used in the production process (along with the machinery and the raw materials) *and* which is paid for. It is the value of labor-power. This is equal to the wages paid for the socially-necessary labor-time required to maintain and reproduce the worker and his family at a socially-accepted level of living. Thus, if a worker, in a 10-hour day, is able to produce enough in 6 hours to maintain and reproduce himself, this is equal to his wage and is Marx's variable capital. It is called "variable" because the use of labor-power by the capitalist results in the worker producing more value than it costs to reproduce him.

Surplus value (*s*), the third portion of gross value, is the unpaid amount of the direct labor—a part of the value of the commodity produced by the worker in the remaining 4 hours of the workday, which is appropriated by the capitalist in the form of surplus value. Thus, if constant capital is 1 hour, the gross value is 11 hours. This gross value less constant capital and variable capital equals the surplus value of 4. The worker produces but does not receive 4 hours of commodities, which become, in money form, profits, interest, and rent.

The three components together make up the gross value of the product. That is, let

$$C' = \text{gross value of the product}$$
$$c = \text{constant capital}$$
$$v = \text{variable capital}$$
$$s = \text{surplus value}$$

then

$$C' = c + v + s .$$

The *net value* of the product omits the using up of the capital goods and raw materials and so is equal to $v + s$. Labor creates the full value of the net product ($v + s$) but receives only v. The capitalist, by virtue of his ownership of the means of production, is enabled to appropriate s, the surplus value.

The *rate of surplus value* (*s'*), or the degree of exploitation, is defined as s/v, the ratio of surplus value to variable capital. Marx also called this the ratio of surplus labor-time to necessary labor-time, the former being that portion of the working day during which the worker creates surplus value, the latter being that portion of the working day during which the worker produces enough to maintain and reproduce himself.

Labor is exploited to the extent that a capitalist class appropriates privately what in fact labor produced.

Does that mean that machines and raw materials are not productive? No, they are productive: they transfer their value to the product. But they are not the creators of surplus value. Machines cannot be exploited by the capitalist. The labor that produced the machines has already been exploited by the previous capitalist who received the surplus value. The machine was then sold at its value (including the surplus value) and so cannot be exploited again at the next stage of production. At this later stage of production, the machine transfers its value, and nothing more, to the commodities. But do not machines raise the productivity of labor and so enable a capitalist to obtain larger surplus value? Machines do raise labor productivity. But, while machines enable the worker to produce more, it is only the labor that produces the surplus value. Only the workers themselves produce value for the capitalist that exceeds the value of their own labor-power. A commodity is produced by direct labor and indirect labor (machines and raw materials); direct labor creates the surplus value, and indirect labor (embodied in c) aids direct labor in so doing.

Surplus value, then, arises in the depths of the production process, not on the surface of circulation, not by capitalists buying cheap and selling dear, not by their cheating. Marx illustrated this in the following way:

$$M \text{------} C \overset{\nearrow L\ (v)}{\underset{\searrow MP\ (c)}{}} \quad . \quad . \quad . \quad . \quad . \quad P \quad . \quad . \quad . \quad . \quad . \quad . \quad C' \text{------} M'$$

Circulation	Production	Circulation
Money-Capital Period	Productive-Capital Period	Commodity-Capital Period

$$C' = c + v + s$$
$$C = c + v$$
$$M' - M = \text{surplus value} = C' - C$$

Starting at the left, the capitalist uses money (M) to purchase the commodities (C) needed in the production process—that is, labor-power (L) and the means of production (MP). These purchases occur in the circulation sphere, where equal values are exchanged, in this case money capital for two "inputs" in the production process. Thus, Marx termed this part of the circulation sphere (where commodities are bought with money and sold for money) the "money-capital period." The result of the production process (. . . P . . .) is the creation of a final commodity (C'), the value of which exceeds that of C by the amount of surplus value incorporated in it. This commodity is then sold for money (C'——M'), a transaction carried out in the other part of the circulation sphere, where once again equal values are exchanged—initiated this time by commodity capital, the money used to buy commodities and thus to complete the circuit. C' minus C represents surplus value, as does M' minus M. The former, however, reflects the *production* of surplus value; the latter, the *realization* of surplus value. After realizing surplus value, the capitalist repeats the process on an enlarged scale with the larger sum of money capital. This means, for instance, that he enlarges the size of his plant and produces a larger volume of commodities.

The Redistribution of Surplus Value

Surplus value includes not only the profits of the industrial capitalists whom we have just considered, but also the profits of commercial capitalists, interest of moneylenders or finance capitalists, and ground rent of landowning capitalists. Marx also noted that directors of business firms and others took shares of the surplus, too. We should further note that the state maintains its bureaucracy and protects the social relations of production with some of the surplus, in the form of taxes.

The rate of surplus value (s'), as we have seen, is equal to s/v. To measure the *rate of profit* (p'), Marx used $p' = s/(c + v)$ on the assumptions (1) that all machinery and raw materials were used up entirely, and labor-power paid for, in the one production period, (2) that capitalists advanced wages to laborers, and (3) that all surplus value was retained by industrial capitalists. Thus, $C = c + v$ is the total capital advanced, and the rate of profit is the percentage that the retained surplus value bears to it. Since the rate of profit ($s/(c + v)$) is computed on a wider base than that used for the rate of surplus value (s/v), the rate of surplus value will be greater than the rate of profit if c is positive— that is, if machinery and raw materials are utilized in production.

A third ratio defined by Marx was that of the *organic composition of capital* (g), equal to $c/(c + v)$, which is a measure for the degree of capital intensity in production. This rate shows the extent to which a capitalist uses constant capital (c) relative to total capital ($c + v$). The organic composition of capital tends to be high when the value of machinery and raw materials is large relative to that of direct labor. This is the case, for example, in highly automated enterprises.

The three ratios—showing the rate of exploitation or surplus value (s'), the rate of profit (p'), and the organic composition of capital (g)— can be combined in one equation: $p' = s' (1 - g)$. This indicates that if g were zero—that is, if only direct labor were used by the capitalist—

then the rate of profit would be equal to the rate of exploitation. As the capitalist uses more and more machinery and raw materials relative to direct labor, g rises and the rate of profit falls relative to the rate of exploitation. That is, the rate of profit then tends to understate the extent to which capitalists are exploiting labor. Thus, even though the rate of exploitation were 40 percent, the rate of profit might be only 10 percent, if the capitalist used a lot of machinery and raw materials relative to labor (enough to make $g = \frac{3}{4}$).

By focusing on the rate of profit, businessmen and their supporters not only understate the rate of exploitation but in fact hide its true source. While surplus value results from the exploitation of direct labor, it appears as though this surplus value comes from total capital $(c + v)$, from machinery and raw materials as well as from direct labor.

Furthermore, industrial capitalists do not retain all of the surplus value. Some of it is channeled to commercial capitalists (merchants), who, using commercial or money capital, buy and sell commodities within the circulation sphere. The activities of these commercial capitalists do not directly produce surplus value—it is produced entirely in the production sphere—but indirectly they contribute to its generation by shortening the time of circulation and by expanding markets. These contributions enable industrial capitalists to produce more surplus value with the employment of less capital. Since all capital, industrial and commercial, in perfectly competitive markets earns the same rate of profit, the industrial capitalists must transfer sufficient surplus value to the commercial capitalists to permit this equality to be achieved. This transfer takes place when the industrial capitalists sell their commodities to merchants at prices below their values, while the merchants resell the commodities to consumers at their values (plus the constant and variable capital employed by the merchants, which they must recover).

In addition to this drain from industrial capitalists' surplus value, the moneylending capitalists also get a slice. These capitalists give up the use value of money, which is its ability to produce surplus value, in return for a portion of that surplus value. The moneylending capitalists loan money to industrial capitalists (and others) at certain interest rates, which are the market prices that serve to redistribute surplus value to them. The portion of the surplus value going to moneylending capitalists is interest, while the portion remaining with industrial capitalists Marx called "profits of enterprise." Clearly, the higher the rates of interest, the higher is financial capital's share of surplus value relative to that of industrial capital. Interest rates are established by competition in the loanable funds markets, and their levels may be high or low depending on the market forces of demand and supply. As Marx saw

Temperance Enjoying a Frugal Meal by James Gillray

it, there is room for much conflict between financial and industrial capitalists over relative shares of surplus value.

Finally, the agricultural capitalists, in the same way as the industrial ones, exploit labor and so obtain surplus value. In this respect, there is no distinction between these two productive sectors of the economy. This surplus value is shared with the landowning capitalists, the latter receiving it in ground rent. The total income of this landowning class includes absolute rent, which reflects monopoly gains from the private ownership of a nonreproducible resource; differential rent, which is based on two equal quantities of capital and labor employed on equal areas of land with unequal results; and an element of interest, which comprises charges for land improvements.

Consequently, productive (industrial and agricultural) capitalists do not retain all of the surplus value generated within their spheres. Some of it goes to commercial capitalists, some to financial capitalists, and some to landowning capitalists. Additionally, Marx claimed, other shares are plundered by private bureaucrats, hangers-on, and just plain swindlers. In any event, the industrial capitalists' profits (after taxes) are only a modest fraction of the total fruits of exploitation. Thus, when these profits are paraded as total income of the capitalist class, they divert attention from the other shares. Further, when these profits are related to total capital $(c + v)$ to obtain a profit rate, both the rate of exploitation (surplus value) and its source are hidden. Finally, when these industrial profits are displayed after taxes have been taken out, the role of the state in supporting the capitalist class is concealed. That is, surplus value includes much of the state's receipts and expenditures, the latter intended to strengthen the class structure and its property relations.

Marxists maintain that the rate of industrial profits after taxes, therefore, is a gross understatement of the extent to which capital exploits labor. In 1974 in the United States, for example, industrial corporate profits after taxes were about $50 billion, but total surplus value (all corporate profits, interest, and rent before taxes) approached $200 billion, or about a quarter of employee compensation (wages and salaries) before taxes. Thus, the rate of exploitation, as Marx would figure it (if prices are used instead of values), was around 25 percent, while the rate of industrial profits on stockholders' equity was only a little over 10 percent.

Values and Prices

The value of a commodity, we have seen, is the socially-necessary labor-time required to produce it. The price of a commodity, on the other hand, is this labor-time valued in terms of money—say, for example, that 100 hours of labor equal $250. This $250 is divided among constant capital (*c*), variable capital (*v*), and surplus value (*s*). If c = $150, and the rate of exploitation is 100 percent, then v = $50 and s = $50 ($s/v$ = 100 percent). In this case, the rate of profit is 25 percent— $s/(c + v)$ = 50/200. If workers are free to move from one job to another to find their best advantage, wage rates for equal work will tend to be the same in each industry. Similarly, if capital is free to move, competition will tend to equalize the profit rates. Thus, following our numerical example, each sphere of production, when competition prevails, should have a profit rate of 25 percent. This would make prices proportional to values when commodities are traded one for another, provided that the organic composition of capital, $c/(c + v)$, is the same in each sphere of production—equal to 150/200, as in our numerical example.

Now, competition *will* tend to equalize rates of profit, but there is no reason to expect organic compositions of capital (the degrees of capital intensity) to be the same from one industry to the next. Suppose that our commodity has a higher organic composition than others on the average. In that event, the profit rate for our commodity would initially be lower than the average, because, while the exploitation rates, s/v, might be the same, the profit rate, $s/(c + v)$, is lower as *c* rises relative to *v*. The price of our commodity, therefore, would have to rise above $250 in order to equalize profit rates. This is accomplished by some capital moving out of this sphere, thereby reducing the supply of the commodity and raising its price. At the other end of the scale, if some commodities are produced with especially low organic compositions of capital, their profit rates will be above average. Consequently, their prices will fall below levels suggested by their values as capital moves into these spheres to take advantage of initially higher profit rates.

Thus, when the organic composition of capital differs among industries, prices will not be proportional to values, though the two will be systematically related to each other in accordance with the structure of the organic compositions of capital. The function of prices, in this case, is to redistribute surplus value among industrial capitalists so as to equalize rates of profit. Those capitalists with low organic compositions of capital, and hence initially with excess amounts of surplus value, lose portions of their surplus to other capitalists who are in the opposite position.

Surplus value is generated in the sphere of production, but it is generated differentially, in excess here and in deficiency there, depending on the organic composition of capital. To redistribute the surplus value so as to equalize profit rates requires that prices differ from values. Marx saw this process not as a weakness but as a decided strength of his analysis: the value-analysis revealed exploitation and its manifestation in surplus value; the price-analysis revealed how the total surplus value was shared within the class of industrial capitalists, in accordance with the laws of competition. At the same time, the price system also redistributed the surplus value among the various classes of capitalists— industrial, commercial, financial, and landed—as we have already seen.

Capital Accumulation

It was Marx's contention that the production of surplus value is "the absolute law" of the capitalist mode of production, that most of this surplus value is continually reconverted into capital—called capital accumulation—and that the system reproduces the capitalist relation: "on the one side the capitalist, on the other the wage-laborer." Capitalism is inherently an expanding system, for capitalists must constantly accumulate and extend their capital in order to preserve it; they must continually expand in order to remain capitalists, for if they did not they would be destroyed by competitors; they would be consumers and not capitalists. This expansion eventually occurs on a worldwide basis, for capitalists must push their mode of production into every nook and cranny of the globe. Nevertheless, capitalists also have an urge to enjoy the consumption of their capital. The overcoming of this urge is supposed to be "abstinence," which is a bourgeois justification, according to Marx, for the private appropriation of surplus value.

Marx asserted that the general law of capitalist accumulation is that it creates *both* wealth and poverty. That is to say, capitalist accumulation has an antagonistic character in that it produces and contains a unity of opposites. "The same causes which develop the expansive power of capital," Marx wrote, "develop also the labor-power at its disposal," including the reserve army of labor (a relative surplus population), whose misery and pauperism grow in step with wealth at the other pole. Furthermore, Marx continued, capital accumulation transforms the workplace into a despotic, degrading, alienating environment, one which mutilates the laborer "into a fragment of a man" and destroys "every remnant of charm in his work." Capital accumulation produces an accumulation of wealth at one pole and an "accumulation of misery, agony of toil, slavery, ignorance, brutality, mental degradation, at the opposite pole." Poverty and misery are not capitalism's negligence but its imperative, its inevitable progenies. This is Marx's principal message about the process of capitalist accumulation.

That message today may sound "wild," and indeed in some respects Marx can now be seen as having incorrectly extrapolated conditions prevalent in his time. However, before the reader plunges in to judge the message too harshly, he should be aware of its depth. For Marx, wealth could not exist by itself, just as a capitalist class could not exist in isolation. Wealth in capitalism has no other meaning than a concentration of much of society's production (its means and its products) in relatively few hands, and there is no way for that to occur without the simultaneous creation of its opposite—poverty, the material deprivation of the many, at least in relative terms. But poverty and misery, Marx contended, must be understood not only as exploitation but as alienation as well—not only materially but also "spiritually."

The Marxian theory of alienation seeks to explain how individuals in capitalist society have lost their understanding and control of the world around them and have, in the process, been stunted and perverted into something less than full human beings. For Marx, the source of all alienation lies in the work process. Alienation means that individuals no longer have an immediate and intimate relationship to the environment; they have been specialized and sorted, made into "the most wretched of commodities," divorced from the products they produce, split into mental workers and manual workers, into town people and rural people, divided into dominant and subordinate classes, thrown into selfish competition with one another. The result of alienation is the loss of personal identity—a transference of an individual's essential powers to others and to "things," even to commodities. Alienation is the negation of productivity, the diminution of one's powers.

Marx saw human beings in capitalistic society as alienated not only from the products they create and from their own labor, but also from others and from themselves. That is, workers under capitalism lose control of their products, produce as cogs in a process they do not understand, are separated from and pitted against their fellow workers, and are deprived of their essential powers. They believe that power resides outside of themselves, in the products they have actually fashioned, and they humble, demean, and almost destroy themselves before the commodity world. In the same way, a religious person might fashion a wooden idol with his own hands, kneel before it, transfer his own powers to it, and thus reduce himself to something less than a full human being. In their manifold alienated states, people lose their inner selves and become passive; they allow themselves to be directed by outside powers that they do not control and do not want to control; they subject themselves willingly to manipulation; they have a sense of powerlessness; they cannot act effectively. Marx did not believe that capitalism was the original cause of alienation—for it existed before that—but under capitalism alienation in all of its forms is maximized.

The proletariat shares with the bourgeoisie every aspect of this commodity-dominated world. But, Marx stated, the latter experiences it as "a sign of its own power," while the former "feels destroyed in this alienation." The bourgeoisie, for Marx, sees no need for piercing the surface of phenomena; indeed it has a special interest in not revealing what is below, and even in deceiving itself on this score. On the other hand, the proletariat, while equally baffled, has a special interest in discovering the true relations and thus in developing a revolutionary consciousness. Productive activity is the catalyst of this transformation.

The capitalist mode of production extracts surplus value from wage-labor for the class of capitalists. The surplus value is used to expand capital, a process which is inherent to this social formation, and which is reinforced by competition. The accumulation process tends to generate increasing demands for labor to work cooperatively with the expanding means of production. However, accumulation leads to *concentration* of capital, which places greater magnitudes of capital in fewer hands and at the same time raises the organic composition of capital—the capital intensity of production—thereby moderating the growing demand for labor. Accumulation is also accompanied by the *centralization* of capital, by the larger capitalists gaining what smaller capitalists lose, by the expropriation of capitalist by capitalist.

The centralization of capital is the dynamic element in the accumulation process. It is furthered by the development of the credit system, which draws together scattered money resources for the use of larger capitalists; by competition, which destroys the weak and bolsters the strong; and by economies of scale (falling average costs), which give increasing cost advantages to the already-large capitals over the smaller ones, enabling the larger capitals to beat the smaller.

If capitalist accumulation is to persist, it requires above all else an ample supply of wage-labor that is continually replenished and available for work at wage levels that ensure the further production of surplus value for the class of capitalists. It is for this reason that Marx considered the reserve army of labor to be an essential ingredient of capitalism, a relatively redundant population of laborers that would expand and contract according to the requirements of the system. As soon as the accumulation process diminishes this surplus population to the point of endangering the further production of adequate amounts of surplus value (by raising wages and other advantages of labor), a reaction sets in: accumulation lags, the introduction of labor-saving machinery is quickened, the reserve army is replenished, and the rise in wages is halted. In these ways, Marx maintained, the foundations of the capitalist system are protected from the dangers of lessened ex-

Diplomacy by Honoré Daumier

ploitation. "The law of capitalistic accumulation . . . excludes every diminution in the degree of exploitation of labor, and every rise in the price of labor, which could seriously imperil the continual reproduction, on an ever-enlarging scale, of the capitalistic relation." According to Marx, the laborer exists to satisfy the needs of capital; material wealth does not exist to satisfy the need of the laborer to develop into a complete human being.

Consequently, capitalist accumulation demands the replenishment of poverty and misery, through the reserve army, to serve its requirements. But, Marx continued, there are other ways that degradation is created by the process of accumulation. First, accumulation and capitalists' pursuit of ever-larger surplus value lead to the geographical concentration of the means of production in industrial urban centers. As Marx and Engels observed, this causes a "heaping together of the laborers, within a given space . . . therefore the swifter capitalistic accumulation, the more miserable are the dwellings of the working-people." Second, accumulation of capital tears apart the fabric protecting individual proprietors, craftsmen, and self-sufficient producers, transforming them into a surplus of dependent wage-laborers. Third, it draws wealth and talent from outlying areas into industrial and urban centers, converting the former into backward, stagnant sub-economies; or it reduces these outlying areas to specialized suppliers of raw materials for industrial capital, thereby increasing their vulnerability to adverse developments; and it transfers wealth from these areas via the price-market mechanism. Fourth, on an international scale, the capitalist mode has augmented its capital through forceful, market control of weaker areas and has drained surpluses from them into the industrial regions. By these means, wealth and poverty are created together, a unity of conflicting opposites.

How Capitalism Is Mystified

Marx alleged that capitalism presents itself on the surface of life in distorted forms—that what it is really like, within its deep recesses, is quite different from what its facial expressions suggest. These surface distortions, Marx contended, lead to illusions about the capitalist mode of production, and the illusions in turn are used by bourgeois ideologists to mystify the workings of the system. Thus, a web of mystification is spun around this mode of production, hindering a clear understanding of its true nature. We are all fooled, Marx said, by capitalism's distortions.

The Distortions of Capitalism

The capitalist mode of production turns labor-power into a commodity, in a world of commodities, to be purchased and exploited by a capital-owning class that appropriates surplus value and is compelled to extend its capital and its mode of production to all corners of the globe. Capitalist relations comprise these two classes existing as a unity of opposites: the capitalist class, owning the means of production, buying the labor-power of a dispossessed proletariat, controlling the work process, possessing the products of labor; and the proletariat, selling its labor-power as wage-labor, working in an environment of alienation, receiving only part of its product, existing to facilitate capital's self-expansion. This, Marx affirmed, is the true substratum of capitalism, its bedrock.

The surface phenomena of capitalism, on the other hand, appear in forms that often distort and falsify the true relationships of this mode of production. Indeed, it was Marx's contention that capitalism, because of its perverted forms, maximizes illusion and mystification, that its essence is more heavily covered by layers of misleading superficial phenomena than that of any previous mode of production, including slavery and feudalism. The outward appearances of capitalism diverge fantastically from its inner laws, which are thereby largely hidden from view. Direct experience, within the capitalist mode, therefore, leads to illusions in the minds of those captivated by its surface data. These illusions can be dispelled only by scientific analysis of the capitalist mode, an analysis that is made possible by the rise of the industrial proletariat (and so of its ideologists) and serves the interest of that class. Thus, both the need for and the possibility of scientific analysis arise together as capitalism develops. Such insights into the workings of the system, however, are strongly resisted by the bourgeoisie and its apologists; furthermore, capitalism makes these insights extremely difficult to comprehend. This explains the continuing coexistence of illusions and their explanation.

In a pre-capitalist, rural patriarchal mode of production, social labor is revealed directly in the social products produced for the family. The work is divided according to age, sex, abilities, and other natural conditions. The different kinds of labor are direct social functions because they are functions of the family—spinning, weaving, growing food, gathering wood, and so forth. The articles produced are family products, not commodities seeking markets, and so they are directly social products. The social relations among the family members appear to them as mutual personal relations, because the labor of each is consciously applied as part of the combined labor of the family. The total products of these labors are social products to be used by the family in ways decided by the members.

Now consider a mode of production that breaks up such families into individual producers, each producing independently of the others, and each producing, not products for the family, but commodities for exchange—a mode that Marx termed "the most embryonic form of bourgeois production." This mode turns social relations between persons into material relations and material relations between things into social relations. In this mode, the social character of private labor, which was obvious and direct in the family situation, is now revealed only indirectly when private products are exchanged—that is, when equal values or labor-times are exchanged. Individual producers now appear to have no relations with one another, but only with their material commodities: "Individuals exist for one another only insofar as their commodities exist." Marx means that individuals, in this mode, make contact with one another only through the exchange of their commodities. For this reason, exchange value appears to be a relation between commodities—this commodity is worth so much of that commodity— but in fact it is a relation between people, between labor-times of workers. As Marx explained:

> A social relation of production appears as something exist-
> ing apart from individual human beings, and the distinctive
> relations into which they enter in the course of production in
> society appear as the specific properties of a thing—it is this
> perverted appearance, this prosaically real, and by no means
> imaginary, mystification that is characteristic of all social
> forms of labor positing exchange-value.

Thus, the social relations of individuals appear in the inverted form of a
social relation between things. This is an actual representation of this
mode of production, albeit a representation which distorts the true relation between human beings.

This distorted form is carried over to the fully-developed capitalist
mode of production. In addition to it, however, the capitalist mode
widens the gap further between its phenomenal appearances and its
essence. Labor and the means of production, for example, are forces
(factors) of production. But, in the capitalist mode, labor becomes wage-
labor, a commodity, a material thing; means of production become
capital, incarnated in the capitalist. Thus, living labor becomes a thing,
and capital, which is dead (embodied) labor, becomes alive in the
capitalist; an inversion of subject and object is accomplished.

The capitalist mode especially presents itself in ways that hide the
fact that surplus value comes from the exploitation of labor within the
sphere of production. Surplus value, in capitalism's fantastic forms,
appears to arise in the circulation sphere or from inherent powers of
capital in its various forms; its very existence is shielded by market expressions of the capitalist mode that misrepresent the real relations of
production.

If these distortions of fundamental bourgeois relations are not recognized as such, but are instead believed to be the true manifestations of
capitalism's inner laws, then illusions are created in the minds of those
deceived. Marx believed that the surface distortions of the bourgeois
mode are so forceful that most people are unable to discover capitalism's underlying mechanism and so remain confused. In fact, the capitalist mode, in its inverted phenomenal forms, generates false consciousness in both capitalists and workers. It produces both the actual
surface distortions and the mental illusions about what lies beneath the
surface. It is on the basis of these illusions that the mystification of
capitalism arises.

The acceptance, as the real thing, of the distortion that transfers
social relations from people to their products, leads to a series of illusions and fantasies. Commodities become fetishes in the same way that

gods, the creation of humans, take on lives of their own, fashioning social relations among themselves and with the human world. In the "religion of everyday life," objects are endowed with life, taking on the powers relinquished by their producers, who, as a consequence, diminish and deceive themselves; the objects come to rule over man. Since "the god among commodities" is gold-money, the possession of money becomes an insatiable desire, the greed of all. This social form of wealth is transformed, under capitalism, into the private power of private persons, who are able, through the power of money, to transform their own personal incapacities into their opposites. According to Marx, "Money is the supreme good, therefore its possessor is good. ... I am *stupid*, but money is the *real mind* of all things and how then should its possessor be stupid? Besides, he can buy talented people for himself, and is he who has power over the talented not more talented than the talented?" Money, Marx claimed, "is the common whore, the common pimp of people and nations."

The Illusions of Capitalism

If the faces of capitalism are distorted, they are powerful and convincing ones which give rise to numerous illusions about this mode of production. The perverted forms of the actual world produce conceptions in the minds of people that diverge drastically from the underlying realities.

The most important of these illusions concerns surplus value—its production, its transformation as profits among industrial capitalists via the price mechanism, its realization in the circulation sphere, and its distribution among industrial, commercial, financial, and landed capitalists.

The origin of surplus value is concealed in many ways. The wage-form, especially when workers are paid by the number of the item produced, extinguishes every trace of the division of the working day into necessary labor and surplus labor, and it therefore creates the illusion that all labor is paid labor. To add to this, wage-labor appears to be "free" labor, even though actually bound to the class of capitalists. This freedom to choose to work for any capitalist reinforces the illusion that labor is not being exploited, that the production sphere cannot be the source of surplus value. Further, industrial profits of enterprise appear to be wages of management, so that both workers and industrial capitalists appear to be rewarded for different kinds of labor, some menial and some managerial. Marx commented that this makes "the labor of exploiting and the exploited labor both appear identical as labor." He added: "Now, the wage-laborer, like the slave, must have a master who puts him to work and rules over him. And assuming the existence of this relationship of lordship and servitude, it is quite proper to compel the wage-laborer to produce his own wages and also the wages of supervision, as compensation for the labor of ruling and supervising him. . . ." The greater the antagonism between the producers and the owners, the greater the role of supervision. This reaches its peak in the slave system. This tenuous claim by "rulers and supervisors" to part of the surplus value is therefore a claim that arises from the antithesis between the laborers and the capitalists, one producing and the other owning the means of production; its antagonistic nature would vanish with the disappearance of classes. Therefore, while in one sense wages of managers are part of variable capital, not surplus value, Marx saw them as largely the latter because they reflected a class relation that would disappear in a "cooperative society of associated labor," Marx's phrase for a classless society.

The source of surplus value is further concealed when values are transformed into prices, thereby redistributing surplus value among the industrial capitalists, some of whom lose a portion of the surplus generated in their production sphere and others of whom gain some—in amounts which in competition equalize rates of profit on total capital. Thus, the average profit of any capital differs from the surplus value which that capital extracted from the laborers employed by it. This transformation process, Marx wrote, "completely conceals the true nature and origin of profit not only from the capitalist, who has a special interest in deceiving himself on this score, but also from the laborer . . . [it] serves to obscure the basis for determining value itself." Each capitalist is therefore under the illusion that his profit comes as much from prices and markets as from his own process of production, and the fact is obscured that all profits are due to the aggregate exploitation of labor by total social capital within the production sphere.

The realization of surplus value in the sphere of circulation creates the illusion that this is its source. Commodities, pregnant with surplus value, are exchanged for more money than the capitalist paid for the constant and variable capital to produce them, the difference being the surplus value itself. Such transactions produce the illusion that the mode of exchange is the dominant sphere and so the basis of the mode of production. The process of production, Marx stated, "appears merely as an unavoidable intermediate link, as a necessary evil for the sake of money-making." Money seems to be made in circulation, in buying commodities below their values and selling them above their values. Surplus value appears to originate from the acumen of capitalists, from their sharp business wits, from their abilities to cut costs, to outguess the market and beat the competition, and from their shrewdness in dealing with money, stocks and bonds, bills of exchange, and the other financial accouterments of capitalism. Marx believed that the entire process by which surplus value is produced is made especially incomprehensible in financial centers, such as London, where "the paper world" distorted everything.

Finally, the origin of surplus value is obscured by the glitter of illusions which emanate from each of its several elements. Interest, a part of surplus value, appears to arise from the inherent powers of money to increase itself, powers that are completely divorced from the production process. The illusion that money-capital has automatic self-expansion powers, occult properties, money generating money, Marx called "the mystification of capital in its most flagrant form." Interest is part of surplus value—unpaid, exploited labor—but it pretends to disavow this source in favor of the innate powers of a thing, of a thing come alive. Similarly, commercial profits appear clearly to come from clever buying and selling within the circulation sphere, and thus to be severed altogether from the productive activities of industrial capitalists. Also, rent seems to arise from the powers of the earth itself, not from social relations of production; from the land or from the presence of that personification of the land, the landlord. The landlord demands his share of the total product that land helped to create. "Just as products confront the producer as an independent force in capital and capitalists—who actually are but the personification of capital—so land becomes personified in the landlord and likewise gets on its hind legs to demand, as an independent force, its share of the product created with its help."

Land is productive but, while it adds to output, it does not "naturally" produce the social form called rent. Similarly, capital is productive but it does not "naturally" produce profit or interest. By the same reasoning, labor is productive but it does not "naturally" produce wages. Interest (profit), rent, and wages are all social forms of the class structure of society that have deep historical roots. They are all components of a total product created by work, and yet each seems to arise from a separate "thing": profit from capital goods, rent from land, and wages from labor. This illusion is played out fully when the capitalist, the owner of capital goods, claims the profit; the landlord, the owner of land, claims the rent; and the worker, the owner of labor-power, claims the wages. Each appears to receive what each is entitled to. Marx called this "the trinity formula," which is "the complete mystification of the capitalist mode of production. . . . It is an enchanted, perverted, topsy-turvy world, in which Monsieur le Capital and Madame la Terre do their ghost-walking as social characters and at the same time directly as mere things."

The Mystification of Capitalism

Marx's analysis that labor is exploited to provide surplus value to a class of capitalists bent on expanding capital was a danger to the ruling classes, especially after the industrial proletariat, responding to the development of capitalism's productive forces, began to gain consciousness of itself as a class. This growing challenge, consciously perceived, stimulated bourgeois theorists to fashion analyses of capitalism that would absolve it of sin. These analyses, Marx stated, were mystifications to the extent that they were based on the perverted surface forms thrown up by capitalism's underlying movements, with the effect of making it doubly difficult for others to understand what was actually going on within the bourgeois mode of production.

The task of the bourgeois theorists was to raise profits to the same moral plane as wages. This could be done if it could be shown that these returns were explainable by some type of real cost or sacrifice incurred by the capitalists or by some special productivity of the capital that they owned. Marx had little respect for these efforts which comprised what he called "vulgar economy." He wrote that vulgar economy "is no more than a didactic, more or less dogmatic, translation of everyday conceptions of the actual agents of production . . . which arranges them in a certain rational order . . . [to] correspond to the interests of the ruling classes. . . ." In another place, Marx pointed out that 'the vulgar economist does practically no more than translate the singular concepts of the capitalists, who are in the thrall of competition, into a seemingly more theoretical and generalized language, and attempt to substantiate the justice of those conceptions." The bourgeois economists who are engaged in this "dirty work for the knights of the moneybag" Marx called "pettifogging ideologists" and other names as well.

One theory in defense of profits is that they are the reward for abstinence—the abstention of the capitalist from present consumption in order to save. This sacrifice—this special pain of the capitalist—it is argued, must be rewarded if it is to be borne. Marx countered that there is no way to relate the abstinence of the capitalist to his profit. But, if there were such a relation, it would probably be an inverse one. As Maurice Dobb has explained: "He [Marx] had only to contrast the profit and the 'abstinence' of a Rothschild to feel that the so-called 'explanation' required no further refutation." The *ability* to save largely determines the volume of saving, which is therefore strongly related to relative affluence and only weakly related, if at all, to some "pain."

As both Dobb and English economist Joan Robinson have pointed out, the sacrifice associated with current saving by the wealthy is more truly a burden or "pain" of the poor whose very poverty allows such wealth, from which most of the saving comes, to continue to exist. If it is true that saving is increased by such an unequal distribution of income, "then it would seem," Dobb says, "that the final incidence of this cost of saving must lie, not upon the rich, but upon the restricted consumption of the poor, which alone permits those high incomes to be earned from which the bulk of the investment is drawn." It is not the abstinence and waiting of the rich that should be rewarded but rather the general deprivation of the poor. "To assert the contrary," Dobb concludes, "is, surely, to be guilty of the circular reasoning of assuming the income of the capitalist to be in some sense 'natural' or 'inevitable' in order to show that what he invests of this income is the unique product of his individual abstinence in refraining from doing what he likes with his own." Joan Robinson has added that, since what the capitalist likes is often a luxurious standard of living, an unequal income distribution is an unnecessarily wasteful way of accomplishing the saving.

Marx's main point about this theory, however, was that capitalists are a historically-determined class, which stands antagonistically against the proletariat, and which, in order to maintain itself as a class, *must* accumulate. Thus "abstinence from present consumption as a sacrifice" struck Marx as a most superficial depiction of a historical process that deeply involved class struggles and that largely determined the scope and direction of people's actions. Capitalists accumulated because they had to. Nevertheless, Marx declared, even at the superficial level, vulgar economists never seem to realize that every human action may be viewed as abstinence from its opposite. "Eating is abstinence from fasting, walking, abstinence from standing still, working, abstinence from idling, idling, abstinence from working." It is true that capitalists, despite the compulsion driving them on to further extensions of their capitals, do develop in their breasts "a Faustian conflict between the passion for accumulation and the desire for enjoyment." But this simply means that the abstention from either may be painful. Why not argue that capitalists deserve a reward for luxurious living, since they have such a passion for accumulation?

Marx also noted, in another connection, that original (primitive) accumulation was hardly a sacrifice for some capitalists in that it came from plunder and theft. The story of capital accumulation, said Marx, is written in blood and fire, and the sacrifices it involved were made by millions of poor and oppressed people the world over, assuredly not by the capitalist class. So whether one considers current accumulation, or the fiery background of these fortunes, it is vulgar to suppose that the capitalist class should be rewarded for such advantages.

Marx believed that interest payments to financial capitalists were simply a portion of the surplus value, a portion which was set by the market forces determining rates of interest. Since Marx, a theory has been developed purporting to explain interest, not in terms of labor exploitation, but in terms of the notion of "discounting the future"—that consumption now is worth more to people than an equal amount of consumption in the future. Therefore, since people feel this way, they must be rewarded for not consuming now, postponing it to the future. Joan Robinson has argued that such a notion is not based on direct observation, "but arises from the desire to represent owning wealth as a 'sacrifice.' " It is true that some people consider it a sacrifice not to consume now, but many others consider it a sacrifice *to* consume now—because they expect a lower income in the future, or their need for consuming power in the future is expected to be very large (as to finance the education of their children), or because they wish to leave an estate for their heirs. The rate of interest is positive, and thus financial capitalists receive interest returns, not because of a subjective rate of discount of the future, but because capitalists are in a position to exploit labor and thereby obtain surplus value—profit. When the rate of profit is expected to be positive, the rate of interest will be positive, because capitalists are willing to pay something for finance capital. Interest payments are based on exploitation, not on a myopic vision of the future.

Another theory in defense of profits is that labor that is aided by machinery can produce a larger total product than it could working without this aid. The difference in the two outputs should therefore be attributed to the productivity of capital. The owner of the capital, it is said, is rightly the recipient of these returns. This was later formulated more elegantly as the marginal productivity theory of capital. Marx's view was that capital goods make labor more productive, a relation that has nothing to do with the production of surplus value. Capitalists exploit both unproductive and productive labor. Joan Robinson has noted that, while capital goods are certainly productive, there is no justification for assigning their productivity to private owners; the bourgeois argument, as Dobb expressed it, "included the illicit link of imputing to the owner the 'productivity' of the things he owned. 'A social relation between men assumes the fantastic form of a relation between things'; and the behaviour of things is not only represented animistically as due to some innate property in them, but imputed to the influence of those individuals who exercise rights of ownership over them." Granted that capital goods are "productive," their private owners are not. It was labor that produced the capital goods, and current labor that uses its own past labor (embodied in the capital goods) to produce more goods. If capitalists actually work, Dobb implied, they can receive a wage like everyone else.

How Capitalism is Transcended

Marx worked out a theory as to how capitalism would be dialectically superseded by socialism. Lenin extended the theory to include the imperialist proclivities of monopoly capitalism and the revolts by colonial peoples against this imperialism. Lenin's extension will be briefly indicated here; a fuller discussion of it must await the next chapter.

Capitalist Crises

Marx did not develop anything approaching a complete theory of capitalist crises that would lead eventually to the overthrow of this mode of production. However, the following chart presents the principal elements of Marx's analysis and of Lenin's extension of it. The chart will serve as a guide to our discussion.

MARXIAN THEORY OF CAPITALIST CRISES

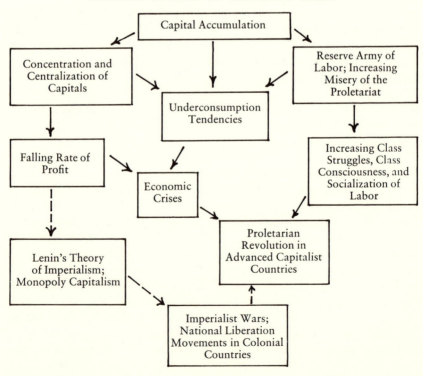

We have previously noted that Marx saw capitalist accumulation as producing the opposites of wealth and poverty, each dependent on the other for its existence: on the one hand, the concentration and centralization of capital in the hands of the bourgeoisie; on the other, the increasing misery of the proletariat. Marx reasoned that the accumulation process would tend to increase the demand for labor and thus to raise wages. This would induce capitalists to substitute constant for variable capital in the attempt to restore the previous level of surplus value. However, this increase in the organic composition of capital, even when accompanied by a rising rate of exploitation, would ordinarily lower the rate of profit. This, in turn, would compel capitalists to reduce the pace of accumulation, which would bring on a crisis, swell the ranks of the reserve army of labor, destroy some of the value of capital, and so tend to reestablish conditions for a later expansion of production.

At the other pole of capitalist accumulation, poverty and deprivation are created. The process of exploitation leaves purchasing power in the hands of the proletariat that enables it to purchase only an inadequate portion of the total products turned out. The large remainder of the output must be fashioned and purchased by capitalists as part of the accumulation process. There is a continual threat, therefore, of too heavy a burden being placed on capitalist accumulation, a "burden" that stems from the exploitation of labor. The underconsumptionist tendencies of the capitalist mode, therefore, refer not solely to the relative poverty of the proletariat but also to the resultant "burden" placed on capitalists to produce and purchase ever-increasing absolute amounts of products if the accumulation process is to continue. "Underconsumption" does not indicate that during phases of rapid accumulation and prosperity wages are depressed. Instead, we have already seen that the opposite occurs. But, while workers in these exhilaration phases are thus enabled to raise their consumption levels somewhat, it is never enough to lighten significantly the "burden" on the capitalist class, which is soon made intolerable by a falling rate of profit. Thus, accumulation slows down until the previously favorable conditions for capitalists have been restored; and this involves principally the destruction of capital values and the replenishment of the reserve army of labor. The former reduces the organic composition of capital (g), while the latter raises the rate of exploitation $(s' = s/v)$, both factors tending to increase the rate of profit $(p' = s'(1-g))$.

Marx contended that, in time, as a result of the above processes, the relations of production would become fetters on the further development of society's productive forces. "This will mark," as economist Paul

Karl Marx

Karl Marx was born May 5, 1818, in Trier, then in the Prussian province of the Rhine, now in West Germany. Probably because his father was a successful lawyer, Marx's initial interest at the University of Bonn (1835), and the next year at the University of Berlin, was in legal studies. But he soon switched his interest to philosophy, joining the group of Young Hegelians—who engaged in radical religious and social criticism—and later receiving the degree of Doctor of Philosophy in 1841 with a dissertation on Democritus and Epicurus.

In October 1842, Marx, after abandoning hopes for a career in university teaching, moved to Cologne to assume the editorship of a new liberal journal, the *Rheinische Zeitung*. This was suppressed by the Prussian government in early 1843. In the summer of that year, Marx married Jenny von Westphalen, his childhood sweetheart who lived next door to his family, and together they moved from the Rhineland to Paris, where Marx became co-editor of the *Franco-German Yearbook* (a device for evading the censorship, which did not apply to larger publications, even when they were issued in serial form). Marx immersed himself in workers' movements, in studying the French Revolution and utopian socialism, and in learning about political economy and capitalism—these last from Friedrich Engels. But Marx's writings eventually got him into trouble again, and he was banished from Paris by the French government, at the instigation of the Prussian government, in January 1845.

He, his wife, and their one-year-old daughter moved to Brussels in February 1845. There he and Engels again participated in workers' movements and continued their writing, which they had commenced in Paris. During these years, they produced, among other works, *The German Ideology* and the *Communist Manifesto*. The revolutions of 1848-49, which started in France and spread rapidly throughout Europe, led to Marx's expulsion from Belgium. He and his family left that country in March to return to Paris, where the new Provisional Government, which contained some socialists, welcomed them. But in April, Marx and Engels left for Cologne to participate in the German uprisings against the crown and the aristocracy, hoping that this bourgeois revolution would quickly be followed by a socialist one. The two friends co-edited a revolutionary newspaper, and Engels even took an active role in some of the fighting in 1849. Early in that year Marx and his associates were tried before a Cologne jury for "incitation to revolt." Marx defended his side before the court and all were acquitted. But, despite this, the government in May ordered the expulsion of Marx (he had previously given up his Prussian citizenship), and after a brief arrest he set off for Paris. The counterrevolution, however, had triumphed in Paris, as elsewhere, and so Marx was ordered to move to Brittany, which he chose not to do, leaving the country instead. This time he and his family made their way to London, arriving in that city in the late summer of 1849. He remained there or nearby until the end of his life in 1883.

Both Marx and Engels were convinced by 1850 that European capitalism was still in the ascendant, and that new uprisings at that time would be fruitless. Marx, therefore, resumed his economic studies, this time in the British Museum Library, and became a correspondent for the *New York Daily Tribune*. Many of these articles were written by Engels, who during the 1850s and 1860s lived in Manchester where he was employed in a training capacity by a textile mill in which his father had a substantial interest, and in which he was a partner from 1864 until his retirement from business in 1870. During these early years, the Marx family was impoverished, living at times on nothing but bread and potatoes, losing three young children, pawning the family silver and some of Marx's clothes, scrounging around for credit, and reduced at times to utter destitution. Engels, besides writing *Tribune* articles, directly aided Marx financially over this period and probably sacrificed his own talents to a great extent to Marx's cause. Marx's greatest economic works were written during the decade from about 1857 to 1867, including his three-volume classic *Capital*, though only the initial volume was published during his lifetime.

Just as Marx had associated himself with the Chartists (the British working-class movement of the first half of the 19th century) upon his arrival in London, so, in 1864, he took a leading role in helping to organize the International Working Men's Association—the First International. He served on its General Council, wrote the inaugural address, and guided its policies until its demise in 1876. In a brilliant work, *The Civil War in France*, Marx supported, described, and analyzed the short-lived Paris Commune of 1871, in which the workers of Paris established for the first time in the world a proletarian government. He continued during these years to take an active interest in the working-class movement in Germany, especially when two prominent factions came together in 1875 to form the German Social-Democratic party. Marx wrote a critique of its draft program (*Critique of the Gotha Program*), which contained some of his few utterances about the future society of socialism. In his last years, he was very much concerned with the possibility of revolution in Russia and in the East. He died 15 months after his wife and was buried in her plot in Highgate cemetery on the outskirts of London.

Marx's Likes and Dislikes*

Your favorite virtue: Simplicity
Your favorite virtue in man: Strength
Your favorite virtue in woman: Weakness
Your chief characteristic: Singleness of purpose
Your idea of happiness: To fight
Your idea of misery: Submission
The vice you excuse most: Gullibility
The vice you detest most: Servility
Your aversion: Martin Tupper
Favorite occupation: Bookworming
Favorite poet: Shakespeare, Aeschylus, Goethe
Favorite prose-writer: Diderot
Favorite hero: Spartacus, Kepler
Favorite heroine: Gretchen
Favorite flower: Daphne
Favorite color: Red
Favorite name: Laura, Jenny
Favorite dish: Fish
Favorite maxim: *Nihil humani a me alienum puto* (Nothing human is alien to me).
Favorite motto: *De omnibus dubitandum* (One must doubt of everything).

* From a manuscript by Marx's daughter Laura, in Erich Fromm, *Marx's Concept of Man* (Frederick Ungar, N.Y., 1965), p. 257.

Sweezy, editor of the socialist journal *Monthly Review*, has written, "the beginning of a revolutionary period during which the working class, at once oppressed and disciplined by its special position in society, will overturn the existing relations of production and establish in their stead higher, socialist, relations of production." The proletariat would be able to carry out this revolution because its prolonged class struggles would awaken it to its task and because the continued development of productive forces would socialize the production process while leaving its ownership in private hands. That is, socialization in the production sphere would increasingly come into conflict with the concentration of private ownership in the relations of production. This growing contradiction would be resolved by the proletarian revolution. The revolution, according to Marx, would occur in the most advanced capitalist countries because it is there that the industrial proletariat and capital centralization would be most developed.

Lenin, while clinging to this analysis for most of his life, nevertheless modified it in several ways, one of which is pictured in the chart. Monopoly capitalism in its highest, imperialist stage, Lenin thought, would be first breached at its weakest links, in the colonial areas. The superprofits of imperialist activity, according to Lenin, would buy off the top layers of labor in the advanced capitalist countries and so delay the revolution there. However, capitalist nations' own wars with each other plus successful national liberation movements on the periphery of international capitalism, Lenin believed, would gravely weaken the imperialist powers in their home bases. Eventually, the worldwide revolution against capitalism would sweep from capitalism's weak edges back to the industrial centers.

Post-Capitalist Society

Marx had much to say in general outline about the higher mode of production which he predicted would succeed capitalism, but he gave few details about how it would operate—for instance, about how the planning mechanism would be organized. He anticipated that society would go through a transition period, after the revolution and overthrow of capitalism, in which the state would take the form of the dictatorship of the proletariat, the means of production would be held in common, but many features of the old society—such as classes, the distribution of income to workers on the basis of their productive contributions, and social differences (mental vs. manual labor, town vs. country, etc.)—would persist for some time. Marx called this transition period "the lower phase of communism." Today this is often referred to as socialism, the higher stage being communism itself, when, with ample productive forces, classes and social differences, as well as the state as an oppressive force, vanish, and, as Marx put it, communism inscribes on its banner: "From each according to his ability, to each according to his needs."

Looking ahead to communism, Marx called post-capitalist society the "cooperative society" or the "associated mode of production," which would be one of freely-associated individuals working with means of production held in common and having a definite social plan; it would be "a society in which the full and free development of every individual forms the ruling principle." Earlier, in the *Communist Manifesto*, Marx and Engels had declared post-capitalist society to be "an association, in which the free development of each is the condition for the free development of all." These pronouncements mean that the ruling principle will no longer be profit making but rather fulfilling the needs of individuals, and such fulfillment for any individual will not demand denial to others, as it does in a class society. Individuals are so associated that either they fulfill their needs together or they do not fulfill them at all.

In the associated mode, the workers own the means of production and thus are not under the discipline of capitalists or their representatives. Rather, they work for their own account and pay their own managers. The antagonistic nature of the labor of supervision thus disappears. The length of the working day would also change, but which way depends on particular circumstances. On the one hand, it would no longer be necessary to produce surplus value for the capitalist class. But, on the other, "means of subsistence" would expand its meaning and a part of what is now surplus value would become necessary labor for accumulation to benefit the working class. Furthermore, the fact that society regulates general production makes it possible for workers to move occasionally from one task to another, thus reducing job specialization and boredom.

In the associated mode, producers do not exchange their products, just as members of a family do not engage in market exchanges, such as "making a bed" for a meal. Hence, "commodities" disappear, and so does labor as the value of these products. Instead, the associated workers determine the amount of time devoted to different products by the products' social utility, and these products are used by society in accordance with its social plan. And, according to Marx, if "commodities" do not exist, neither does money as a particular social form, as a social relation. What exists are products of a classless society and the means of distributing the products.

Marx believed that in post-capitalist society the "general costs of administration not belonging to production" would decline, while expenditures on schools, health services, and other worker welfare programs would rise. Moreover, for the first time, human relationships would be direct and not perverted by money and market relations. As Marx expressed this, there would be "the complete emancipation of all human senses and qualities." Power would not come from the possession of money, as in bourgeois society, but would instead emanate from specific expressions of an individual's life: love becomes potent "if through a living expression of yourself as a loving person" you make yourself a loved person. No longer will love be bought.

As a reminder that a still higher stage lay beyond the associated mode of production, Marx declared that this mode still represents "the realm of necessity," and beyond it lies "the true realm of freedom." Marx concluded:

> In fact, the realm of freedom actually begins only where labor which is determined by necessity and mundane considerations ceases; thus in the very nature of things it lies beyond the sphere of actual material production. Just as the savage must wrestle with Nature to satisfy his wants, to maintain and reproduce life, so must civilized man, and he must do so in all social formations and under all possible modes of production. With his development this realm of physical necessity expands as a result of his wants; but, at the same time, the forces of production which satisfy these wants also increase. Freedom in this field can only consist in socialized man, the associated producers, rationally regulating their interchange with Nature, bringing it under their common control, instead of being ruled by it as by the blind forces of Nature; and achieving this with the least expenditure of energy and under conditions most favorable to, and worthy of, their human nature. But it nonetheless still remains a realm of necessity. Beyond it begins that development of human energy which is an end in itself, the true realm of freedom, which, however, can blossom forth only with this realm of necessity as its basis. The shortening of the working-day is its basic prerequisite.

The principal aim of society, as Marx saw it, is the full development of human beings—the free unfolding of their human powers, the full realization of their potentials in all their dimensions, the achievement of the rational regulation of their natural and social environment, the overcoming of alienation. The aim is the emancipation of man, the development of a truly human person who *is* much, as contrasted to one who *has* much. This emphasis on human beings was expressed by Marx in many ways, including the following: "A critique of religion leads to the doctrine that the highest being for man is man himself, hence to the categorical imperative to overthrow all relationships in which man is humbled, enslaved, abandoned, despised." Or, as Engels saw man in the new society: "Man, at last the master of his own form of social organization, becomes at the same time the lord over nature, his own master—free." Marx looked forward to the day when each person would become "the fully developed individual, fit for a variety of labors, ready to face any change of production, and to whom the different social functions he performs are but so many modes of giving free scope to his own natural and acquired powers."

The denial of this free scope for human development under capitalist society, Marx asserted in a variety of ways, is one of its most damning failures. That was Marx's most penetrating critique of a society that he came, more and more, to despise.

Hail the Socialist Revolution by V.D. Kalensky

CHAPTER FOUR

LENIN AND THE REVOLUTION AGAINST CAPITALISM

IN HIS MAJOR ECONOMIC WRITINGS, Marx analyzed the capitalist mode of production, finding the source of surplus value in the exploitation of labor by the capitalist class at the point of production. His work was a thorough investigation of the economics of this mode of production. It was also a critique of capitalism that encompassed not only the material aspects of life but the psychological as well, a critique that contrasted the full potentialities of human beings with their stunted existence under capitalism.

Lenin mastered and accepted Marx's economics works, but he was not principally interested in devoting his life to an extension of these economic analyses. Although some of his work in these theoretical areas was highly original, Lenin's persistent concern was not with economic theory but rather with the development of a revolutionary movement that would overthrow Russian Tsarism and capitalism. Lenin felt that Marx had already proved the exploitative, oppressive, alienating properties of capitalism; the task was now to overthrow this system. For that purpose, both revolutionary theory and practice were needed.

In the final years of his life, after the Bolsheviks had come to power in 1917, Lenin was engrossed in building socialism in Russia. While he contributed many interesting ideas to this problem, he did not have much opportunity to develop them in practice, for his life was cut short at the age of 53, only a few years after the old regime had been swept away.

This chapter, then, presents Lenin more as a revolutionary and less as an economic theorist or economic planner.

Marx and Engels on Revolution

Marx and Engels were also absorbed with the theory and practice of revolution against capitalism, not simply with criticizing it. Indeed, it was Marx, as a young man, who wrote: "The philosophers have only *interpreted* the world, in various ways; the point, however, is to *change* it." These two critic-revolutionaries, however, believed that the proletarian revolution against capitalism had the best chance of occurring in the most advanced capitalist countries, where the proletariat had reached maturity. "No social order ever perishes," Marx declared, "before all the productive forces for which there is room in it have developed." Thus, at various times, Marx and Engels looked to France, England, the United States, and a few other industrial capitalist nations for the outbreak of revolution.

If nothing more were said, however, their full views on this matter would be distorted. First of all, as early as 1848 in the *Communist Manifesto*, Marx and Engels announced that the Communists were turning their attention chiefly to Germany, not to the more advanced capitalist countries of France and England. Germany, they said, was "on the eve of a bourgeois revolution . . . [that] will be but the prelude to an immediately following proletarian revolution." They based this expectation on the belief that Germany's proletariat was more developed than was England's in the 17th or France's in the 18th century, and so, unlike the latter two, would be able to carry through a double revolution.

In 1850 Marx elaborated on this view, stating that the German workers had a dual task: to support the bourgeoisie in its democratic struggles and to prepare for the socialist revolution. He suggested that the first stage of the German revolutions could lead to proletarian revolutions elsewhere, which would in turn support the completion of the revolutions in Germany. Thus, Marx and Engels indicated that proletarian revolutions in advanced capitalist countries, instead of being ignited from within, could be sparked by bourgeois revolutions in relatively backward, adjacent areas. These areas in turn could develop, in a continuous motion, into armed proletarian victories—if backed by the peasantry, Marx later added.

About a decade later, in a letter to Engels, Marx turned his attention to Russia, asserting that "the impulse for the European revolution can scarcely come from anywhere but Russia. In Russia the movement is advancing faster than in all the rest of Europe." Later, Engels voiced the same thought: "Russia is the France of the present century. To her belongs rightfully and lawfully the revolutionary initiative of a new social organization." Russia, in fact, occupied much of Marx's time during the last decade of his life. He mastered the language, studied its history, read its novelists and poets, conversed for long hours with its revolutionary émigrés, and immersed himself in its peasant and agricultural problems. "It would give me pleasure," Engels once wrote to him, "to burn up the Russian publications on the condition of agriculture, which for several years have kept you from finishing *Capital*."

During these years a group of Russian intellectuals, the Narodniks, was promoting the view that the Russian peasant commune (*mir*) was unique in its egalitarian and communal institutions and was the foundation on which socialism could be built, without Russia having to go through the stage of capitalism. In these communes, land was held in common but was periodically redistributed among the peasants for individual family cultivation. Marx noted this dualism of common ownership but divided petty cultivation—a collective element and a property element. The Narodniks believed that Russia's historical role was to lead the rest of the world into socialism. In 1875, Engels stated that the emancipation of serfs in 1861 had dealt a heavy blow at communal property in Russia, which was being broken up by the encroachment of bourgeois forms. However, Engels surmised that if proletarian revolutions quickly succeeded in the advanced capitalist countries of Western Europe, they would enable Russia to move directly to socialism by way of the transformation of the village communes into higher forms. A few years later, Marx elliptically backed Engels in a letter written (but never sent) to a Russian journal: "If Russia continues to pursue the path she has followed since 1861, she will lose the finest chance ever offered by history to a people and undergo all the fatal vicissitudes of the capitalist regime."

In 1882, Marx and Engels, in the preface of a new Russian translation of the *Communist Manifesto*, wrote: "If the Russian revolution serves as a signal for a workers' revolution in the west, so that the two complement each other, then contemporary Russian land tenure may be a starting point for communist development." A decade later, after Marx's death, Engels retreated from this position, declaring that the peasant communes had already been mostly dissolved by capitalist agriculture and that Russia was inescapably progressing through her capitalist phase. Engels renewed his and Marx's belief that socialism demanded large-scale agriculture, not divided petty-bourgeois cultivation.

Thus, Marx and Engels were drawn into Russian revolutionary questions, which necessarily engaged them in the problems of the Russian peasantry. They had looked upon the peasants in Western Europe as backward and reactionary — comprising a class left over from pre-capitalist societies that was destined to disappear during capitalist development. However, when Marx and Engels turned their attention to the East, it was immediately obvious that bourgeois revolutions were not likely to succeed without the active support of the peasantry, for the alliance of the bourgeoisie and the proletariat appeared to be too weak to prevail against strong absolutist and feudal forces. Consequently, they explored and rethought the revolutionary potential of the peasantry. But, while peasants eventually found a niche in Marx's and Engels' revolutionary outlook, it remained for Lenin to fashion for them a more influential revolutionary role.

Marxism and the Russian Revolutions

Marx's works began to appear in Russia in the 1870s. In the year Marx died (1883), the first Russian Marxist group, the Emancipation of Labor, was founded in Geneva by G.V. Plekhanov, a Russian who came to be widely regarded as the father of Marxism in his country. This group, for the next 15 years, attacked the theories of the Narodniks, arguing that capitalism was already fast making inroads on the communes, and that socialism would come to Russia not by a leap over capitalism but by the development of the capitalist mode in industry and agriculture, and as the achievement, not of the peasantry, but of the industrial proletariat.

In 1895 Lenin, after having visited Plekhanov in Switzerland, organized a new Marxist group in St. Petersburg, the League of Struggle for the Liberation of the Working Class, which was the first Russian organization to bring factory workers and socialism together. This led to Lenin's arrest in that year and to his Siberian exile. During Lenin's banishment, the First Congress of the Russian Social-Democratic Labor party was held in Minsk in 1898, attended by nine delegates. Although this was the formal beginning of a Marxist political party in Russia, most of the participants were immediately arrested by the police, and none played a leading role in the party after that.

When Lenin was released in early 1900, he again sought out Plekhanov in Geneva with the aim of starting a Marxist weekly (*The Spark*) and a journal (*The Dawn*) in order to set forth a party program and eventually to summon a new party congress. This Second Congress of the Russian Social-Democratic Labor party was held in London in the summer of 1903 (after the Tsar's spies chased it out of Brussels), and it was there that the famous split occurred between the Mensheviks (members of the minority) and the Bolsheviks (members of the majority), appellations based on a single series of votes at that Congress.

During these early years, Lenin not only battled the Narodniks, along the lines that Plekhanov had established, over their views on peasants and agrarian socialism, but he was also embroiled in a controversy with the so-called legal Marxists ("legal" to the Tsarist censorship), who believed that Russia would first have to go through the stage of capitalist development before socialism could be established. In Lenin's view, the legal Marxists concentrated so heavily on this first stage as to lose sight of and interest in the proletarian revolution itself. They were, Lenin charged, reformers and not revolutionaries.

Lenin had essentially the same view of the Economists, a group of Social-Democrats who advocated a sharp separation of economics from politics. The former, they argued, should be the province of workers, the latter the province of the liberal bourgeoisie. The workers should press for higher wages and better working conditions, and the liberal bourgeoisie should strive to carry out the bourgeois-democratic revolution. Lenin's heated response, which we shall turn to in a moment, is contained in his book *What Is To Be Done?*

Lenin also, at this time, began his long argument with the Mensheviks. He promulgated his views that revolutionary theory was needed for a revolutionary movement, and that such theory should be imparted to the working class by a tightly-knit party of professional revolutionaries—in effect, by a Communist party. This party, Lenin insisted, must be secretive, select, professional, centralized, and disciplined. The Mensheviks, who advocated a more open and democratic party, charged Lenin with proposing a dictatorship, not *of*, but *over* the proletariat—and also over the party itself.

Political commentator Isaac Deutscher, in his book *Stalin*, has clearly presented the basic differences between the two sides on this organizational issue:

> The Mensheviks saw the party as a rather broad, and therefore somewhat loose, organization which should strive to embrace the working class and the Socialist intelligentsia and in the end to become identical with them. That conception was based on the belief that socialism was so congenial to the proletariat that the whole proletariat could be looked upon as the potential Social-Democratic party. To Lenin's mind, this was naïve. He saw the working class as a vast heterogeneous mass, divided by differences of origin and outlook and split by

sectional interests. Not all sections of the proletariat could, in his view, achieve a high degree of Socialist enlightenment. Some were deeply sunk in ignorance and superstition. If the party tried to embrace the whole, even most, of the proletariat, it would become heterogeneous like the proletariat itself—it would embrace its weakness as well as its strength, its ignorance as well as its Socialist longing, its backwardness as well as its aspirations. It would become an inert image of the working class instead of being its inspirer, leader, and organizer.

An underlying issue in all of these early controversies was whether, to reach socialism, Russia had to go through a bourgeois-led revolution, which would remove the remnants of feudalism and overthrow Tsarism for the purpose of opening the way for the full development of capitalism and of its major classes—the bourgeoisie and the proletariat. The Narodniks said no, while the legal Marxists and Economists answered yes. As their views developed, the Mensheviks sided with the ideas of the latter two groups. Lenin's response was that all were wrong: the two revolutions, democratic and socialist, were necessary, but they would be linked together by the revolutionary proletariat assuming the dual task of leading the bourgeoisie to the completion of its revolution and then carrying through its own. These views had strong implications for party organization; hence, Lenin's debates with the Economists and the Mensheviks over this issue were grounded in fundamental differences about the theory of the Russian revolution.

E.H. Carr, the noted Cambridge historian, in his multi-volume work *A History of Soviet Russia*, has neatly identified the deeper theoretical basis of this organizational debate:

> The dispute between Bolsheviks and Mensheviks, though it appeared to turn on esoteric points of Marxist doctrine, raised issues fundamental to the history of the Russian revolution. The Mensheviks, clinging to the original Marxist sequence of bourgeois-democratic and proletarian-socialist revolutions, never really accepted Lenin's hypothesis, thrown out as early as 1898, of an indissoluble link between them. The bourgeois revolution had to come first; for it was only through the bourgeois revolution that capitalism could receive its full development in Russia, and, until that development occurred, the Russian proletariat could not become strong enough to initiate and carry out the socialist revolution. . . . Narrowing their horizon to the bourgeois revolution, the Mensheviks found difficulties in imparting to their political program

any socialist or proletarian appeal. . . . Wedded to the cut-and-dried thesis that Russia was on the eve of a bourgeois, but not of a socialist, revolution, the Mensheviks followed the legal Marxists in their emphasis on revolutionary theory and in their postponement of revolutionary action to some still remote future; they followed the Economists in preferring the economic concept of class to the political concept of party and believing that the only concrete aim that could be offered to the workers at the present stage was the improvement of their economic lot.

The Third Party Congress, an exclusively Bolshevik affair, was convened in London during April and May 1905, in the midst of revolutionary eruptions by Russian workers which had been kindled earlier that year by Russia's military defeat by the Japanese. The Bolsheviks, from afar, called for an armed insurrection by the proletariat against the autocracy and for "a democratic dictatorship of the proletariat and the peasantry," while the Mensheviks warned the party against seizing power itself, advising it instead to "remain the party of extreme revolutionary opposition."

The revolution of 1905 commenced with a massacre of striking workers by the Tsar's troops in front of the Winter Palace in St. Petersburg. The workers had marched to the Palace to present a petition to the Tsar; they were gathered there peacefully, unarmed, when the troops opened fire. Their petition asked for fair wages, civil liberties, a gradual transfer of land to the people, and other moderate reforms. According to Lenin, it began:

> We workers, inhabitants of St. Petersburg, have come to Thee. We are unfortunate, reviled slaves, weighed down by despotism and tyranny. Our patience exhausted, we ceased work and begged our masters to give us only that without which life is a torment. But this was refused; to the employers everything seemed unlawful. We are here, many thousands of us. Like the whole of the Russian people, we have no human rights whatever. Owing to the deeds of Thy officials we have become slaves.

And it ended:

> Sire, do not refuse aid to Thy people! Demolish the wall that separates Thee from Thy people. Order and promise that our requests will be granted, and Thou wilt make Russia

happy; if not, we are ready to die on this very spot. We have
only two roads: freedom and happiness, or the grave.

They got the grave.

The massacre set off waves of economic and political strikes that
swept over the cities of Russia. Many peasants were aroused by these
strikes to fight the landowning nobility and their other oppressors,
to burn and pillage. Mutinies broke out in the armed forces. The intensity of the revolution reached its peak in late 1905, the climax coming
in the December uprising of workers in Moscow, which was quickly
but bloodily suppressed. That October the Tsar had introduced reform
measures in an attempt to quell the rebellion, including a Parliament
based on limited suffrage and limited powers. These measures helped
draw support to his side. Although revolutionary ferment continued
during 1906 and 1907, the back of any concerted effort had been
broken in the defeat of the Moscow workers.

Twelve years later in a lecture on this revolution Lenin noted that its
peculiarity lay in the fact that it was a bourgeois-democratic revolution
in its social content (its demands), but a proletarian revolution in its
methods of struggle (economic and political mass strikes). He attributed
its failure partly to the inability of the scattered, isolated Russian peasantry to organize itself into a strong revolutionary force, partly to the
fact that the broad masses "were still too naïve, their mood was too
passive, too good-natured, too Christian."

It is pertinent to note, however, that, except for Trotsky, not one of
the important émigré leaders, Bolshevik or Menshevik, took an active
role in this revolution. Lenin himself did not leave Switzerland for
Russia until almost ten months after the Winter Palace massacre, and
by that time there was little that he could do. Trotsky alone was on the
firing line almost from the beginning.

The revolution was in full retreat when the Fourth Party Congress
assembled in Stockholm in April 1906. The meeting was called to sanction a merger that had been worked out a short time before between
the Bolsheviks and the Mensheviks. As it turned out, the resolutions of
the Congress largely reflected Menshevik views regarding their clear
distinction between the democratic and socialist revolutions. At the next
Congress, in London in May 1907, Lenin was a determined, relentless
fighter for his own program. The Bolsheviks were able, after bitter
controversies with the Mensheviks and with Trotsky (who stood apart
from both factions, in "beautiful uselessness" according to Lenin),
to carry most of the decisions and resolutions. But these verbal tugs-of-
war themselves did seem beautifully useless in the presence of the

reality of counterrevolution in Russia. The Tsar's troops had triumphed, the working classes were silent, Tsarist reforms disappeared one by one, and repression again bore down on Russia.

A few signs of the revival of revolutionary fires became visible in 1910, and a few years later workers once again were striking in many sections of the country. The beginning of the World War in 1914 saw Russia as a belligerent on the side of France and Britain, but by the winter of 1916, after several severe military defeats at the hands of the Germans, she was badly weakened. Poland very early had been lost to the Germans, and with it went much of Russia's industrial output. The entire transportation system, especially the rail network, was falling apart; nearly one-fifth of the locomotives were out of action by the end of 1916. Millions of peasants were called into military service—a mobilization of manpower that was intensified to compensate for grave shortages of military equipment—and the peasants also entered war industries in droves. This depletion of labor in the rural areas, along with the destruction of cropland from the fighting and hoarding of food in parts of the countryside, soon resulted in growing food shortages elsewhere. Hardship and hunger multiplied, strikes spread across the land, riots broke out everywhere, and finally in early 1917 the Tsarist government fell.

The new Provisional Government, made up predominantly of the liberal bourgeoisie, instituted a series of reforms, which Lenin, then in Zurich, denigrated as nothing but empty promises. Lenin managed to return to Petrograd in April, and he immediately called on the workers to unite against the Provisional Government. He announced that the present situation represented the transition from the bourgeois revolution to the socialist revolution; the second revolution was coming. The Bolsheviks, he urged, must support and gain leadership of the workers' and peasants' Soviets (Councils) and prepare for the proletarian revolution.

Soviets—"people's parliaments"—had sprung up everywhere, in factories, in workshops, in soldiers' barracks, in cities and towns and villages. Having initially appeared in the revolution of 1905, they were the representative, grass-roots assemblies of the people, and as such they were a potent political power alongside the Provisional Government. Although the Soviets were dominated by the Mensheviks and others, and not by the Bolsheviks, it was nevertheless the Bolsheviks who shortly raised the cry "All power to the Soviets." This slogan was later withdrawn when the Provisional Government captured leadership of the Soviets.

Bolshevik strength in Petrograd grew rapidly during the summer months. In July, however, hundreds of thousands of demonstrators in Petrograd urged the seizure of power by the Soviet leaders from the Provisional Government. Lenin did not believe that power could be held by the Bolsheviks for very long at that time, so, compelled by circumstances to lead the demonstrators, Lenin's Bolshevik party guided their ardor into nonviolent but revolutionary channels. Nevertheless, troops opened fire on the workers and soldiers and there were desperate clashes. The turmoil and bloodshed of those July days were shortly turned against the Bolsheviks, some of whom were arrested, their printing presses smashed. Lenin was forced to go into hiding, and he remained underground until the month of the revolution. Despite this setback, by October the Bolsheviks had gathered so much support in the capital, and the Provisional Government had become so isolated, that Lenin's charges had only to step in to claim power, for little opposition remained.

Lenin's Theories of the Russian Revolution

Marx's dialectical conception of the role of individuals in history had degenerated, by the time Lenin was a youth, to a mechanical explanation of the inexorable forward march of History (with a capital *H*). This interpretation reduced human beings to passivism and engendered in them a fatalism that sapped their strength. Lenin's contribution was to return to Marx's own dialectical approach and thus to revive practice or productive activity as the means by which individuals not only change the world but also come to know it and, in the process, change themselves. Lenin restored will, action, and initiative into a Marxism that had gained a machine but had lost its soul. But this "voluntarism" in Lenin was, at times, carried beyond Marx, with exaggerated emphasis on the first part of Marx's dictum, to the relative neglect of the second: Men make their own history, but not exactly as they please. Although, at other times, Lenin shifted almost the entire weight to the other side of the equation, his controlling disposition was to stress the active, initiating side. It was people who made revolutions, not History.

In *What Is To Be Done?* (1902), Lenin argued that workers, if left to themselves, develop only trade-union consciousness, whereas socialist consciousness is formed by intellectuals. The task was to bridge the gap by means of a revolutionary party that would reach out from the intellectuals to the workers, and by so doing raise the political consciousness of the workers to the level of the intellectuals.

Lenin described trade-union consciousness as an awareness by workers of the necessity to fight an employer for better wages and working conditions, but an unawareness of how these individual actions fitted

Long Live the Third Communist International!, anonymous

into the whole. On the other hand, socialist or political consciousness was rational knowledge of how the system as a whole works, the interests of workers as a class, and the revolutionary means to achieve those interests. Lenin called for a small, secretive revolutionary party of dedicated professionals who could impart this political consciousness to the workers through political education. Our task, he said, "is to combat spontaneity, to divert the working-class movement from this spontaneous, trade-unionist striving to come under the wing of the bourgeoisie, and to bring it under the wing of revolutionary Social-Democracy."

Thus, Lenin was the first to declare, not simply that radical intellectuals and workers live in separate worlds, but that the two worlds could be merged, with the aid of a vanguard party, into a revolutionary entity. This was his answer to the Economists' challenge that workers' economic interests could be satisfied by economic (trade-union) struggles and that, in this process, they would eventually gain socialist consciousness. No, Lenin said, "the fundamental economic interests of the proletariat can be satisfied only by a political revolution that will replace the dictatorship of the bourgeoisie by the dictatorship of the proletariat." And for that, the workers require political education which can be imparted only by professional revolutionaries.

In a work written in the heat of the 1905 revolution, *Two Tactics of Social-Democracy in the Democratic Revolution*, Lenin conceived of a Russian revolution in two stages: first, a bourgeois-democratic revolution, and, then, a socialist revolution. The book's title, therefore, refers to the tactics of the Bolsheviks, on one side, and the tactics of other Marxists, on the other side, in the first stage of this series of two revolutions.

The bourgeois revolution would sweep away remnants of serfdom, including autocracy and monarchy. It would establish bourgeois democracy and freedom, and at the same time clear the path for the full development of capitalism. These steps not only express the interests of the bourgeoisie, Lenin said, but also those of the proletariat, for they were all advances toward socialism. Capitalist development, Lenin thought, is inevitable in Russia, but it is being retarded and distorted by the old social relations of production—by Tsarist despotism. "In countries like Russia, the working class suffers not so much from capitalism as from the insufficient development of capitalism."

The bourgeois revolution cannot be carried through resolutely by the big bourgeoisie (owners of large means of production) and landlords, because they are "caught between two fires"—the autocracy and the proletariat. They will fight only up to a point for the democratic revolution. "We know that owing to their class position they are incapable of waging a decisive struggle against Tsarism; they are too heavily fettered by private property, by capital and land to enter into a decisive struggle. They stand in too great need of Tsarism, with its bureaucratic, police, and military forces for use against the proletariat and peasantry, to want it to be destroyed."

Lenin believed that the bourgeois revolution could be decisively led only by the proletariat, who would ally itself with the peasants, with some help from other classes. After the decisive victory over Tsarism, there would be established the "revolutionary-democratic dictatorship of the proletariat and peasantry" which would be a class, not a personal, dictatorship. It could not be a dictatorship of the "inconsistent" and "self-seeking" bourgeoisie, for that class would eventually come to terms with Tsarism and turn on the proletariat; once it faced the dangers of the proletariat, the bourgeoisie would prefer to negotiate with Tsarism rather than to crush it. "The bourgeoisie, in the mass, will inevitably turn towards counterrevolution, towards the autocracy, against the revolution, and against the people, as soon as its narrow, selfish interests are met. . . ."

The democratic revolution, Lenin asserted, if led properly by the proletariat, "may bring about a radical redistribution of landed property in favor of the peasantry, establish consistent and full democracy, including the formation of a republic, eradicate all the oppressive features of Asiatic bondage, not only in rural but also in factory life, lay the foundation for a thorough improvement in the conditions of the workers and for a rise in their standard of living, and—last but not least—carry the revolutionary conflagration into Europe." Therefore, it was Lenin's hope that the bourgeois revolution in Russia would intensify the revolutionary energy of the world proletariat and so quicken the socialist revolutions. Russia could provide the spark to ignite the revolutionary tinderbox of Europe.

About this initial revolutionary stage Lenin succinctly stated: "The proletariat must carry the democratic revolution to completion, allying to itself the mass of the peasantry in order to crush the autocracy's resistance by force and paralyze the bourgeoisie's instability." Thus, it would be the workers and peasants together against Tsarism, supported up to a point, but only up to a point, by the bourgeoisie—all in a struggle for bourgeois-democracy.

The second revolution would be the socialist one. It would be carried through by the proletariat in alliance with "the mass of the semi-proletarian elements of the population"—including rural workers and poor landless peasants. The peasantry, at this stage, especially the richer ele-

ment, would be unstable and incapable of resolutely supporting socialism, for they would have achieved their petty-bourgeois aims of private
ownership of land. The bourgeoisie, having already turned against the
proletariat, would now resist determinedly. "The proletariat must accomplish the socialist revolution," Lenin declared, "allying to itself the
mass of the semi-proletarian elements of the population, so as to crush
the bourgeoisie's resistance by force and paralyze the instability of the
peasantry and the petty bourgeoisie." So the proletariat would end up,
almost by itself, as the ruling class after the socialist revolution.

The tactics of Lenin's opponents grew out of the belief that the bourgeois revolution had to be played out fully and that the socialist revolution was quite a separate thing and lay some distance into the future.
Alfred Meyer, in his book *Leninism,* has described these views as
follows:

> The next revolution which has to be fought in Russia is the
> bourgeois revolution; the principal force that will fight it is
> the bourgeoisie. The bourgeoisie will fight it more enthusi-
> astically if it is not at the same time troubled by forces further
> to the left. For this reason, the proletariat should refrain from
> disturbing the bourgeoisie in its fight against autocracy. . . .

Lenin's retort was that the bourgeoisie was too frightened to carry out
its own revolution against an autocracy that it needed for protection
against the proletariat. But even if the bourgeoisie did manage to lead
the way to victory, Lenin thought, the workers would be in no position
at that point to prepare to carry out their own socialist revolution.
They would have been engaged in nothing but trade-union issues,
and so could not have developed the socialist consciousness necessary
for their assumption of power.

Immediately after the February 1917 revolution which toppled the
Tsar, Lenin wrote that it was not surprising that the revolutionary
crisis should have broken out first in Russia, "where the disorganization
was most appalling and the proletariat most revolutionary." He thought
that the Russian proletariat was highly revolutionary because of its vivid
experiences in the revolution of 1905 and in the counterrevolution of
1907-14. The February revolution (1917) was a result, he said, of a
unique historical situation. He called the newly formed Provisional
Government a lackey of French and British imperialism, a government
that "*cannot* give the people *either peace, bread, or freedom.*" It was
a government, he charged, that was already negotiating with the Tsar
for the restoration of the monarchy. The proletariat, allied with the
semi-proletarian elements and with the world proletariat, must achieve

a truly democratic republic and a complete victory of the peasants over the landlords—neither yet achieved—*then* press on to socialism.

Upon returning to Russia in April 1917, Lenin propounded what have since been known as his April Theses. In these, he declared that the bourgeois-democratic revolution that had just taken place must be developed into the proletarian-socialist revolution, and he proposed a Republic of Soviets as the political form of the dictatorship of the proletariat.

The first stage of the revolution, he said, put power into the hands of the bourgeoisie, "owing to the insufficient class-consciousness and organization of the proletariat." The second stage must place power in the hands of the proletariat and the poorest sections of the peasantry. No support should be given to the Provisional Government, or to its pleas to continue the war for the defense of the country. The entire state power should be transferred to the Soviets. Abolish the police, the regular army, and the bureaucracy; arm the whole people and establish a state like that of the Paris Commune. All landed estates must be confiscated; banks should be amalgamated into a single national bank. The immediate task is not to introduce socialism, but rather to bring production and distribution under the control of the Soviets. The bourgeois-democratic revolution, Lenin indicated, must be thoroughly completed by the proletariat before moving on into the proletarian-socialist stage.

Lenin warned his followers that it was necessary to educate those who were fooled by the empty phrases and false promises of the bourgeoisie, that this persuasion must be carried to workers, soldiers, everyone. "The crisis," he cautioned, "cannot be overcome by violence practiced by individuals against individuals, by the local action of small groups of armed people. . . . Today's task is to explain more precisely, more clearly, more widely the proletariat's policy. . . ." But, he later added: "We are for civil war, but only for civil war waged by a politically conscious class." By August, Lenin had given up whatever hope he had had for a peaceful assumption of power by the Bolsheviks. In September, he wrote that only the urban working class can lead the people to victory, "provided all state power passes into its hands and provided it is supported by the peasant poor." Lenin was now breathing and living insurrection. Victory for the Bolsheviks, in fact, came easily about a month later, when on the morning of October 25 their forces occupied the key points in Petrograd, and members of the Provisional Government either fled or were made prisoners. That afternoon Lenin announced the victory of "the workers' and peasants' revolution." It was almost bloodless.

Immediately afterward, Lenin saw the October revolution as "only the beginning of the world socialist revolution." He believed that socialism could be achieved in Russia only if the European proletariat carried out its own socialist revolutions. Russia was not entering socialism, he thought, but only the transition period to socialism. However, even this could not be completed without the aid of the international proletariat. In early 1918, in his report to the Third All-Russia Congress of Soviets, Lenin stated: "The final victory of socialism in a single country is of course impossible"; it requires the international socialist revolution. He went on: "Things have turned out differently from what Marx and Engels expected and we, the Russian working and exploited classes, have the honor of being the vanguard of the international socialist revolution; we can now see clearly how far the development of the revolution will go. The Russian began it—the German, the Frenchman and the Englishman will finish it, and socialism will be victorious."

Lenin, a few months later, still obsessed with the same thought, stated that the Bolsheviks carried out their revolution only because they believed it would be followed by revolutionary movements in other countries. "Regarded from the world-historical point of view, there would doubtlessly be no hope of the ultimate victory of our revolution if it were to remain alone." Lenin believed that the difficulties faced by the Bolsheviks could be cleared up if there were an all-Europe revolution. "Without a German revolution," he said more pointedly, "we are doomed."

In March 1918, he doubted that the revolution in Europe would come quickly. The revolution was easy in Russia—"as easy as lifting a feather"—because the workers had not been bribed by the superprofits of imperialism, and most of the people were indifferent to what was happening elsewhere. But revolution in Europe would be much more difficult, Lenin observed, because there many of the workers have been bought off with reforms, and there are powerful organizations poised against the working classes.

As Lenin's expectations for European proletarian revolutions evaporated, he turned his attention to the East. India, China, and other Asian countries, he said, had been jolted out of the rut by the imperialist war, and their development is proceeding along European capitalist lines. The European countries are not consummating their revolutions as we expected, he admitted, not directly but rather indirectly through the exploitation of other countries, which draws them into the world revolutionary movement. Revolution will occur in these outer reaches of the world capitalist system and will then spread back to Europe. "In the last analysis, the outcome of the struggle will be determined by the fact that Russia, India, China, etc., account for the overwhelming majority of the population of the globe." These pronouncements, we shall now observe, emerged from Lenin's theory of capitalist imperialism.

The Theory of Imperialism

Lenin admitted that colonial policy and imperialism existed before capitalism. Rome, after all, was an imperial power, and there have been others down through the ages. But different modes of production generate imperialism in different ways. Lenin was not interested in imperialism in general, in the abstract, but rather in imperialistic activities during the latest stage of capitalist development.

The briefest definition of this type of imperialism, Lenin explained, is "the monopoly stage of capitalism." Imperialism is not a *policy*, Lenin insisted, but rather a *stage* of development. He added that imperialism is the epoch of finance capital as well as of monopolies, and that such capitalism strives everywhere for domination, not for freedom. When capitalism was in its competitive stage, Lenin asserted, in which many small firms competed vigorously with one another, imperialism and domination were weak forces within an economic environment of competition and expanding freedoms for trade and expression. However, when competitive firms were transformed into giant monopolies, capitalism entered its stage of decaying freedoms. Imperialism, in this stage, became the spread of capitalism, by any means foul or fair, to all corners of the earth in search of superprofits.

Lenin pointed to several basic features of capitalist imperialism. First, he wrote, industrial competition has turned into monopoly, the change having come in the last decade or two of the 19th century. Production has become so large-scale that the work processes are now in effect socialized, in sharp contrast to the continued private ownership of the means of production. Thus, he claimed, monopoly capitalism is a transition stage to socialism. Capitalist crises are intensified in monopoly capitalism because monopoly in one sector of the economy comes into conflict with competition in other sectors and so increases the anarchistic tendencies of the system—that is, the disparity is increased between the advanced and backward sectors of the economy. At the same time, growing crises foster concentration and monopoly. Thus, crises and monopoly feed on each other.

Second, Lenin observed, financial (bank) competition has also turned into monopoly. He assembled data to show that in Western Europe only a few huge banks in each country dominate financial business. Further, increasingly close links have developed between monopoly finance and monopoly industry. More and more, the banks are providing capital to industry, and so they are coming to control this sector. In fact, Lenin asserted, imperialism is really the domination of finance capital over all other forms of capital, which can partly be seen in the extremely rapid growth of securities and debts in these economies. Industry no longer relies so heavily on obtaining funds through the stock exchanges but has increasingly borrowed from the banks and other financial institutions. Finance capital, according to Lenin, is characterized by the separation of owners of capital from managers, money capital from industrial capital, and rentiers from entrepreneurs and managers. Finance capital, in other words, breeds coupon clippers, financial manipulators, and managers of industrial processes appointed by the increasingly parasitic capital-owning class. Swindles, speculation, and fraud, Lenin charged, abound in this stage of decaying capitalism.

Third, Lenin argued that the export of capital had become more important than the export of goods and services from the advanced capitalist countries. Monopoly capital generates enormous surpluses of capital, and it concentrates these surpluses in fewer hands. It becomes more and more difficult to invest these surpluses domestically at prevailing profit rates. Therefore, rising portions of the capital seek overseas opportunities that promise higher returns. Monopoly capital not only has the profit incentive to penetrate one area after another throughout the world, but it also has the means to do this in the forms of huge capital, power, and knowledge of conditions abroad. Thus, monopoly capital was seen by Lenin as imperial capital seeking fortunes abroad where labor is cheap, raw materials amply available, natural resources invitingly abundant, and markets potentially large. Monopoly capital advances its power beyond national boundaries to the globe's farthest reaches.

The fourth feature of imperialism noted by Lenin is that the industrial-financial monopolies divide up the world economically. The monopolies of one nation, either by themselves or combined with those of other nations in super-monopolies, try to obtain exclusive rights to markets and raw materials in designated areas of the world, free from the competition of other foreign monopolies. Lenin explained that imperialism is the age of international cartels:

> Monopolist capitalist combines—cartels, syndicates, trusts —divide among themselves, first of all, the whole internal market of a country, and impose their control, more or less completely, upon the industry of that country. But under cap-

italism the home market is inevitably bound up with the foreign market. Capitalism long ago created a world market. As the export of capital increased, and as the foreign and colonial relations and the "spheres of influence" of the big monopolist combines expanded, things "naturally" gravitated towards an international agreement among these combines, and towards the formation of international cartels. . . . The capitalists divide the world, not out of any particular malice, but because the degree of concentration which has been reached forces them to adopt this method in order to get profits.

A fifth feature cited by Lenin, complementary to the previous one, is that the imperialist governments divide the world *politically* to protect and guarantee the success of their enterprises' economic penetration. Thus, capitalist countries establish colonies, gaining political control of an area that is required for the protection of their corporations' profit-making ventures. Lenin saw the connection between the economic and political divisions of the world in this way:

The principal feature of modern capitalism is the domination of monopolist combines of the big capitalists. These monopolies are most firmly established when *all* the sources of raw materials are controlled by the one group. And we have seen with what zeal the international capitalist combines exert every effort to make it impossible for their rivals to compete with them; for example, by buying up mineral lands, oil fields, etc. Colonial possession alone gives complete guarantee of success to the monopolies against all the risks of the struggle with competitors, including the risk that the latter will defend themselves by means of a law establishing a state monopoly. The more capitalism is developed, the more the need for raw materials is felt, the more bitter competition becomes, and the more feverishly the hunt for raw materials proceeds throughout the whole world, the more desperate becomes the struggle for the acquisition of colonies.

This political division of the world, Lenin announced in 1917, is now complete. Henceforth, there can be only redivision, and this will necessarily occur by force. In fact, Lenin pointed out, the World War is nothing but an attempt by capitalist latecomers (notably Germany) to grab territory from the older powers. The uneven development of capitalism around the world, nation by nation, insures imperialist wars, once the world has been divided, between the rising and the declining capitalist states, for the young can expand only at the expense of the already-established imperialists.

Lenin emphasized that there are several motives that compel monopoly capital to expand into every available space. As already noted, monopoly capital generates huge clusters of capital, all of which cannot be invested profitably at home, for such concentrated investment would tend to produce oversupplies of commodities and overdemands for labor, both of which would threaten monopoly profits. Further, monopoly capital must continually control its raw materials, not only those already known to exist but potential sources as well. Lenin noted: ". . . finance capital in general strives to seize the largest possible amount of land of all kinds in all places, and by every means, taking into account potential sources of raw materials and fearing to be left behind in the fierce struggle for the last remnants of independent territory, or for the repartition of those territories that have been already divided." These territories, even though of uncertain future worth to monopoly capital, would nevertheless protect the claimant against the future possibilities of the area furnishing unusually rich and cheap supplies of raw materials to competitors. Moreover, Lenin stated, the export of capital has become the means of encouraging the export of commodities, especially military weapons. The imperialist powers fight for colonies partly because they provide potential markets for their own exports. Finally, Lenin believed that one driving force behind imperialism was the attempt by these countries to relieve domestic tensions, unemployment, and other social maladies at home. While Lenin did not place great weight on this factor, he did accept its validity and demonstrated it with a journalist's interview of Cecil Rhodes, the British politician and initiator of the Boer War of 1899-1902, in which Rhodes stated:

> I was in the East End of London yesterday and attended a meeting of the unemployed. I listened to the wild speeches, which were just a cry for "bread! bread!" and on my way home I pondered over the scene and I became more than ever convinced of the importance of imperialism. . . . My cherished idea is a solution for the social problem, i.e., in order to save the 40,000,000 inhabitants of the United Kingdom from a bloody civil war, we colonial statesmen must acquire new lands to settle the surplus population, to provide new markets for the goods produced in the factories and mines. The Empire, as I have always said, is a bread and butter question. If you want to avoid civil war, you must become imperialists.

Lenin pointed to a final feature of imperialism: it reduces the revolutionary fervor of workers in the imperialist countries. The top strata of the working class, including many labor leaders, are bribed with the superprofits that the capitalists extract from colonial areas. Moreover, workers are caught up in the intensification of nationalism during the age of imperialism. The frequent clashes arising among imperialist powers engender nationalist ardor in workers, which weakens their dedication to revolutionary causes and to the international brotherhood of all working classes. Imperialism, by establishing colonies, is also able to split the working class at home by importing cheap colonial labor to oppose local labor. Super-exploitation of foreign labor, at home and abroad, demands justification which is found in racist ideology that intensifies the fragmentation of labor and augments conflicts among various segments of the working class. Imperialism, Lenin summarized, increases opportunism at home.

Lenin concluded that, because of imperialism's super-exploitation of the poor in colonial areas and its oppressive control over colonial peoples generally, the beginning of the world revolution against capitalism would occur first in these impoverished areas, on the periphery of the international capitalist system, at its weakest links. These revolutions would initially take the form of national revolutionary movements, in which broad masses of the population would participate. After that, these movements might develop their own momentum, according to specific circumstances, into higher forms leading *directly* to socialism, provided that, in the initial phases of the revolution, the proletarian movement had maintained its vigor and kept the initiative in its own hands. As Lenin later expressed this point more fully: "If the victorious revolutionary proletariat conducts systematic propaganda among [the backward nations], and the Soviet governments come to their aid with all the means at their disposal—in that event it will be mistaken to assume that the backward peoples must inevitably go through the capitalist stage of development."

The imperialist powers themselves, situated in the heart of global capitalism, would gradually be weakened by their efforts, increasingly more demanding and increasingly more futile, to halt these national liberation movements. They would be further debilitated by the decline of their superprofits, as costs and risks associated with overseas exploitation rose. Imperialist wars would add the finishing blows to an already reeling system. The long-term decline in monopoly capital's profit rates from these hostile forces would drive the capitalist classes to extract further surplus value from their own laborers in order to make up for what was lost abroad. Oppressive measures, therefore, would be directed by capital at the workers in its attempt to crush workers' resistance to accepting the major burden of the nation's diminution of economic and political power. In desperation, democracy would be scrapped and a type of fascism imposed on the nation. "But this development," as Alfred Meyer put it, in his book *Leninism*, "would mean a renewal of the revolutionary spirit among the working classes of the Western industrial nations, and thus the inevitability of socialism would be reestablished." Thus, the proletarian revolutions in the advanced capitalist countries would occur only after the grip of monopoly capital had been loosened by the revolutionary poor in the colonies.

Lenin's Economic Policies

During Lenin's few remaining years after the October revolution, he helped to initiate and carry out three sets of economic policies: some initial measures designed to consolidate power in the hands of the working classes (October 1917 to June 1918); the policies of War Communism (June 1918 to February 1921); and the New Economic Policy (March 1921 to Lenin's death [1924] and beyond).

Initial Policies

Lenin analyzed the October revolution as the completion of the bourgeois-democratic revolution in which power had been transferred from the bourgeoisie to the proletariat and the peasantry. Socialism was not on the current agenda, but rather the immediate task was to establish a controlled, directed capitalism—a state capitalism—and to consolidate the power of the working class. "The proletariat . . . should not think of improving its position at the moment, but should think of becoming the ruling class."

Lenin's initial preoccupation was to establish conditions that would make it impossible for the bourgeoisie to regain power. Economically, he said, this called for the confiscation of landed estates, the introduction of limited workers' control in factories, the nationalization of banks and some factories, the organization of the whole population in consumers' societies, and a state monopoly in the trading of necessities. In short, Lenin proposed to satisfy the immediate land demands of the peasants, to transfer power to the workers and their managers, and to gain control generally over the production and distribution of goods and services, especially over grain, fuel, and a few other essential items.

Accordingly, the day after gaining power, the Bolsheviks issued a land decree which abolished all private ownership of land without compensation to former owners, placed it in the hands of local Soviets and land committees, prohibited hired labor and the buying and selling of land, and established an egalitarian use of the land. Lenin reluctantly accepted these small units of cultivation with the resulting postponement of the Bolsheviks' program of large-scale, collectivized cultivation by agricultural workers and technical experts. Socialism in the countryside was for the future.

However, in May 1918, the Bolsheviks, responding to severe food shortages in the cities, began a drive against the richer peasants in an attempt to split them from the rural poor and to ferret out speculators and hoarders of grain. Workers from towns and factories were dispatched to the countryside to lead the newly organized committees of poor peasants against the rural bourgeoisie. Lenin saw these actions not only as solutions to an immediate problem, famine, but also as a long step toward socialism. "It was when the peasantry split," E.H. Carr wrote of Lenin's perspective, "and the poor peasants, linked with the industrial workers and led by them, took the offensive against the petty bourgeois *kulaks* that the socialist revolution in the countryside could be said to have begun."

On other fronts, the Soviet state quickly took over. There was some nationalization during the first few months. In mid-1918, the sugar and oil industries were nationalized, and state monopolies were established over all foreign trade and over domestic trade in such products as coffee and yarn. Some mining, manufacturing, and armament firms were nationalized during these months. In addition, government control bodies were created to oversee and guide the activities of private industries. Protective labor legislation was passed.

While the Bolsheviks favored moving slowly on nationalization—and in fact nationalized only when unusual circumstances compelled them to—many of the workers themselves, following syndicalist lines, took over "their" firms during 1917-18, and most of these were nationalized on the initiative of local organizations. These syndicalist actions, as seen by Maurice Dobb, were predicated on "the notion that factories should be run directly by the workers in them, and for the benefit of those workers." The Bolsheviks opposed syndicalism on the ground that it was antithetical to a national planning system run in the interest of the entire proletariat. The Bolsheviks favored a system in which individual managers, after consultations with workers and representing the workers, would have final responsibility for factory decisions and would report to higher economic bodies. Lenin also promoted the Taylor system (as he presumably understood it) of scientific management through time-and-motion studies, workers' payments on the basis of their productivity, and generous salaries to technicians and specialists, many of whom had bourgeois leanings. However, the essence of the Taylor system (founded by Frederick W. Taylor near the end of the 19th century), which was famous in the United States and probably inadequately analyzed by Lenin, was to complete the subjection of labor to capital by stripping the worker of whatever control over the work process he might still possess, under the name of "scientific management."

During the first half of 1918, Lenin's program was to try to institute the strictest accounting and control of production and distribution. He urged the party and workers to suspend the war on capital. We have expropriated enough, Lenin said, and it is now time to organize what we have. He further insisted that the productivity of labor be raised on a national scale, to be accomplished by (1) the imposition of tight labor discipline, an "iron rule," by (2) raising the educational and cultural standards of the working classes, and by (3) the introduction of scientific management. Lenin explained that labor discipline in older class societies was enforced by oppression and starvation, and that it must be reestablished in Soviet society on a new, comradely basis within the context of strict accounting and control.

Lenin theorized that in Russia the march to socialism would have to take place through a state-controlled capitalism, and that this march would be disrupted repeatedly by petty-bourgeois forces. The basic problem, he claimed, was that there existed in Russia at that moment five elements of the mode of production, a complication that did not exist in the advanced capitalist countries but which was prevalent throughout the underdeveloped areas because imperialism had imposed its social relations there on top of pre-capitalist ones. Russia not only had these multiple social relations but also a socialist one in that state power was in the hands of the workers. Thus, there existed in Russia:

(1) patriarchical production: rural family production for own use;
(2) small commodity production: rural production for sale on a small scale;
(3) private capitalism: private ownership of the means of production and the production of commodities;
(4) state capitalism: state-controlled enterprise in private hands; and
(5) socialism: state power in the hands of workers.

Lenin reasoned that the petty-bourgeois element, contained in (2), predominated and in fact pervaded every pore of society. Out of this petty-bourgeois capitalism sprang not only these small owners and traders themselves but also their criminal counterparts—profiteers, hoarders, embezzlers, swindlers, bribe-takers, and the like. All of these types, Lenin believed, combined with the larger capitalists in a war against both state capitalism and socialism. To begin with, Lenin announced, state capitalism must be established on a firm footing in order to crush the opposition. The current problem was not one of capitalism against socialism but rather that of a progressive state capitalism, of large, efficient units, at war with the millions of small, self-seeking, individual bourgeois operators throughout the society. Politically, Lenin pointed out, once state power was held by the working class there would be to that extent socialism. But, economically, a country infested with petty-bourgeois capitalism could not be transformed overnight into socialist forms. The path to full socialism must lead through state capitalism.

This strategy, however, was abandoned in the summer of 1918 when civil war, supported by foreign intervention, broke out. For the next two and a half years, the Bolsheviks plunged into an ever-widening net of compulsory measures, nationalization decrees, and direct controls that swept them far afield from the transitional road mapped out in the early months of their rule.

War Communism

War Communism was ushered in not only by the outbreak of civil war but also by (1) widespread syndicalist movements, which forced the Bolsheviks into the extension of nationalization, by (2) growing criticisms by the "left" about the slowness with which the Bolsheviks were moving toward socialism, and by (3) hyperinflation, which as time went on made it necessary for the Bolsheviks to replace monetary transactions with barter. A characteristic feature of the policies of War Communism was that they quickly moved the economy toward what many Bolsheviks believed to be true communism—common ownership of the means of production, the elimination of "commodities," markets, and money, payment to workers according to need rather than work done, work incentives based on revolutionary enthusiasm, the growth of egalitarian standards in all facets of life, and the extension of planning to all sectors of the economy.

The core of War Communism was the direct compulsory requisitioning of agricultural surpluses from the peasants and the centrally-organized distribution of these surpluses by the government to the cities, army, and industry. In poor exchange, the peasants received grossly inadequate supplies of manufactured goods. This was the government's policy response to the growing danger of famine in non-rural areas,

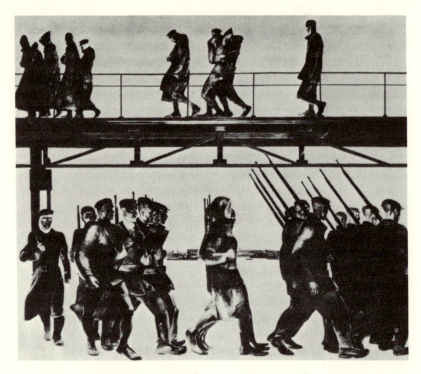

The Defense of Petrograd by Alexandr Deineka

especially in Petrograd and Moscow, and to the necessity of feeding an increasing number of army troops. All production above essential needs was taken by coercion from the peasants, and they responded by hiding whatever surpluses they had and, over the longer run, by producing less. The effect of this, Dobb explained, "was to rupture that alliance between the industrial working class and the peasantry upon which the Soviet Revolution had been based."

Settlements between government bodies were increasingly made without the use of money. Workers were more and more paid in kind, and they received a growing list of necessities as free supplies. Private trade was abolished and put into government hands. Centralized planning and control developed rapidly from the fertile soil of fixed prices, rationing, compulsory deliveries, labor allocation, and nationalization of all industries. As a result of the hyperinflation, money as a means of exchange was almost eliminated, and barter transactions spread everywhere. The Soviet economist E.A. Preobrazhensky welcomed this disappearance of money as a sign that Soviet society was entering into communism, its entry facilitated by the printing presses that poured forth tons of paper money. "Honor to our printing presses," he exulted.

None of the above policies worked well, and they all tended to break down over time. Peasants cheated the requisitioners, black markets were prevalent, large areas of the economy could not be controlled or even observed, excess demands and supplies were not brought together, labor absenteeism grew and strikes spread, and peasant dissatisfaction deepened. Nevertheless, the policies of War Communism got some of the basic jobs done—those most directly associated with winning the civil war and turning back all foreign invaders.

Later, after these policies had been scrapped, Lenin stated that "it was the war and the ruin that forced us into War Communism." And he added: "It was not, and could not be, a policy that corresponded to the economic tasks of the proletariat. It was a makeshift." A few months later, he suggested that War Communism was a mistake, that the country could not in fact reach communism without going through the preparatory stages of state capitalism and socialism. "We expected . . . to be able to organize the state production and the state distribution of products on communist lines. . . . Experience has proved that we were wrong." It was not possible, he concluded, to leap from petty-bourgeois capitalism, over state capitalism and socialism, into the arms of communism.

The New Economic Policy

The end of the civil war saw the breakdown of central controls, outbreaks of unrest in urban and rural areas, widespread banditry by discharged soldiers, and an increase in violence. According to E.H. Carr:

> The economic consequences of war communism, whose bankruptcy was revealed by these events, formed a vicious circle offering no defined starting-point for analysis. A catastrophic decline in industrial production, due in part to the destruction of plant, in part to the disorganization of labor, in part to the cumbrous system of centralized administration . . . had been followed by a virtual breakdown of state or state-controlled distribution of commodities at fixed prices, leading to a rapid growth of illicit private trade at runaway prices and a wild currency inflation; and this in turn had prompted the refusal of the peasant, in the face of a goods famine and a worthless currency, to deliver necessary supplies of grain to the towns, so that population was progressively drained away from the industrial centers, and industrial production brought still nearer to a standstill.

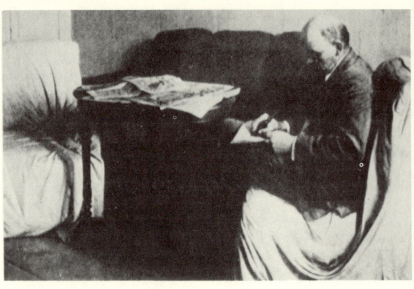

Lenin at the Smolny Institute by Isaac Brodsky

Lenin

Vladimir Ilyich Ulyanov, later known by his pen name of Lenin, was born on April 22, 1870, 13 years before Marx's death and a quarter century before Engels'. He never met either. During these years he was geographically far removed from them, for Simbirsk, his birthplace and home for his first 17 years, lies on the Volga river over 350 miles southeast of Moscow. When Lenin was 17, his older brother, a Marxist, was hanged for plotting the assassination of Tsar Alexander III. The next year Lenin began to study law and Marxian literature. Without having attended a university for longer than a few months (he was expelled for participating in a mild student demonstration against the dismissal of liberal professors and similar actions of the Minister of Education), he passed the law examination in 1892. At about the same time that he became an assistant to a St. Petersburg attorney, he also became a revolutionary.

Lenin's initial writings in the mid-1890s attacked the Russian Narodniks, who believed that Russia could skip capitalism through the socialist development of the village *mir* (commune), a subject that had greatly interested Marx during the last years of his life. At this time, Lenin began a long study to prove that Russian capitalism was in fact developing rapidly and that Russia was following the path of Western Europe, not the path to agrarian socialism. Lenin was jailed in late 1895 for revolutionary activities and a year later was exiled to Siberia for three years, where he married Nadezhda Krupskaya, whom he had met in St. Petersburg and who was now in exile too. Lenin's exile ended in early 1900 and shortly thereafter he traveled to European centers for the purpose of contacting and involving himself with Russian revolutionary exiles and their activities. For five years he moved about Europe's capitals; helped to launch various revolutionary newspapers and a magazine that were smuggled into Russia; wrote an important work, *What Is To Be Done?*, which called for a professional, vanguard party to lead the workers to socialism; and organized the Bolshevik wing of the Social Democratic party to do exactly that.

The impoverishment and oppression of Russian workers and peasants combined with Russia's military defeats by Japan to spark revolutionary uprisings in St. Petersburg, Moscow, and other Russian cities and villages early in 1905, and these uprisings drew Lenin back to Russia later in the year. During this period, Lenin formulated a theory of the stages of the Russian revolution, which included roles for the bourgeoisie, the proletariat, and the peasantry. This is discussed in his work, *Two Tactics of Social-Democracy in the Democratic Revolution*. The revolts were quelled by the government, and in late 1907 Lenin settled in Switzerland, not returning to Russia until April 1917. He spent these years in Geneva, Paris, Cracow, and back to Switzerland, watching, waiting, writing, and organizing—much of this surrounded by boredom. Notable among his writings at this time was *Imperialism: The Highest Stage of Capitalism*. Shortly thereafter, he completed *The State and Revolution*, which sets forth the role of the state under capitalism, socialism, and communism.

Russia's agony in World War I led finally, as in 1905, to revolutionary uprisings in February 1917. The Tsar abdicated in the following month, and a Provisional Government was established. Lenin left Zurich in April for Petrograd (so renamed in 1915 from St. Petersburg), and on arrival there immediately announced his program. He believed that Russia was going through a transition from the February bourgeois revolution to the coming proletarian one led by the Bolsheviks. The new government would be based on the Soviets of workers and peasants, which would nationalize land and banks and create model agricultural settlements. Socialism would not be immediately introduced but the production and distribution of social goods would be controlled.

The Winter Palace, the Provisional Government, and Petrograd fell to the Bolsheviks in October 1917. Lenin became the President of the Soviet of People's Commissars, and within a few months he pulled Russia out of the war, hoping by so doing to save the revolution in Russia and so to encourage the workers in Europe to carry out revolutions against their own bourgeoisie. Lenin believed that the Russian revolution would spark proletarian revolutions in the West which would then serve to support and protect the Russian socialist state. For the next two years and more, Lenin battled against the counterrevolutionary White armies, which were aided by the British, French, Japanese, Americans, and others. When this foreign-supported civil war was won by the Bolsheviks, and after Poland had turned back the Red Army at Warsaw and had herself met defeat in the Crimea, Lenin turned his full attention to long-term economic development of the country. He abandoned the tight economic controls and compulsory measures imposed from 1918 to 1921 and introduced the New Economic Policy, in which private ownership and initiative, open markets, and profit making were allowed in agriculture, small industry, and trade—a form of state capitalism.

During December 1921, Lenin became seriously ill and was unable to work for several weeks. Between May 1922 and March 1923 he suffered three strokes, the second removing him from effective leadership of the government, and the third from public life. During his final months, he proposed making scores of workers and peasants members of the Central Committee, warned the party about Stalin's coarseness, intolerance, capriciousness, and rudeness, recommended that more power be given to the State Planning Commission (as Trotsky desired), decried Great Russian chauvinism against minority peoples, deplored the low cultural level of the people, and called for a cultural revolution. He lingered on for ten months after his third stroke, dying on January 21, 1924, at the age of 53.

Lenin's solution was the New Economic Policy (NEP), which began in March 1921 with the abolition of grain requisitioning and its replacement by a tax in kind. This tax, which had been briefly tried in October 1918, was set as a given percentage of production above subsistence, meaning that the more the peasants produced, the more in absolute amounts they could retain. The surpluses left to the peasants could then be exchanged by them on markets for manufactured goods. Thus, markets were revived and money transactions restored. Retail trading was opened wide to individual profit making (wholesale trading less so), and petty-bourgeois capitalism was allowed to flourish once again in the agricultural and trade sectors. In the industrial sectors, there was some denationalization in 1921, though not much. Large and important industries remained in government hands. However, the NEP introduced a new decentralized system for industrial firms, in which many were given complete commercial and financial independence. At the same time, monetary and banking reforms were carried out to finance the increasing amount of private trading under way.

Inasmuch as markets once more served as links between agriculture and industry, between town and country, the alliance between the proletariat and the peasantry was being reestablished. Lenin called this alliance fundamental if socialism was to be attained. "Our party," he wrote, "rests upon two classes, and for that reason its instability is possible, and if there cannot exist an agreement between those classes its fall is inevitable." An agreement could be reached, he said, on the basis of free exchange—unrestricted trade between the two classes—a turning back to capitalism. We frustrated and even prevented such exchanges, Lenin confessed, especially local exchanges. "In this respect, we are very much to blame for having gone too far; we overdid the nationalization of industry and trade, clamping down on local exchange of commodities. Was that a mistake? It certainly was." Our new policy, Lenin declared, will give rise to many new kulaks and all sorts of petty-bourgeois activities. But if this is not done it will be impossible, "in view of the delay in the world revolution, to preserve the rule of the proletariat in Russia."

Our program, Lenin explained, should be to retreat to petty-bourgeois capitalism, channel it into state capitalism, and finally transform state capitalism into socialism. Concessions to foreign capitalists are the simplest way to implant state capitalism in Russia. Cooperatives are also capable of becoming elements of state capitalism, and there are other possibilities as well. Since the state is proletarian, Lenin said, the state capitalism that we shall develop will not be a bourgeois capitalism but a workers' capitalism. It will be a state capitalism *under communism*.

Lenin also, at this time, outlined a long-run economic policy that would build up the productive forces in the agricultural sector. The only way to eliminate the rural petty-bourgeoisie, he predicted, "is through the material basis, technical equipment, the extensive use of tractors and other farm machinery and electrification on a mass scale." In fact, Lenin became infatuated with the possibilities of rural electrification, to the extent that he equated socialism itself with Soviet power plus electrification—which was his shorthand expression for socialist relations of production plus huge gains in the productive forces of society.

Lenin's Last Thoughts

Lenin became ill during December 1921 and was ordered by his doctors to stop work for several weeks. He suffered his first stroke in May 1922, the second in that December. During much of 1922 he worked in spurts with long periods of rest in between. His third stroke in the following March left him without speech, incapacitated, until his death in January 1924. It was during the last months of his active life that Lenin hurriedly expressed his deepest concerns in a few speeches and articles and in a journal that he dictated for several days after his second stroke. While he covered a great variety of subjects, we shall limit ourselves to his thoughts about the building of socialism in the U.S.S.R.

In these communications, Lenin was clearly worried about the appropriateness and the possible efficacy of the NEP. Although it was obviously required to end the stagnation and prevent the possible collapse of Bolshevik power, it would inevitably strengthen bourgeois elements throughout the countryside and thus increase the danger of splitting the peasants from the urban proletariat. If this alliance were ruptured, Lenin warned, Bolshevik rule would be finished.

> [I]n the final analysis the fate of our Republic will depend on whether the peasant masses will stand by the working class, loyal to their alliance, or whether they will permit the "Nepmen," i.e., the new bourgeoisie, to drive a wedge between them and the working class. The more clearly we see this alternative, the more clearly all our workers and peasants understand it, the greater are the chances that we shall avoid a split, which would be fatal for the Soviet Republic.

To reduce the chances of a split and to accelerate generally the march toward socialism, Lenin proposed that the cultural level of the population, especially that of the peasantry, be raised. The people, he said, were largely illiterate and ignorant, had little desire for learning, and were bureaucratic, extravagant, uneducated. A cultural revolution was urgently needed—not to achieve proletarian culture, for that would be too ambitious, but only to attain the bourgeois culture of Western Europe. That would indeed be a great advance, he declared. "For a start, we should be glad to dispense with the cruder types of pre-bourgeois culture, i.e., bureaucratic culture or serf culture, etc." To accomplish this, Lenin recommended an improvement in the system of education and the upgrading of school teachers. In addition, the education of peasants could be furthered by setting up cooperatives throughout the countryside, so that every peasant could participate in the building of socialism. Urbanites and factory workers, Lenin said, should establish contacts with the peasants so as to raise the latter's cultural level—not their communism (that must wait) but their culture. He recognized that higher culture depended on improvements in the material base. Hence, the two efforts had to be combined.

At the other, upper end of society, the burgeoning, inept, bourgeois bureaucracy worried Lenin. The many foolish things done by the Bolsheviks, he charged, were partly the fault of "our machinery of state," which often operates against us.

> In 1917, after we seized power, the government officials sabotaged us. This frightened us very much and we pleaded: "Please come back." They all came back, but that was our misfortune. We now have a vast army of government employees, but lack sufficiently educated forces to exercise real control over them. In practice it often happens that here at the top, where we exercise political power, the machine functions somehow; but down below government employees have arbitrary control and they often exercise it in such a way as to counteract our measures.

In the last article that he wrote, Lenin returned to this theme, urging the party to strive for the utmost degree of economy and to remove all traces of extravagance in the state structure, "of which so much has been left over from Tsarist Russia, from its bureaucratic capitalist state machine."

Lenin was preoccupied for much of this period with "foreign concessions"—that is, obtaining, on Soviet Russia's terms, foreign capital for its heavy industrialization program. In early 1923, he pointed out that "the practical purpose of our New Economic Policy was to lease out concessions." In fact, such concessions were a large element in Lenin's definition of state capitalism, but they failed to materialize. It may be that the foreign concessions were a substitute, in Lenin's mind, for European proletarian revolutions. The failure of the latter to take place would therefore not mean the failure of Russia to obtain foreign capital.

But another substitute for proletarian revolutions in the West were anti-imperialist revolutions in the East, which would weaken the co-lonial powers and perhaps ultimately spark internal proletarian revolu-tions against them. The imperialist World War, Lenin thought, had jolted China, India, and other Asian countries out of their ruts and put them on the track of capitalist development. Thus, they have been drawn "into the general maelstrom of the world revolutionary move-ment." The final outcome of the world struggle "will be determined by the fact that Russia, India, China, etc., account for the overwhelming majority of the population of the globe."

Lenin expressed confidence in the ultimate ability of Russia to attain socialism. It is true, he said, that our productive forces are weak; and there is no doubt that the capitalist powers, during the civil war, hin-dered our progress toward socialism. "They failed to overthrow the new system created by the revolution, but they did prevent it . . . [from de-veloping] the productive forces with enormous speed . . . [that] would have produced socialism." However, he asserted, socialism does not have to wait on the full development of the productive forces. We can, in a revolutionary way, first create the social and cultural prerequisites for socialism and then "proceed to overtake the other nations."

Thus, Lenin argued that the social relations of production and parts of the superstructure could be revolutionized, transformed the socialist way, before the productive forces were fully developed. We shall observe, in the next two chapters, how Stalin and Mao Tse-tung, each in his own way, responded to that summons.

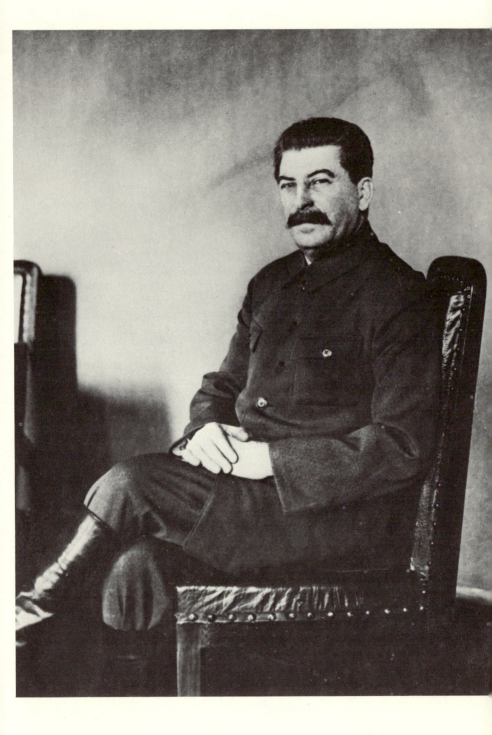

CHAPTER FIVE

STALIN AND THE DRIVE FOR SOVIET POWER

IN HIS DYING MONTHS, Lenin tried to alert the party about the dangers of permitting Stalin to occupy a commanding position. "Comrade Stalin," Lenin wrote in a series of letters to the party Congress, which were later considered his last testament, ". . . has unlimited authority concentrated in his hands, and I am not sure whether he will always be capable of using that authority with sufficient caution. . . . Stalin is too rude and this defect, although quite tolerable in our midst . . . becomes intolerable in a Secretary-General. That is why I suggest that the comrades think about a way of removing Stalin from that post and appointing another man in his stead who in all other respects differs from Comrade Stalin in having only one advantage, namely that of being more tolerant, more loyal, more polite and more considerate to the comrades, less capricious, etc." But this counsel came too late, for, more than a year before Lenin's death, Stalin had, almost silently, gathered much of the political power in his own hands. By 1929, he had all of it.

Indeed, even earlier, he was secure enough to speak openly about Lenin's "will." "It is said," Stalin boldly reminded the Central Committee and other notables, "that in that 'will' Comrade Lenin suggested to the congress that in view of Stalin's 'rudeness' it should consider the question of putting another comrade in Stalin's place as General Secretary. That is quite true. Yes, comrades, I am rude to those who grossly and perfidiously wreck and split the Party. I have never concealed this and do not conceal it now. . . . It is characteristic that there is not a word, not a hint in the 'will' about Stalin having made mistakes. It refers only to Stalin's rudeness. But rudeness is not and cannot be counted as a defect in Stalin's *political* line or position." The members gave him prolonged applause for this speech.

The events that propelled Stalin toward these heights can be briefly related. (See also the biographical sketch of Stalin on pages 125-26.) In 1912, Lenin appointed Stalin to the Central Committee of the party, launching him on a course that ultimately led to the top of the revolutionary movement. He became temporarily one of the leaders of the party after the February 1917 overthrow of the Tsar, until Lenin's return in April from Zurich. A day after the Bolsheviks' revolutionary triumph, Lenin appointed Stalin as Commissar for Nationalities, a post that gave him some control over almost half of the population—the ethnic minorities. In 1919, Stalin was appointed to the Political Bureau and to the Organizational Bureau, the highest bodies of the party. In the same year, he became Commissar of the Workers' and Peasants' Inspectorate, which was charged with scrutinizing every branch of government with the aim of improving efficiency, reducing bureaucracy and corruption, and transforming the old state into a new socialist one. This position gave him general supervision over government administration and an opportunity to build up his personal authority within both the state and the party machines. In 1922, a few months before Lenin had his first stroke, Stalin's appointment to the new office of Secretary-General of the Central Committee opened the way for him to control the daily affairs of the party.

Thus, when Lenin issued his warning in December 1922, it was probably already too late to dislodge this artful administrator. Nevertheless, throughout the remainder of the 1920s, many attempts were made from inside the party to unseat Stalin. All were unsuccessful. As it turned out, at the time of Lenin's death, Stalin was to have thirty more years of life, and a quarter of a century as personal dictator of his vast realm.

The New Economic Policy after Lenin

The New Economic Policy (NEP), introduced by the party in March 1921 at Lenin's instigation, persisted through Lenin's death and the political turmoil that followed, until Stalin abruptly halted its course in 1929. The NEP, as we saw in the previous chapter, meant a return to private agriculture, private retail (and, to a much lesser extent, wholesale) trade, and small-scale private manufacturing, along with the continuation of publicly-owned large-scale industrial, banking, transportation, and foreign-trade enterprises. It was thus a mixed economic system of private and public (nationalized) undertakings, though the latter represented the crucial industrial and financial areas of the economy. These nationalized industries were divided into two groups: those centralized under the state budget and those decentralized and placed on a commercial basis. Firms in the second group were allowed to federate into trusts, to give them the advantages of larger size and to make them easier to oversee. Throughout the economy, markets were increasingly utilized to allocate resources.

Economy Recovery under the NEP

National output had dropped sharply after 1913: industrial production declined by the early 1920s to only a fifth of its prewar level, and agricultural production fell to two-thirds of its previous standard. The end of the civil war and the introduction of the NEP permitted recovery to occur, so that by 1928, production indexes generally were somewhat higher than their prewar levels. These and other data are in Table 1.

Table 1. *Production Indexes, U.S.S.R.: 1913 to 1928*

Year	Production Indexes (1913 = 100)		
	Industry	Agriculture	Transportation
1913[a]	100	100	100
1920	20	64	22
1928	102	118	106

[a] The 1913 figures refer to interwar territory of the U.S.S.R.

Source: G.W. Nutter, "The Soviet Economy: Retrospect and Prospect," in David Abshire and Richard V. Allen, *National Security: Political, Military, and Economic Strategies in the Decade Ahead* (New York: Praeger, 1963), p. 165.

The economic recovery of the 1920s was based mostly on the re-utilization of pre-revolutionary capacity and only secondarily on new investment. However, with the former source of growth largely depleted by 1926, the burden for further expansion shifted over to capital formation. Thus, as the party leaders saw the situation at the time, if growth was to continue, a higher rate of saving and investment would be required, and, in addition, if industry was to expand, rising agricultural surpluses would be needed to feed the growing industrial cities and to purchase capital goods from abroad.

The Bolsheviks' land reform of 1917, however, had resulted in many small, inefficient private holdings of land, with the consequence that technical progress, gains in agricultural productivity, and the accumulation of marketable surpluses were retarded. Total agricultural output responded sluggishly to the demands placed on it, and, at the same time, large portions of the harvests were consumed on the family farms, leaving insufficient amounts for the domestic and foreign markets. Moreover, to upset most of the party leaders even more, a relatively well-to-do peasant class (the *kulaks*) flourished throughout this decade, worsening inequalities of income and wealth distribution and implanting a rural bourgeoisie that threatened the socialist aims of the party.

The Great Debate

During the second half of the 1920s, a spirited debate took place among the top leaders about the future course of the economy. In late 1925, the party supported the principle of industrialization for the coming years, and it overwhelmingly resolved "that the Soviet Union be converted from a country which imports machines to a country which produces machines. ..." This, however, implied a stepped-up industrial investment program, which in turn required additional saving. Since foreign credits are generally unavailable, the burden would have to be thrown on domestic sources of saving. In real terms, this meant that some economic resources, including labor, would have to be diverted from production of consumer goods and re-employed in investment activities. Also, much unemployment during these years could be absorbed, thereby alleviating the reallocation problem. But which class or group would be compelled to reduce its consumption, and how could this be achieved?

During the debate, left-wing and right-wing positions developed, the former calling for important and radical changes in current policies (that is, in the NEP) and the latter either defending these policies or proposing only mild reforms. The left was identified with internationalism, the right with isolationism and nationalism. Between these extremes a center position was formed, which Stalin and his entourage occupied and utilized to good advantage.

The leading economic theorist of the left was Evgenii Preobrazhensky, who advocated rapid industrialization—a big push—financed by "primitive socialist accumulation," a concept first used with effect in 1922 by Trotsky. By this phrase, Preobrazhensky meant that since, in a backward economy, socialist industry could not generate nearly enough saving to finance its own rapid growth, the bulk of saving had to come from the private sector, from the "internal colonies," so to speak, of the socialist sector. And in Russia, the finger pointed to agriculture and the peasants. Thus, "primitive socialist accumulation" was intended to be analogous to the primitive accumulation in the early stages of capitalism, so brilliantly described by Marx in the first volume of *Capital*. (This is discussed in Chapter 2.)

Preobrazhensky proposed that such saving be obtained through differential pricing of commodities that would turn the terms of trade against the peasants, or by direct taxes on them. He thought that while the peasants' real incomes would have to fall relative to others' incomes during the rapid industrialization period, they could nevertheless rise absolutely (*i.e.*, relative to the peasants' former incomes) upon the swells of growth that the industrialization program would generate. He left no doubt that, in one way or another, the expansion of industry would have to be at the heavy expense of the peasants. (His opponents, however, attributed to him a more extreme position of wanting to exploit and impoverish the peasants.) It also followed that such an all-out industrialization effort would require centralized national planning, which Preobrazhensky enthusiastically endorsed.

He further believed that this pattern of saving and investment in a backward country asserted itself as an objective law of accumulation. Whatever the subjective wishes of the party's leaders might be, this law would impose itself during the transition period, compelling the party to follow its dictates. Although it would obtrude most harshly on a backward country trying to attain socialism on its own, it would also impose its terms on a backward country that had proletarian allies in other countries. Thus, he believed that even if the proletarian revolution did spread to Western Europe, as he and his left-wing colleagues assumed it would, there was a necessarily difficult transition period ahead for the young socialist society.

Associated on the left with Preobrazhensky was Leon Trotsky, a superstar of the Bolshevik revolution, organizer of the Red Army, and Commissar of War. By the spring of 1926, they were joined by G. Zinoviev, party leader in Leningrad, and L. Kamenev, Commissar of Trade, both of whom, frightened by Stalin's power plays, deserted him to form with Trotsky a "joint opposition" to Stalin and the right-winger Bukharin. Trotsky maintained, in his theory of permanent revolution, that the revolution in Russia would have to pass from its bourgeois to its socialist phase, and from its national (*i.e.*, Russian) to its international (*i.e.*, mainly Western European) phase. If the second passage did not occur, the first would necessarily remain incomplete—that is, in the absence of world revolution, Russian socialism would become distorted, truncated. There was no way, Trotsky thought, to achieve a flourishing socialism in the absence of the economic and social integration of many proletarian states around the world.

Nevertheless, even in isolation, the Soviet Union should establish full-scale national planning, principally to strengthen the socialist industrial sector in its struggle, within the framework of the NEP, with the private agricultural sector. He thus advocated industrialization, but he believed, contrary to Preobrazhensky, that the urban workers would have to shoulder much of the burden of this program, through lower real wages. By these means, some progress could be made toward socialism while awaiting the world revolution; the latter, indeed, might be hastened by socialist success in the Soviet Union.

While Trotsky's main objective was similar to Preobrazhensky's, he did not advocate the frenetic pace of industrialization envisioned by the latter. Neither did he single out the peasants to bear the burdens of industrial expansion. He also objected to what he felt were Preobrazhensky's exaggerated notions about "objective" laws and to his view that the backward Soviet society, even working in isolation, could eventually catch up with the advanced capitalist countries. Trotsky saw this feat as impossible.

In mid-1926, the joint opposition to Stalin and the right-wing presented a left-wing program that defended the interests of the workers over the new bourgeois classes (rich peasants, NEP bourgeoisie, and the bureaucracy that reflected their interests), calling for a rise in industrial wages and for tax reforms that would shift burdens from the poor to the wealthy. The program also called for more rapid industrialization and more thorough national planning, and it urged the collectivization of agriculture, on a gradual, voluntary basis. Finally, the program attacked the center and right on their insistence that socialism could be completed in a single country and on their failure to allow inner-party democracy.

The most prominent theorist on the right was N. Bukharin, a member of the Politbureau in the mid-1920s; he was joined by two other Politbureau members, M. Tomsky, the trade union leader, and A. Rykov, Premier of the government. Bukharin argued for gradual expansion of all sectors simultaneously, within a general policy of moderate capital accumulation financed by the voluntary saving of the peasants, and with a large role for the foreign sector. He advocated a rather slow rate of growth with prices set in favor of the peasants at large, and other concessions and incentives, to encourage their voluntary saving. What he proposed, his opponents alleged, was the abandonment of class struggle in the countryside.

The rural demand for industrial goods, Bukharin thought, should dictate the pace of industrial expansion. The more prosperous the agricultural sector became, the faster this pace would be. Thus, at one point, Bukharin called on the peasants to enrich themselves, in a slogan that his opponents later used, with much profit, against him. But even a slow pace of growth, he argued, should be accepted: ". . . we shall move ahead by tiny, tiny steps, pulling behind us our large peasant cart."

Bukharin can be called the coauthor with Stalin of the doctrine of "socialism in one country," which was diametrically opposed to Trotsky's conception of socialism within the context of world revolution. The revolutionary period in Europe had come to an end, Bukharin proclaimed, and the Soviet Union would be isolated for some time to come. Even so, socialism could gradually and completely be achieved. Bukharin also railed against Preobrazhensky's peasant proposals, claiming that such policies would destroy the alliance between the workers and the peasants, an alliance that was absolutely essential for the building of a socialist society. He argued that a lenient policy toward the wealthier farmers would enable them to increase substantially their marketable grain surpluses (the less wealthy ones could not do this) and so provide the wherewithal for the expansion of industry.

The center position was secured by Stalin. His outlook, first formulated in the autumn of 1924, was that socialism could be built *completely* in a single country, but its *final victory* could not be guaranteed in the absence of widespread proletarian revolutions abroad—a doctrine that borrowed from the revolutionary and internationally-minded left and from the nationalist and isolationist right. Furthermore, Stalin said, foreign revolutions would actually be accelerated if socialist construction was carried out successfully in the Soviet Union. So Stalin managed to present an optimistic program that exuded great confidence in Russia's ability to go it alone, while at the same time he appealed to those who still looked abroad for final salvation. Trotsky's perspective, on the other hand, was described as being pessimistic and demeaning in that it looked—vainly, many thought—for ultimate strength outside of the Russian people.

In the meantime, Stalin declared, it was important to maintain the alliance between the working class and the peasantry. He accused Trotsky and the left-wing of hostility not only toward the *kulaks* but toward the middle peasants as well, and he criticized the right-wing for favoring the *kulaks*. Stalin presumed to speak for the peasants, and so he allied himself in general with Bukharin and the right-wing, but he established a little distance from them by confining his good will mainly to the poor and middle peasants, and by advocating (in late 1927) collectivization of farming—to be achieved by persuasion rather than pressure. Moreover, though he lashed out at the super-industrializers of the left, he did advocate industrialization in his own program.

His position was therefore a centrist or eclectic one, from which he contributed clarity but little of substance to the debate on economic development, preferring instead to play off one side against the other, and in the interim to consolidate his power within the party and the state.

From this vantage point, Stalin at first extended a friendly hand to the right in order to defeat Trotsky and the left-wing. Once this had been largely accomplished, by late 1926, he began his turn leftward, isolating the right more and more. During 1928-29, Bukharin and his supporters were attacked and finally removed from the Politbureau, which Stalin instead loaded with his own supporters. He was then in a position to pursue a new direction without opposition from prominent Bolshevik leaders. The new course not only incorporated much of the left-wing's basic program, but carried those policies far beyond the limits prescribed by the left's former leaders.

Stalin's Abandonment of the NEP

Stalin's abandonment of the NEP may have been partly a political maneuver to consolidate his power, but it was also heavily influenced by both domestic and international forces. Because the economic recovery was expected to slow down, the party in 1926 called for a speed-up of industrialization and thereby an expansion of the country's industrial capacity. In the next year, a resolution of the Central Committee stated: "Taking into account the possibility of military aggression of capitalist countries against the first proletarian state in history, it is necessary to work out the Five-Year Plan in such a way as to give maximum attention to those branches of the national economy in general, and of industry in particular, that will play the main part in assuring the defense and economic stability of the country in time of war." Thus, the threats of domestic stagnation and of war both played important roles in the decision to expand industry, even though Stalin and his associates probably exaggerated the war scare for domestic political purposes.

Investment rates began to rise in 1926-27, and two years later they were soaring. These capital expenditures led to increases in aggregate demand for goods and services, which began to put upward pressure on prices. By this time, however, price ceilings had been imposed for several years on state industrial goods, and in 1927, very low procurement prices were set on agricultural products, so that increasingly at the controlled prices excess demands developed. By the same token, supplies to regular markets were discouraged, especially supplies of grain, and this curtailment for a time threatened to bring about urban famines. Consequently, shortages of goods, including agricultural output, became increasingly widespread and severe. These developments induced the Bolshevik leaders to stress direct planning as opposed to indirect market processes, and general rationing in cities had to be imposed on consumers in 1929.

While price controls, which assumed a key role in this drama, conflicted with the purposes of the NEP, they accurately reflected the contradiction in the aims of the party: to allow private initiative and incentives more room, but at the same time to prevent undue enrichment, speculation, and anarchic outcomes. Private profit incentives were thus hemmed in by price ceilings, surcharges for transporting private goods, taxes on super-profits, jail sentences for "evil-intended" price increases, and other punitive measures, and this combination of opposites was the outer manifestation of the inner struggle going on. Stalin and members of his faction also, for political purposes, wanted to lower prices by means of controls, to counter the demands for higher industrial prices (from the left) and for higher agricultural prices (from the right).

The developing situation of "shortages," which was at least partly the result of interference with market processes by the party leaders, led Stalin to strike hard at the *kulaks* and speculators, who were accused of causing the "goods famine" by withholding supplies from official markets. The rough measures against the richer peasants—raids, illegal searches, and the like—may have reduced production and official supplies even more. Stalin then launched an even harsher attack against the speculators and hoarders: peasants were menaced with jail if they failed to deliver grain. In effect, the compulsory requisitioning of grain and other War Communism measures were reimposed. The continuation of worsening conditions led to the final step—all-out enforced collectivization of agriculture—which eventually eliminated the *kulaks* as a class and increased the marketed surplus of grain. Thus, step by step, Stalin was drawn toward a total program of central planning, nationalization, all-out industrialization, and enforced collectivization, which no one, left or right, had advocated, and much of which Stalin himself in previous years had rejected.

Socialism and Soviet Power in the 1930s

The pillars of the first Marxian-socialist society began to rise in 1928-29, the initial year of the first five-year plan (FFYP). These pillars consisted of national planning itself, the social ownership of the means of production (nationalization of industry and collectivization of agriculture), and the utilization of these institutions to achieve rapid economic development and substantially higher living standards.

Between 1928 and June 1941, when the Germans invaded the Soviet Union, there were three five-year plans. The first was completed almost a year ahead of schedule; the third was cut short by the invasion. The largest industries had been nationalized shortly after the revolution, and the others were brought under social ownership and control during the FFYP. Collectivization of agriculture started in 1929 and was mostly completed in the next six or seven years. Finally, impressive gains were made in industrial production and in the overall growth of national output during the 1930s, but family living standards, especially for rural families, did not rise significantly until after World War II.

An Outline of Achievements and Failures

The Soviet economy expanded rapidly but unevenly during the FFYP, October 1928 to December 1932. Famines, transportation bottlenecks, and other difficulties made 1933 a very poor year. Exuberant growth, somewhat more balanced than before, resumed in 1934 and continued for three years. In 1937, the final year of the second five-year plan, despite an outstanding agricultural harvest, the economy began faltering—at least in the civilian industrial sectors. The remaining years before Hitler's invasion were satisfactory but far from outstanding.

Military production was emphasized early by the Soviet government, because of perceived threats from major capitalist countries during the 1920s. It was accelerated in the early 1930s, when Japan moved into Manchuria and Hitler came to power, announcing the Nazis' intention to stamp out communism. By the mid-1930s, the Soviet government was devoting 10 to 15 percent of its budget to defense expenditures, and near the end of the decade, the proportion reached 25 to 30 percent. Such an escalation in arms spending made necessary periodic modification of the five-year plans, so that consumer and other vulnerable civilian sectors saw their target figures reduced from time to time. The slowdown of the civilian economy after 1936 was owing to the gathering war clouds, to the waves of terror during 1936-38, when many of the top party and military leaders were tried and executed in the great purges, and to planning errors and difficulties.

Although there were many failures and much terror associated with these five-year plans, it must be recognized that the entire effort represented the first time in the history of the world that a country had utilized national planning and social ownership of the means of production to transform radically its society and to elevate its economy so rapidly. There were many social gains during these years. Illiteracy was almost completely wiped out, major improvements were made in health services, increasing numbers of children were educated, social services were extended to many more families, unemployment was eliminated, work opportunities for women were greatly expanded, many poor peasants improved their standard of living in urban-industrial jobs, and tens of thousands of young people were inspired by the lofty aims set forth by the party for the transformation of their motherland.

With regard to economic achievements, Maurice Dobb, in his classic work, *Soviet Economic Development Since 1917,* has written:

> If we survey the changes wrought in the economy at large by this decade of grand construction, we must inevitably be impressed by the extent to which the transformation had been qualitative as well as quantitative. The quantitative growth of industry can be epitomized in such indices as these: that the output capacity of the iron and steel industry had been expanded by four times over the decade between 1928 and 1938, of coal by three and a half times, oil nearly three times, and of electrical power by some seven times; while at the same time a whole range of new industries had been established, such as aeroplanes, heavy chemicals, including plastics and artificial rubber, aluminium, copper, nickel, tin. The U.S.S.R. had become the largest producer of tractors and railway locomotives in the world, and the second largest producer of oil and gold and phosphates.

And, it must be remembered, these accomplishments were recorded at a time when most of the rest of the world was in a deep economic crisis, in which massive unemployment, widespread poverty, and despair prevailed almost everywhere.

There were failures as well. Economic growth was quite lopsided, because of the persistent emphasis on heavy industry, and many families, particularly in rural areas, failed to benefit from this growth. Even in the favored sectors, economic planning often went awry. And the economic gains were accompanied by tremendous human costs, including those associated with purges, forced labor, and the imposed impoverishment of some groups.

Collectivization of Agriculture

One of the urgent problems faced by the Soviet leaders was how to achieve more rapid industrialization in the face of a backward and recalcitrant agricultural sector. Some of the leaders had suggested collectivization of the land and equipment; this would result in larger, more efficient units, in which class differences would be reduced and hence a more concerted effort to raise production and agricultural surpluses could be achieved. Always, however, collectivization was thought of as being gradual, voluntary on the part of the peasants, who, it was hoped, would become convinced of the advantages of such cooperation through persuasion and example. Those on the right-wing of the debate envisaged even the *kulaks* slowly but surely coming around and "growing into socialism." In any case, the phlegmatic pace of this process promised relief to industry only after some years of earnest effort in the rural areas.

Stalin cut through this problem with the blade of coercion. In the latter half of 1929, he ordered some local officials to carry out mass collectivization in their areas. This involved, for each collective, the bringing together of several dozen families and their equipment, tools, animals, and other capital goods. In the new institution, the capital was owned and managed collectively and peasants were paid according to the work points they earned at the job. The success of these initial experiments encouraged Stalin to broaden the movement and to accelerate its tempo. In some localities, persuasion went out the window: "He who does not join a kolkhoz [collective] is an enemy of Soviet power," it was announced. At about the same time, Stalin made up his mind to liquidate the *kulaks* as a class. Before long, their property was expropriated by the Soviet state, and millions of them, with their families, were uprooted and driven into exile. Others were given the poorest land in their areas to cultivate, and still others were delivered into the hands of the political police. In March 1930, Stalin suddenly called for restraint, for persuasion and not coercion, and he brazenly blamed local officials for the "excesses" committed during the past several months, referring to the perpetrators as "dizzy with success." During this respite, many peasants left the collectives—but not for long, for there was soon a resurgence of the feverish campaign to increase the number of collectives. By 1933, two-thirds of the peasant households and over 80 percent of the crop area had been collectivized. In the next three years, the process was virtually completed.

There was widespread, panicky resistance, by *kulak* and non-*kulak* alike, to these radical policies. Large numbers of farm animals were killed by their peasant owners, others died from lack of fodder, and still others perished of neglect in the collectives. Many peasants obstinately held out for some time before finally being driven into the new units. Thousands fled into towns and to other sanctuaries. But in the end, collectives and, to a lesser extent, state farms (state enterprises, in which peasants worked for wages as rural laborers) dominated the countryside, leaving only marginal activities for private enterprise. However, within the collectives, peasants were permitted to own household goods and some animals and to work privately a small percentage of the crop area. The state now had better control of both production and marketable surpluses, though the initial success of collectivization lay not so much in raising production as in enlarging the share of that production going to the state.

By the close of the 1930s the collectives were solidly-established institutions, in which peasant families pooled their means of production in order to produce in common, and, at the same time, engaged in private production on their own plots of land.

National Planning and National Results

Marx and Engels did not say much about the nature of the coming socialist society. But they left little room for doubt that there would be a planned mode of production, vastly superior to the anarchic, market-oriented capitalist mode. "Only conscious organization of social production," Engels wrote, "in which production and distribution are carried on in a planned way, can lift mankind above the rest of the animal world as regards the social aspect, in the same way that production in general has done this for men in their aspect as species." History ought to be produced, Marx and Engels proclaimed, like any other product, for a purpose; but since planlessness was the essence of capitalism, up to now human beings had been prevented from consciously organizing their own development.

The Bolsheviks, like all other Marxists, had adopted this view of the possibilities and purposes of planning. Accordingly, shortly after the revolution, the party called for "the greatest possible concentration of the whole economic activity of the country in a unified plan worked out for the whole State," and the Council of Labor and Defense was established for this purpose. Despite these intentions, there was in fact very little national planning in the Soviet Union until the latter half of the 1920s. But there were, very early, many partial plans.

The first of these was drawn up by the State Commission for Electrification, which outlined the projected power development of the country for the next 10 to 15 years. This Commission in 1921 became the famous State Planning Commission (Gosplan); it was at that time an advisory body attached to the Council of Labor and Defense. Gosplan grew during the next few years. At first it engaged in piecemeal planning, especially in those areas of the economy most in need of attention. Then, gradually it began coordinating the various partial plans. In 1925, it established branches throughout the country and so was in a position to produce and oversee a national plan: in 1925-26 it began to issue annual "control figures," which for the first time gave a comprehensive view of the interrelationships among key economic variables. These were considered guides to action, not directives. Trotsky ecstatically called these control figures "the glorious historical music of growing socialism." While he seems to have been carried away—the figures represented only the first tentative steps toward full-scale planning—it is nevertheless true that nothing like this had previously been seen in the world. Improvements and extensions were made in these figures during the next few years, until Gosplan's 1928-29 work became in fact the data for the initial year of the FFYP.

In 1931, Gosplan was removed as an advisory body to the Council of Labor and Defense and put directly under the Council of People's Commissars (in effect, the Council of Ministers, the highest government body), and after that its role in national planning was pre-eminent.

Should planning merely extrapolate tendencies of the past, leaving basic structures unchanged, or should it try to chart the unsailed seas? Each side of this issue had ardent spokesmen during the 1920s. The former were generally conservative, appealed to objective conditions, carefully calculated the costs of development, and looked to agriculture to set the pace for industry. The latter were more daring, were willing to change circumstances rather than adapt to them, and relied more on political will and less on economic laws. Stalin turned out to be the supreme venturer of the group. He set forth for the unknown seas, and the plans that comprised the FFYP were his navigation charts.

The FFYP stressed investment over consumption, industry over agriculture, heavy industry over light industry, and urban development over rural. It set out to establish an industrial base that could, within a short time, produce the machinery, chemicals, iron and steel, electricity, and other goods required for the Soviet Union to become a first-rate economic and military power. "We are fifty or a hundred years behind the advanced countries," Stalin announced in early 1931. "We must make good this distance in ten years. Either we do so, or we shall go under." Ten years later, Hitler invaded Russia.

During the FFYP, a "Great Leap" mentality developed, a forerunner of the state of mind in China a quarter of a century later. Anything became possible, all ramparts could be scaled, and moderate voices were accused of making a fetish of figures. There was also a brief resurgence of War Communism fever: the expectation of soon abolishing money, the idealization of communal living (one Western author guesses that this arose from overcrowded conditions in the cities!), the hope of substituting "products" for "commodities," and so on. In 1934, Stalin referred to this as "Leftist petty-bourgeois chatter" from "Left freaks," but at the time he was part of it.

Needless to say, the Soviet Union did not attain communism in those years, nor did it even reach some of the crucial production goals set in the five-year plans. Nevertheless, the economic transformation of the country between 1928 and 1941, when Hitler attacked, was epic. Some of the highlights of this stupendous effort are shown in Table 2.

Table 2. National Planning and National Results, U.S.S.R.: 1928 to 1940
(1927-28 = 100)

	1927-1928 Actual[a]	1932 Planned Minimum Version	1932 Planned Maximum Version	1932 Actual	1937 Planned[b]	1937 Actual	1940 Actual	1928-1940 Annual Rate of Growth
National income	100	182	204	135[c]	297	207[de]	230	7.2%
Personal Cons.	100					117[e]	134	2.5
Investment	100	254	338			405[e]	363	11.3
Defense	100					1431	3802	35.4
Industrial Output	100	208	236	150	321	245	263	8.4
Intermediate Goods	100			184		298	343	10.8
Civilian Machinery	100		257	270		567	486	14.1
Consumer Goods	100	184	204	109	255	163	180	5.0
Agricultural Output (crops only)	100	144	155	109	302	149	123	1.7

[a] The "actual" figures throughout the table are Western, not Soviet, estimates.
[b] These data are Soviet planned amounts reduced to conform to lower Western estimates of Soviet performance. Each figure is equal to the Soviet planned amount multiplied by a ratio of the Western estimate of actual Soviet performance in 1932 to the Soviet estimate of actual performance in 1932.
[c] The assumed annual growth rate is 7.8 percent.
[d] The assumed annual growth rate is 8.9 percent. This and the preceding growth rate are consistent with the average of 8.35 percent shown by Cohn for 1928-37.
[e] These are averages for the ranges given by Cohn.
Sources: Alec Nove, An Economic History of the U.S.S.R. (London: Penguin Books, 1972), pp. 145, 225; and Stanley H. Cohn, Economic Development in the Soviet Union (Lexington, Mass.: D.C. Heath, 1970), pp. 28, 39.

The FFYP specified both minimum and maximum goals, but the actual results in 1932, as measured by Western experts, were in fact below the minima for many key items. However, this was probably not true for machinery or defense output, two of the most crucial areas. National income as a whole appears to have fallen short of plans, and certainly both agricultural output and the production of consumer goods were far behind schedule. Over the full period, a spectacular annual growth rate was recorded for defense output, and there were exceptionally high rates for those commodities that fed the industrial base—industrial intermediate goods and machinery; in general, investment expenditures throughout the economy were consistently high. On the other hand, those commodities destined for consumers did relatively poorly (though production of consumer goods did rise by 5 percent a year), and the growth rate of agricultural output was very low (the figure in the table would be even lower if livestock were included).

It is clear that economic growth over these years was rapid, unbalanced, and variable. The growth rate of national income reflects a doubling in a decade; this would have been a great performance at any time, but was particularly sparkling during the 1930s, when real GNP in the United States and other advanced capitalist countries barely rose at all. The Soviet performance, however, was unbalanced in the ways previously described. Moreover, it was variable, with the highest rates coming in the middle years, the slowest toward the end, and more average ones occurring near the beginning.

Inequalities and Incentives

Socialism is a transition period between capitalism and communism. As such, it contains the "poisonous weeds" of capitalism and the "fragrant flowers"—or, at least, their seeds—of communism. Among the poisonous weeds are material and individual incentives (rather than moral and collective ones) and inequalities resulting from payment according to work (rather than need). However, if a socialist society is making good progress toward communism, the poisonous weeds should be wilting and the fragrant flowers beginning to thrive. More prosaically, this means that the working class will continue to work hard even though payments are increasingly divorced from individual effort and distributed collectively.

During these years, the incentives used by Stalin to motivate hard work were both material and moral, individual and collective. In using the individual, material incentives, moreover, he did not hesitate to order distended wage structures, in which the skilled and managerial individuals received many times the wages of the unskilled and subordinate. Neither did he hesitate to open wide gaps between the incomes of peasants and of urban workers, or between wages in one geographical area and in another. Indeed, Stalin did not for a moment attempt to hide these growing disparities. "Marxism," he said in 1934, "is an enemy of equalization." Equality for Marxists, he went on, means the abolition of classes, nothing more and nothing less. He lashed out at the "Leftist blockheads, who idealize the poor as the eternal bulwark of Bolshevism under all conditions," and who wish to have workers, skilled and unskilled, pool their wages in a common fund and then share equally. He called the equalization of wages and salaries a "reactionary, petty-bourgeois absurdity worthy of a primitive sect of ascetics but not of a Socialist society organized on Marxian lines."

At the same time, Stalin promoted moral and collective incentives by dramatizing the production records established by teams of workers and individuals (the so-called Stakhanovites) who were presumably driven by revolutionary spirit rather than the hope of monetary rewards, though the latter apparently found their way into these areas as well.

The combination, however, was heavily weighted toward the individual and material incentives, and throughout the decade income inequalities grew, as did special privileges for bureaucrats, scientists, technicians, artists, and others. Masses of rural families, starting at the bottom, ended at the bottom, where deprivation and despair reigned. Stalin's incentive structure was no doubt highly successful in eliciting hard work from the proletariat, but its cost in terms of growing inequities was enormous.

Preparing for War

In early 1939, in a report to the 18th Party Congress, Stalin noted the imminence of another world war—a new imperialist war that was in a sense already well under way:

> In 1935 Italy attacked and seized Abyssinia. In the summer of 1936 Germany and Italy organized military intervention in Spain, Germany entrenching herself in the north of Spain and in Spanish Morocco, and Italy in the south of Spain and in the Balearic Islands. In 1937, having seized Manchuria, Japan invaded North and Central China, occupied Peking, Tientsin and Shanghai and began to oust her foreign competitors from the occupied zone. In the beginning of 1938 Germany seized Austria, and in the autumn of 1938 the Sudeten region of Czechoslovakia. At the end of 1938 Japan seized Canton, and at the beginning of 1939 the Island of Hainan.

We are witnessing, he stated—in a conclusion based on Lenin's analysis—an open redivision of the world by force, a redivision that has not yet spread into a world war. But he had little doubt that it would.

The third five-year plan, which started in 1938, was developed with this danger in mind. Military expenditures were sharply increased, so much so that improvements in living standards were forgone for the remaining years of peace. By 1940, investment and defense expenditures consumed about half the national output. In that same year, labor discipline was strengthened with harsh measures, including the imposition of criminal charges for absenteeism. The working day was lengthened, specialists were made subject to labor assignments, and there was a compulsory call-up of about a million young school graduates for training in "labor reserve schools." Some social insurance benefits were cut. A 1940 decree made poor-quality production a criminal offense.

Thus the civilian retrenchment, labor discipline, and stepped-up military outlays demanded by the approaching conflict began to go into effect just a few years before a capitalist-imperialist war engulfed the Russian land and the world for the second time in a quarter of a century.

The Soviet Economy in War and Its Aftermath

The Soviet Union suffered terrible losses during its four years of fighting, and required another three or four years to recover prewar levels of production. Thus, at least seven years of economic growth were sacrificed to the war. By the time of Stalin's death in March 1953, the country was in the middle of its fifth five-year plan and setting records. And by that time, the Chinese communists had swept to victory and were in the first year of their initial five-year plan, the priorities of which were strongly guided by the Soviet Union.

The War and Economic and Social Losses

Hitler struck in June 1941. By the end of November, vast territories had been lost and with them more than half the nation's production of coal, steel, and aluminum, a quarter of the nation's engineering production, over a third of the grain lands and railway lines, and most of the pigs and horses. Leningrad was cut off from the rest of the country and blockaded—the ordeal was to last for 900 days—and Moscow was besieged. As Dobb put it: "Scarcely more than twenty years after the wars of intervention had been terminated, the Russian land, the fair new towns, the new mills and factories and collective farms, were to be ravaged by an invader more ruthless than any since the days of the Tartars."

Despite the swiftness of the Nazis' march, the Soviets managed to evacuate more than a thousand large-scale enterprises and 10 million people—to the Urals, West Siberia, Central Asia and Kazakhstan. Much had to be left behind, including many firms producing consumer goods, and much was abandoned as Soviet troops retreated in disarray. In November 1941, the level of industrial production was only about half what it had been a year earlier.

In the summer offensive of 1942, the German armies occupied the northern Caucasus and Don River areas and approached the industrial center of Stalingrad, on the southern Volga. By these moves, Germany took away from the U.S.S.R. almost all of its remaining grain lands and much else besides. In the meantime, plants and industries, moved to the eastern regions, were beginning to produce; by the end of the year they were in high gear, and there was new capital formation as well. In the summer of 1943, Stalin announced that the Soviets had surpassed the Germans in the production of tanks and aircraft; and in the course of the war they greatly increased their output of electric power, coal, railway mileage, arms and ammunition, steel, and most of whatever else was needed. The Soviets' total supplies of war necessities were also enlarged by aid from their allies.

The Soviet armies began a successful counter-offensive against the Germans on the Moscow front in the winter of 1941-42. The battle for Stalingrad—called the greatest battle of World War II—took place in the summer, autumn, and early winter of 1942. By December, Hitler's troops were in retreat and surrendering. In the summer offensive of 1943, the Soviet armies recaptured almost two-thirds of the territory previously lost. In the following year, the German armies suffered one defeat after another, starting with Leningrad and ending in Budapest. Unconditional surrender came in 1945.

As the Germans retreated, they leveled the land. Dobb reports:

> When the Germans retreated the deliberate devastation was extraordinarily thorough. Mine-shafts were not only flooded but systematically wrecked; iron works, steel furnaces and factories demolished; and railway tracks so extensively destroyed by means of special devices as to be unusable without extensive relaying. The countryside in the path of the German retreat for hundreds of miles was made a wasteland, devoid of livestock and buildings and often of inhabitants. Nearly 2000 towns, 70,000 villages, and factories employing 4 million persons were partially or wholly destroyed, according to official calculations, and 25 million persons were rendered homeless. Contemporary Soviet estimates placed the sum of this appalling devastation at half the material devastation in Europe.

The Soviet nation lost 20–25 million people as a result of the war, a horrible fact that Stalin never could bring himself to divulge to friend or foe. It was uncovered only in 1959, in the first postwar population census.

The Postwar Economy, 1945 to Stalin's Death

The principal item on the economic agenda in 1945 was the reconstruction of a devastated economy. This task was specified in Gosplan's fourth five-year plan, which covered the years 1946-50. The plan once again gave high priority to railway building, heavy industrial investment, and producers' goods—steel, oil, coal, chemicals, machinery—and once again consumer goods, housing, and agriculture were relatively downplayed.

By 1948, most of the key industrial goods had regained their 1940 levels of output, and two years later the plan was overfulfilled for the production of coal, oil, electricity, and steel. The planned target for tractors was exceeded by more than 100 percent. On the other hand, the grain harvest did not quite meet expectations, nor did the output of such consumer items as wool and cotton fabrics and shoes.

State prices for buying grain from the collectives (*i.e.*, compulsory-procurement prices) remained so low that there was very little income available to the members. In addition, the collectives were taxed more heavily, and several years later, they were compelled to set aside larger amounts of revenue for capital investments. Still other burdens were placed on the rural areas. The costs of production of the collectives often exceeded the revenues, sometimes by very large margins. This must have greatly reduced the incentives of peasants to produce for the collectives and induced them instead to turn toward their own private plots and animals. But even in the latter area the state levied heavy taxes. As a consequence of Stalin's seemingly hostile policies toward the peasants, along with a terrible drought in 1946, the flight of population from the rural areas, and some disruptive reorganizations in the countryside, agriculture was little better off in 1950 than it had been in 1940.

However, toward the end of the fourth five-year plan, and during the next plan (1951-55), the output of consumer goods began to rise more rapidly, and their prices were reduced several times in these years. Wages rose sharply, too, especially those at the lower end of the pay scale. As a consequence, living standards began moving up briskly, no doubt for the first time since the mid-1920s. By the time of Stalin's death, urban families were substantially better off than they had been in 1940. Rural families, although sharing to some extent in the general improvement, were even yet struggling at markedly lower living levels. Almost everyone was still short of housing space.

The Economy after Stalin

It is not my intention to review in any detail the performance of the Soviet economy after Stalin's death, for his successors have thus far not been giant figures in the world communist movement, and I am eager to move on to Mao Tse-tung, who was a giant. Still, the Soviet picture would remain incomplete without at least a few indications of the economy's course over the past quarter of a century. These are also needed for an assessment, later in this chapter, of the Soviets' grandiose experiment.

G. Malenkov (party head 1953-55), Nikita Khrushchev (1955-64), and Leonid Brezhnev (1964-present), Stalin's successors, all attempted to rectify at least in part Stalin's neglect of consumers, peasants, urban dwellers, and the aged. The output of consumer goods was greatly augmented; compulsory-procurement prices and over-quota delivery prices for agricultural products were raised; and several other measures were refashioned to the benefit of peasants, among them the stepped-up production of agricultural machinery. Millions of hectares of new crop lands were opened up, and hundreds of thousands of people moved to these frontiers; more resources were allocated to housing; and pensions and other sources of income for the retired were boosted.

Between 1950 and 1975, the Soviet economy grew rapidly, but it did not have the buoyancy and élan of the prewar period. The somewhat slower rate of postwar growth was a result of the greater attention paid to consumers and to housing, the continuing onerous military requirements (though note the spectacular technical advances made in this field), the dwindling of the surplus rural population available for industry, and increasing planning difficulties. Yet, as Table 3 indicates, overall growth was still very good, agricultural performance showed a big improvement over the 1930s, and consumption per capita rose smartly, by 3½ to 4 percent per year. Furthermore, the data in the table show that Soviet postwar growth was substantially higher than that of the United States. Consequently, the ratio of GNP per capita in the U.S.S.R. to that in the U.S. rose from 28 percent in 1950 to 44 percent in 1975.

Table 3. Economic Performance, U.S.S.R. (1928-1940, 1950-1975) and U.S. (1950-1975)

	Average Annual Rates of Growth		
	Soviet Union		United States
	1928-1940	1950-1975	1950-1975
GNP	4.5-9.8% (av.7.2)	5.2%	3.3%
Industrial Output	8.4	7.6	3.9
Agricultural Output	1.7	2.5	1.9
Steel Production	13.5	7.0	2.5-3.0
Consumption per capita	−0.6	3.5-4.0	1.9

Sources: *Economic Report of the President*, January, 1977; Joint Economic Committee, U.S. Congress, *Economic Prospects for the Seventies*, p. 393; Joint Economic Committee, U.S. Congress, *Soviet Economy in a New Perspective*, pp. 246, 275, 631, 646, and 653; and Table 2 above.

Stalin's successors have greatly narrowed income disparities. This is attested to by many outside observers, including one author who titled his article on this topic "The Soviet Income Revolution." This revolution was achieved through a series of measures, extending over 15 years, that raised wages of the lowest income groups, especially in the services sector, boosted the minimum wage rate of urban workers by more than a third and of rural workers by about a half, raised by more than a third the minimum pensions of disabled workers and the minimum benefits of survivors, established a national social insurance system for peasants, similar to the one for workers, lowered taxes on low-income families, promoted greater geographical equality through state investments, and in general considerably narrowed the gap between urban and rural living standards. In the last 25 years, real disposable income per capita in the Soviet Union has risen by about 6 percent per year, which is well over twice the rate in the United States, and many of these gains have gone to the lower income groups. Immediately after the war, the top 10 percent of income receivers had 14 times the income of the bottom 10 percent. Two decades later, the ratio was under 5. (These data exclude collective-farm families.)

These achievements have been accompanied by some failures, or at least ominous signs. The Soviet GNP growth rate has been on a long-run downward trend throughout the postwar period. It was over 6 percent in the 1950s, around 5½ percent in the 1960s, and close to 4 percent in the 1970s (through 1978). The economy badly needs modern technology in many crucial areas, and it is struggling to achieve this and other means of raising the lagging productivity of its labor force. The Soviets no longer have ample supplies of under-utilized labor and other resources to throw into the breach, so they must try to improve the performance of what they have. However, while the growth rate has been declining, the economy has not been subjected to cyclical ups and downs, and even the lower growth rate of the 1970s is still fairly high by capitalist standards.

There is also evidence of increasing privileges for the elite, in the form of better housing, special clinics and hospitals, better education for their children, and access to foreign travel and special stores and automobiles, as well as bloated bonuses, dachas, hunting lodges, and the like. Bourgeois values and culture often seem to be spreading throughout the society. There are also growing signs of petty bribery, black marketing, wholesale thieving from the state, illegal underground private manufacturing, and illicit scalping. According to many foreign observers, the drug culture, alcoholism, political and social indifference of the population, the low prestige of manual labor, and rampant materialism complete the picture of "socialism on the skids."

Is the Soviet Union Socialist?

The vital question therefore arises of whether the Soviet Union is still a Marxian-socialist society. Its supporters and even many of its detractors would say that it is. The communist Chinese and their adherents claim that it is not—that a type of capitalism has been restored there. I cannot hope to resolve this issue, but the salient arguments can be clearly set forth. The Chinese case is presented first.

Chinese Criticisms of the Soviets

The Chinese critics of the Soviet Union first point to some early difficulties encountered by the Bolsheviks, which compelled them eventually to overstress the productive forces to the neglect of production relations and the superstructure; they put heavy industry before light industry and agriculture, investment ahead of consumption, urban before rural areas. In overemphasizing technology, Stalin had to promote bourgeois incentives with large wage differentials, piece-rate wage systems, and generous bonuses, which resulted in marked economic and social inequalities within the working class. This led to the playing down of class struggle and the rejection of a dialectical outlook.

According to Mao Tse-tung, the restoration of capitalism did not occur under Stalin. Stalin maintained socialist forms by "clearing out quite a gang of counterrevolutionary representatives of the bourgeoisie who had wormed their way into the Party." Hence, Mao implied, Stalin's policies tended both to revitalize the bourgeoisie, through the use of capitalist incentives, and to eliminate them, through purges. Considering everything, Stalin was a staunch revolutionary who fought for the proletariat and who created the first Marxian-socialist state.

After Stalin's death, the Chinese say, Khrushchev and his supporters usurped party and state power (in 1956) on behalf of a bureaucrat-monopoly-bourgeoisie that now runs the country as a fascist dictatorship. The restoration of capitalism occurred at that time. This clique no longer believes in class struggle and revolution and has espoused peaceful coexistence with imperialism (belief in the peaceful intentions of imperialists), peaceful transition from capitalism to socialism (opposition to armed revolution), peaceful transition from socialism to communism (opposition to the dictatorship of the proletariat and to class struggle), and economism (opposition to bold measures for social transformation).

The restoration of capitalism in the U.S.S.R., according to the Chinese, has seriously disrupted the development of Soviet productive forces, and has opened the door to graft, theft, depraved social morals, alcoholism and drugs, and juvenile delinquency. The new capitalist class controls all monopoly capital in the country and obtains much surplus value through its exploitation of the Soviet and other working peoples. This is the economic base of Soviet social-imperialism, the Chinese allege, which seeks world hegemony and "is the most dangerous source of war."

Soviet and Other Responses

The Soviets and their supporters, of course, deny all of these claims. To begin with, they point to their revolution, during which the proletariat captured political power. They then direct attention to their establishment of the very foundations of a socialist society—national planning and the social ownership of the means of production. Next, they say, with this much accomplished, they pursued the correct path of gradually and steadily building up their productive forces, which is the only method of guaranteeing further changes in the relations of production. Socialism can be built only through resolute long-range planning and a continuous development that emphasizes large-scale, heavy industry and utilizes the advantages of building on the progressive forces inherent in urban areas and the industrial working class. Moreover, the correct socialist principle is payment according to work, and significant wage differentials are needed as incentives for hard and better work. Piece-rate payments and bonuses contribute to this end.

The Soviets also believe that in this new nuclear age war would devastate everyone, comrades and enemies alike; furthermore, the socialist bloc is now strong enough to begin to attract third-world countries into its camp. It is now likely that gradually, peacefully, through economic competition, the vigorous growth of the socialist camp's productive forces will win the day against imperialism and allow a peaceful transition to socialism by increasing numbers of underdeveloped countries.

The Soviets have also alleged that continuing class struggle is necessary only in the transition period between capitalism and socialism, when the dictatorship of the proletariat is required, but that the socialist period itself is classless, as is the next stage of full communism. In these final two stages, therefore, the state represents all the people and there is no need for the dictatorship of one class over another. Thus, the Chinese preoccupation with the dictatorship of the proletariat and with class struggle during the socialist phase is unwarranted.

An Assessment

Most Marxists agree that the restoration of capitalism is possible in a country that has previously achieved socialism. Such a country either progresses toward communism or retrogresses back to capitalism. There is no standing still. If it retrogresses, the capitalism that is restored is not competitive or even private monopoly capitalism but state-bureaucratic monopoly capitalism.

An underdeveloped country starting out to attain socialism will ordinarily commence from some combination of feudal and capitalist relations of production and superstructural elements. During the course of economic development, the feudal elements become weaker, the capitalist elements become potentially stronger (though perhaps actually weaker), and the socialist elements gain dominance. If the transition is successful, socialism will be reached, despite the growing potential strength of bourgeois components within the socialist society.

The class basis for the restoration of capitalism consists of various groups left over from the old regime and enlarged by the program for the development of the country's productive forces. The groups consist of enterprise managers, industrial technicians and experts, engineers, planners, scientists, and in general the intelligentsia. Under certain circumstances, they will be joined by small-scale producers, speculators, and traders. All of these strata will be aided by bourgeois ideology that hangs on and is daily recreated, and by imperialism—by the weight of the world capitalist system. The forces on the side of capitalist restoration are potentially powerful.

However, restoration can be successful only when this bourgeoisie is adequately represented in the state and party bureaucracies, where the restoration has to be organized and implemented. If restoration occurs, the social property of the working class becomes the collective property of the state bourgeoisie. That is, the bourgeoisie recapture the power to control and profit from the means of production, through the state and party bureaucracies. The bourgeoisie link up with the bureaucracies to take political power away from the proletariat. The monopoly bourgeoisie and the bureaucrats then share in the spoils.

Capitalist restoration apparently can be averted by a socialist country only if class struggle by the proletariat against the bourgeoisie is continued and carried out in such a way as to enhance the political power of the proletariat and to strengthen and extend socialist relations while weakening bourgeois ones—both in the economic base and in the superstructure.

If capitalism has been restored in an erstwhile socialist country, one would expect to observe the reappearance of capitalist economic crises (Marx's "capital accumulation crises"), accompanied by periodic widespread unemployment and an enduring reserve army of labor. These capitalist features would be revived through the debilitation of centralized planning and the transfer of planning powers to enterprise managers operating with profit incentives and through a widening network of commodity markets. One would also expect to find increasing economic inequalities within the working class, and increasing hierarchical arrangements within the work-places, brought on by the resuscitation of labor-power as a commodity and the extension of material incentives. The restoration of a type of monopoly capitalism and its capital accumulation crises should lead to imperialist behavior and the militarism required to support it. One would also look for the revival of the ideology opposing class struggle and advocating the primacy of productive forces. Finally, many bourgeois superstructural elements would be restored, such as bourgeois art, literature, and education, and the values of individualism and consumerism.

When these criteria are applied to the Soviet Union, the picture is seen to be somewhat mixed. On the one side, capitalist crises have definitely not reappeared there, for Soviet real GNP has increased every year since 1950. Of even more significance, over that same period there has not been one year of downturn of fixed-capital investment expenditures; they have risen steadily for 27 years, in sharp contrast to investment performance in the advanced capitalist countries. This is clear indication that the central planning system is intact and that the capital-accumulation process has not been subject to swings by enterprise managers operating in terms of the profit motive. Adding to this strong evidence is the absence of deep unemployment problems; there is in the Soviet Union nothing like the capitalist reserve army of labor. It is also true, as we have seen, that since Stalin's death income inequalities have been reduced substantially, and workers' real wages and living standards have risen markedly, which is evidence (though not conclusive) against the view that labor-power has become a commodity and material work incentives and capitalist work relations have spread without restraint.

On the other side, critics point to the superpower and imperialist behavior of the Soviets as evidence that monopoly capitalism has been restored there. That the Soviet Union is a superpower is beyond dispute. However, "superpower behavior" implies that the U.S.S.R. is primarily interested in the division of the world between itself and the United States, and in maximizing its share for its own benefit. Its recent behavior is ambiguous here. Some observers interpret its actions this way, but others believe that it is principally concerned with proletarian internationalism—that is, with the worldwide diffusion of Marxism. Either way, the Soviet Union is an expanding military power, coming into collision with the United States wherever vital resources are at stake.

Properly speaking, capitalist-imperialist actions mean that capital is being exported for the purpose of generating surplus value out of the exploitation of the working classes of other lands. Even if the U.S.S.R. is acting out of self-interest, and has little or no concern to spread proletarian revolutions, applying this definition of capitalist imperialism to it would be difficult, for it has exported very little capital to other countries, and then mainly through foreign-aid programs with fairly generous terms. Generally speaking, the Soviet Union does not build *Soviet* factories in foreign countries. The very basis for imperialism—surplus capital that cannot find profitable employment at home—does not appear to exist there. Furthermore, some evidence exists—from southern

Africa, Ethiopia, Vietnam, Cuba—that it is on the revolutionary side, that it is willing to upset the status quo and thus endanger itself in the interest of extending Marxism. However, there is also evidence pointing in the other direction—from India, Egypt, Iraq, and elsewhere, where anti-Marxist regimes have been handsomely supported.

Some critics further contend that the restoration of capitalism in the Soviet Union is indicated by its full retreat from class struggle at home, its acceptance of the overriding importance of productive forces (to the neglect of the transformation of its relations of production and its superstructure), the alarming diffusion of bourgeois values and institutions throughout Soviet society, and the degeneration of socialist morality among the population. There is much evidence in support of these arguments and very little on the other side. The problem is to judge how important these arguments are compared with the others previously discussed.

Looking back, we can see that Stalin, in subordinating almost everything else to the rapid growth of his country's productive forces (which he narrowly interpreted to exclude human agents), fostered growing inequalities in wealth and status, inflicted brutalities on many of the people, and allowed the erection of a huge bureaucracy and the fashioning of a labor aristocracy and a managerial elite. Stalin failed to rely on the working classes and the masses generally in the struggle against the forces of capitalism, and in effect he depoliticized the masses. As a consequence, workers' and peasants' concerns and motivations were turned inward, and private affairs came to rule the daily lives of the people. Without a high level of political and class consciousness among the workers, without their continuing participation in the building of a socialist society, the planning mechanism went awry and work incentives increasingly had to take compensating capitalist forms. In the process, the working class lost much direct political power and came to be represented more and more by an expanding state bureaucracy.

Stalin's successors set out to reverse some of the developments associated with his name—income inequalities, geographical imbalances, urban-rural disparities, and lopsided priorities. However, the Stalinist era had generated so many bourgeois tendencies within the economy that they came to be represented by growing numbers of Soviet leaders. After Stalin's death, these tendencies coalesced into a revisionist Marxism, akin to Bernstein revisionism. The tenets of original Marxism, however, continued to coexist with, and stand in opposition to, revisionism—an ideological opposition reflecting the enduring struggle between the new bourgeoisie and the proletariat. This struggle has generated both revisionist and revolutionary actions by the Soviet leadership.

Although it is doubtful that a conclusive answer can be given, I believe that the evidence against capitalist restoration is weightier than the evidence for it—in other words, that the Soviet Union is still a socialist country. But there is also sufficient evidence to suggest that its socialism falls far short of traditional Marxian standards and that it may currently be in a process of transition from socialism to capitalism. This issue is particularly difficult to resolve because, as we now know, Marxian socialism, wherever it has appeared, has taken strong national forms, each differing significantly from the others. A single set of fixed standards cannot be used to judge the purity of all these forms of socialism. What are needed are flexible standards that reflect the historical process of worldwide socialist development and the different national traditions within which the global movement occurs. But these still remain to be worked out.

Stalin and Marxian Theory

Stalin's major contribution to the theory of Marxism lies not so much in his writings as in the actual policies that he designed and that came to define a Marxian-socialist society—national planning, nationalization of industry, collectivization of agriculture, and an all-out, forced march toward industrialization and modernization, attended by both impressive gains and heavy costs. By the end of the 1930s, and then on into the 1940s and 1950s, this combination of measures and aims was widely regarded among Marxists as *the* socialist development model. Only after China's Great Leap Forward in 1958-59 shook the ground on which these beliefs rested did Marxists seriously reassess the matter.

Stalin's first theoretical work, written in 1913 at Lenin's suggestion, was on the Marxian view of the problem of nationalities (*Marxism and the National Question*). In this essay, Stalin held that nation-states were created by the bourgeoisie and served as an instrument of its class purposes. Nationalism forced the masses to fight for "their" bourgeoisies against other oppressed peoples; therefore the final aim of the proletariat should be to rid the world of nationalism. At the same time, in the age of modern imperialism, when a nation-state itself is oppressed, it is proper for the proletariat to ally itself with the bourgeoisie and other classes to lead the fight for national liberation. Hence, Stalin said, Marxists should fully support the right of nations to self-determination, including the right to secede from a larger union. Consequently, the ultimate elimination of nationalism called for the short-term support of many nationalist movements. "The aim of Social-Democracy [Marxism]," he concluded, "is to put an end to the policy of national oppression, to render it impossible, and therefore to remove the grounds of strife between nations, to

Stalin

Joseph Vissarionovich Djugashvili (later Koba, and still later Stalin) was born on December 21, 1879, in the town of Gori, situated in the province of Georgia not far north of the Turkish border. His parents had been born into serfdom, and he himself grew up in squalor and poverty; his three brothers died in childhood.

He attended the local school from 1888 to 1894, after which he entered the theological seminary in Tiflis (Tbilisi), capital of the Caucasus; there he studied until July 1899, when he was expelled, probably for dangerous ideas and uncooperative behavior. Several months earlier, he had joined a secret socialist organization. At the end of 1899, he obtained a job in the Tiflis observatory, and in his free time, he supported workers' movements and wrote for a new Marxist journal. He lost his job in 1901 and turned his attention fully to socialist activities.

In late 1901, Stalin went to Batum, on the Turkish border, to organize oil-field and other workers. He was arrested in 1902, jailed for a year and a half, and then exiled to eastern Siberia. However, in a few months, he escaped and returned to Tiflis and Batum. In March 1903, while in jail, Stalin was elected a member of the executive of the All-Caucasian Federation of Social Democrats—a Marxist group. By 1905, he considered himself a supporter of Lenin and hence a Bolshevik—one of a few among a majority of Georgian Mensheviks.

He first met Lenin in December 1905 in the Finnish town of Tammerfors, at a national congress of Social Democrats. His initial glimpse of Leon Trotsky occurred in London in 1907 at another congress. During the following decade, Stalin spent seven years either in jail or in exile. Consequently he was not able to take more than minimal advantage of his appointment in 1912 to the Central Committee of his party.

Stalin returned from Siberian exile to Petrograd (St. Petersburg before 1915) in March 1917, shortly after the Tsar was deposed. For three weeks, until Lenin's arrival from Switzerland, he was the leader of the party. On the day after the October revolution, Stalin became Chairman of the Commissariat for Nationalities—a position deriving from his first theoretical work, written in 1913 at Lenin's suggestion, on the Marxist view of national states and nationalist movements. He shortly became a member, along with Lenin, Trotsky, and Jacob Sverdlov, of the executive of the Central Committee.

By 1922 Stalin had most of the political power in his hands. (He did not obtain absolute rule until 1929.) As Commissar for Nationalities, he supervised almost half of the nation's population. As Commissar of the Workers' and Peasants' Inspectorate—a position he got in 1919—he was in charge of inspecting every branch of government for corruption and inefficiency. In April 1922, he was appointed to the new office of Secretary-General of the Central Committee, which enabled him to manage the party's affairs on a day-to-day basis.

After Lenin's third stroke, in March 1923, a triumvirate of Stalin, L. Kamenev, and G. Zinoviev was formed in the Politbureau to prevent Trotsky from succeeding Lenin. (The other members of the Politbureau, besides Trotsky and the triumvirate, were N. Bukharin and M. Tomsky.) In January 1925, Stalin forced Trotsky to resign his position as Commissar of War. A few years later, Trotsky was ousted from the party, and in early 1928 he was exiled to Alma Ata (about 1,800 miles southeast of Moscow). In the following year, he was deported to Turkey, and after short stays in France and Norway, he arrived in Mexico in

1937. There, three and a half years later, he was murdered by one of Stalin's followers.

Stalin's victory over Trotsky owed something to his more ruthless and tenacious propensities and to the latter's aloofness and his almost stupid behavior in the face of fierce opponents. It had more to do, however, with two objective conditions that strengthened the one man and weakened the other. The first was the Bolsheviks' loss of domestic support, which made a strong centralized party machine necessary for the retention of their power and brought on the degeneration of the party from a body of theorist-activists to a burgeoning bureaucracy of administrators. Stalin's position within that changing structure was strengthened daily. The second was the failure of foreign revolution, which supported Stalin's thesis of "socialism in one country" and weakened Trotsky's thesis of "permanent revolution."

As soon as Stalin had Trotsky on the run, he no longer required the triumvirate. For a time, Kamenev and Zinoviev, frightened by Stalin's moves, joined with Trotsky against Stalin. Operating from the center, but now drawing his support from the right-wing (Bukharin, Tomsky, and A. Rykov), Stalin from 1925 to 1928 promoted "right" policies, which stressed harmony, steady progress, a pro-peasant outlook, and a belief that this was a period of capitalist stability in the West.

But because serious grain shortages developed in early 1928, and for other reasons, Stalin suddenly abandoned this conservative set of policies and called for tough measures against the *kulaks*. This was quickly followed by the Soviets' first five-year plan, which included programs for the collectivization of agriculture and the full nationalization of industry. Thus, after routing the leading leftists of the party, Stalin now more or less adopted their radical program, and, from this vantage point, began his attack on the rightists.

For the next twelve years, Stalin fashioned an economic-development program that emphasized extraordinarily high rates of saving and investment, the promotion of heavy industry and huge enterprises, the growth of urban areas, and military production. By the time Hitler invaded the Soviet Union in June 1941, the economy was strong enough to withstand the initial assaults and eventually to turn defeats into victories—aided by Stalin as Supreme Commander of the armed forces.

The murder of Sergei Kirov (a high-ranking party leader) in Leningrad in December 1934 sparked Stalin's drive of oppression that led to the great purges of 1936-38. He focused first on his own staff, then on the party in Leningrad, next on lower levels of the party and administration throughout the country, and finally on the very top levels of the party and armed forces.

After World War II, Marxism came to Eastern Europe, partly by conquest (by the U.S.S.R.) and partly by revolution from within. China's revolution followed in 1949, despite Stalin's efforts to delay Mao's all-out offensive against Chiang Kai-shek.

The Soviet economy recovered rapidly after 1945. The first Soviet atomic bomb was detonated in 1949; Stalin carried out an anti-Titoist purge of Eastern Europe's Communist parties, 1949-52; and the Soviets supplied war materiel to the Chinese and to North Korea during the Korean War.

In Stalin's last years, the cult of the leader reached its peak, and the country descended into megalomania, xenophobia, and anti-Semitism. Stalin died, at the age of 73, on March 5, 1953.

take the edge off that strife and reduce it to a minimum. . . . The final disappearance of a national movement is possible only with the downfall of the bourgeoisie."

Eleven years later, immediately after Lenin's death, Stalin published *The Foundations of Leninism,* which helped to establish his leadership of the party, and at the same time established "Marxism-Leninism" as the relevant body of knowledge for Marxists. Stalin defined Leninism as the further development of Marxism in the era of imperialism—the theory and tactics of the proletarian revolution and the dictatorship of the proletariat. This definition has been widely accepted by Marxists, even up to the present day, although those Marxists who support China would broaden it to include "Marxism-Leninism and Mao Tse-tung Thought."

As early as 1925, Stalin hinted at his opposition to equality of wages, but he made it explicit for the first time in a speech in 1931. Three years later, in his report to the 17th Party Congress, he went on to state that Marxism is an enemy of egalitarianism. He defended inequalities in the short-term as necessary for building the nation's productive forces, which were the only basis for the final elimination of poverty. Thus, just as the short-term support of nationalism was necessary for its ultimate demise, so the acceptance of poverty and inequalities was required for their long-term elimination. Stalin's denunciation of egalitarian tendencies has not been widely accepted within Marxist circles, and in recent years the doctrine has been roundly denounced by Mao, who, while agreeing with Stalin that perfect equality was not desirable or attainable in the socialist stage of development, believed that narrowing wage differentials whenever feasible was essential.

In his report to the 18th Party Congress in 1939, Stalin announced that Soviet society was at last free of class conflicts and presented "a picture of friendly collaboration between workers, peasants and intellectuals." It no longer contained antagonistic, hostile classes, since the exploiting classes had been eliminated. This pronouncement opened the way for Stalin's successors to declare that the Soviet state, and likewise the Communist party, were the state and party for all the people. Mao vigorously challenged this thesis in the late 1950s, maintaining that the class struggle would necessarily continue throughout the entire era of socialist development.

Stalin's essay *Dialectical and Historical Materialism* appeared in 1938. Many communist leaders have felt compelled to publish something on the philosophical foundations of Marxism, and Stalin evidently could not resist this urge. His effort, however, was rather humdrum, and only a few points stood out. Following Engels, Stalin extended the dialectical method from human societies to all of nature, an interpretation much disputed by Marxists today. He discussed historical materialism with little attention to the dialectical relation between human beings and their environment—*i.e.*, to people changing their world and being changed at the same time. Instead, his emphasis was on "the laws of development," the conditions of material life of society. Similarly, his account of the dependence of relations of production on forces of production amounted almost to technological determinism, with the human factor largely missing from the picture. Thus, he approvingly quoted Marx's statement that the handmill gives you a feudal society and the steam-mill an industrial-capitalist one. (See page 13.) While recognizing the revolutionary role of the proletariat, he gave no attention to the manner in which the proletariat, on the basis of revolutionary consciousness, transforms itself by engaging in revolutionary movements. Stalin's treatment of this subject lent itself rather easily to a more-or-less mechanical or non-dialectical interpretation of the historical movement of societies.

In 1950, Stalin's essay *Marxism and Problems of Linguistics* appeared in *Pravda*. He declared that language is not an element of the superstructure, and hence does not correspond to, or change with, the economic base; it is not an element or a product of the base. "It was created not by some one class, but by the entire society, by all the classes of the society, by the efforts of hundreds of generations." There are, of course, class dialects, jargons, and so on, but these are not class languages. There are also class cultures, he said, but culture is not language, for the latter may be common to two or more cultures. Stalin then observed that language might be analogous to machines in the economic base, in that both manifest "a kind of indifference toward classes and can serve equally different classes of society, both old and new." (The implication that the march of technology is inexorable, unaffected by the class struggle, has been heatedly denied of late by a group of young Marxists.) In the end, Stalin dismissed the analogy—but not the inexorable march of technology—and so set language outside of Marx's framework.

In the Stalin-directed Soviet society of yesterday, this shift in the view of language opened the way for identification of other "independent elements," such as mathematics, the facts of science (but not their interpretation), and logic, and so freed many researchers from the narrow Stalinist versions of their subject-matter. It allowed the sciences more freedom to develop, inasmuch as they were no longer considered to be class-related.

Marxist doctrine generally holds that the economic base of society determines the superstructure. A few years before his treatise on linguistics was published, Stalin put forward the view that in a socialist society, such as the Soviet Union, the superstructure assumes a much more active role than it does in a capitalist society and becomes increasingly influential on the economic base. In pre-socialist societies, Stalin pointed out, the laws of social development are unknown, and so those societies develop blindly. In socialism, the Communist party can consciously guide social development in terms of known laws and so can act as a motor of social progress. Thus, the party, through its five-year plans, has a primary role to play in directing society through socialism and toward communism.

Perhaps Stalin's major work was his last, *Economic Problems of Socialism in the U.S.S.R.*, written in 1952, just a year before his death, and intended to serve as a basis for discussion in the 19th Party Congress. In the discussion of his initial topic, the character of economic laws under socialism, his main points were that economic laws, as against scientific (natural) laws, do not last indefinitely, but belong only to historical periods; and that people cannot abolish either scientific or natural laws, but they can control, manage, and harness them. However, "unlike the laws of natural science, where the discovery and application of a new law proceeds more or less smoothly, the discovery and application of a new law in the economic field, affecting as it does the interests of obsolescent forces of society, meets with the most powerful resistance on their part." This distinction has been used by Marxists in recent years to explain the difficulties of transforming people's consciousness from bourgeois to proletarian forms.

Stalin next turned to the question of whether all "commodities" (as distinct from "products"—see page 00) are eliminated under socialism. His answer was that ordinarily they are not, because not all the means of production are socialized (that is, nationalized, or owned by all the people)—the rest being collectivized (that is, owned by the members of a collective only) or in private hands. The goods turned out and "exchanged" within the nationalized sector are truly "products," but in all other transactions they are "commodities," inasmuch as they are produced by one set of owners and bought by another. "Of course, when instead of the two basic production sectors, the state sector and the collective-farm sector, there will be only one all-embracing production sector, with the right to dispose of all the consumer goods produced in the country, commodity circulation, with its 'money-economy,' will disappear. . . ." Stalin went on to claim that commodity production under socialism is confined within strict bounds and so is not likely to lead back to capitalism. Finally, the existence of commodity production implies the existence of the law of value—that is, the exchange of commodities in terms of the socially-necessary labor-time embodied in them. When socialism is transformed into communism, both commodities and value will disappear, for only products will be produced and they will be distributed according to the needs of the people.

For a socialist society to attain communism, Stalin wrote, at least three main preliminary conditions have to be satisfied. First, there must be a continuous expansion of all social production, but the means of production must expand even faster. Second, collective-farm property must be raised to national property and commodity circulation replaced by a system of products-exchange. In this sense, he said, the Soviet Union's relations of production were lagging behind the seven-league strides of its productive forces. Third, there must be an all-around cultural and educational advancement of society, so that its members may lead fuller, happier, and more varied lives. "Only after *all* these preliminary conditions have been satisfied in their entirety will it be possible to pass from the socialist formula, 'from each according to his ability, to each according to his work,' to the communist formula, 'from each according to his ability, to each according to his needs.' "

As we have already seen, there are reasons for believing that the Soviet Union is no longer progressing toward communism, but may in fact be slipping backward. It is evidently much more difficult to close in on communism than most Marxists believed several decades ago. In the next chapter, we shall observe how Mao and the Chinese Communist party approached this formidable task.

CHAPTER SIX

MAO AND THE BUILDING OF SOCIALISM

MAO TSE-TUNG was a Marxist revolutionary his entire adult life. But, unlike Marx, Mao did not pursue the economic theory of exploitation and capitalist processes. And, unlike Lenin, he applied his talents over long periods of time not only to revolution but also to the task of building a socialist society. For almost half a century—ever since he first took to the hills in 1927 to found a revolutionary base area—Mao combined revolution against an old society with construction of a new one. His base areas in the years 1927-49 contained not only guerrilla armies but also economic development programs to improve the lives of the people residing in them. Thus, before gaining national power in 1949, Mao and his party, unlike Lenin and his, accumulated a wealth of experience on the design and implementation of economic policies, such as land reforms and agricultural development. After becoming the guiding spirit of his nation, Mao continued his search for a Chinese model of economic development—a Chinese path to communism.

Today, China is a rapidly developing country that has been freed of the worst afflictions suffered by its people over the centuries. This transformation in a few decades from the old to the new China has been noticed by many of the world's poor and in time is likely to change their own lives. What Marx and Engels started and Lenin and Stalin continued, Mao carried forward.

It required a few centuries and several revolutions for capitalism to establish itself on the ashes of feudalism in Western Europe. Socialism has had an equally difficult time in the world at large. The Russians and Chinese have carried out the two largest proletarian revolutions to date, and several smaller nations have followed in their wakes. It is likely that some of these socialist buds will die out or be crushed—a few already have—and some will no doubt flower. The ultimate outcome of these attempts to fashion socialist societies depends on too many factors to be easily handled here. However, it is useful, before turning to China's efforts at socialist development, tó compare the starting points from which the two socialist giants—the U.S.S.R. and China—set out to establish socialism. These starting points were so dissimilar that this fact alone offers valuable insights into why the two countries took such divergent paths in their pursuit of presumably the same end.

Starting Points: Russia and China

As we have seen, the Chinese Communists contend that the U.S.S.R. has failed to achieve socialism and has in fact retrogressed to a form of state capitalism. Whatever one's judgment about this, facts confirm that the Bolsheviks, during their first few years in power, encountered enormous problems in their efforts to establish a transition between capitalism and socialism. These early difficulties may have proved so redoubtable as to make it extremely laborious for them to produce and then retain socialism in their land. A discussion of these difficulties will throw much light on Chinese development.

Lack of Socialist Theory and Practice

First, in contrast to the Chinese Communist party (CCP), the Bolsheviks had no experience and very little theory to assist them in the building of a socialist society. They had carried out no land reforms, no programs of income redistribution, no development policies. Indeed, most of the Russian Marxist leaders had lived in European cities much of the time prior to the revolution, a background totally different from Mao's life in the mountains among the peasants of his own country. Lenin and the other Bolsheviks gave little systematic thought to what things would be like after the revolution, with the result that when the time came to move forward they did not have a clear conception of the path that should be followed. Lenin in 1923 virtually admitted that the party, with its attention riveted on the revolution, had followed Napoleon's dictum: "First engage in a serious battle and then see what happens." Further, Bolshevik ideas about economic policies were often mutually contradictory, for the party was seriously split on these issues. In this respect, the CCP was ideologically more unified by the time it assumed power in 1949, and by then it knew a great deal about peasants' miseries and how to alleviate them, though it had inadequate knowledge about urban, industrial problems.

Added Difficulty of Being First

Second, in addition to their lack of theory and practice in this area, the tasks before the Bolsheviks were exceedingly difficult. Lenin pointed this out in early 1918: "The more backward the country which, owing to the zigzags of history, has proved to be the one to start the socialist revolution, the more difficult is it for that country to pass from the old capitalist relations to socialist relations. New incredibly difficult tasks, organizational tasks, are added to the tasks of destruction." These "incredibly difficult tasks" included the major one of mobilizing the people to raise quickly the country's productive forces—without at the same time nourishing bourgeois values, incentives, and institutions that in time would transform the society back into a capitalist one. The building of bourgeois societies in the past, Lenin said, was a relatively easy job, for much had been formed within the womb of the previous societies, as the resistance of workers and peasants to the rising bourgeoisie had been weak, and the spontaneously growing national and international markets had been enormous aids to the new class. But the task of the proletariat was now much harder, as Lenin explained:

> ... the principal task of the proletariat, and of the poor peasants which it leads, is the positive or constructive work of setting up an extremely intricate and delicate system of new organizational relationships extending to the planned production and distribution of goods required for the existence of tens of millions of people. Such a revolution can be successfully carried out only if the majority of the population, and primarily the majority of working people, engage in independent creative work as makers of history. Only if the proletariat and the poor peasants display sufficient class-consciousness, devotion to principle, self-sacrifice and perseverance, will the victory of the socialist revolution be assured. By creating a new, Soviet type of state, which gives the working and oppressed people the chance to take an active part in the independent building up of a new society, we solved only a small part of this difficult problem. The principal difficulty

lies in the economic sphere, namely, the introduction of the strictest and universal accounting and control of the production and distribution of goods, raising the productivity of labor and *socializing* production *in practice.*

Of course, the Chinese faced much the same problem from equally depressed economic conditions, but they did have the experience of the U.S.S.R. to draw upon. They had learned from the mistakes made and the economic victories won by the Soviets. They knew, or could quickly learn, about five-year plans, investment programs, and other economic operations.

Narrow Political Base

Third, the Bolsheviks' strength was narrowly confined to the cities. They came to power not on the basis of having organized the peasants, not on the wings of socialist demands by this numerous class, but because of the support of the poorer industrial workers of Petrograd and Moscow plus spontaneous uprisings of peasants who called for land to the tillers, a petty-bourgeois demand. The party was city-based and hardly knew the countryside. Even as late as 1924, G.E. Zinoviev, a prominent Bolshevik leader, could admit that "the party is still too much an urban party, we know the country too little." To cover up this weakness, symbolic appointments of "peasants" were made, an example being Kalinin as president of the All-Russian Central Executive Committee, who, as Lenin explained (with perhaps some irony), "still keeps up his connection with the country . . . and visits it every year." Thus, the Bolsheviks did not have roots among the great majority of the people who, consequently, were largely ignorant of anything approaching socialist ideology or goals. It was this gluey mass of rural petty-bourgeoisie that quickly enveloped and then immobilized the Bolsheviks.

By contrast, Mao and the CCP worked with and mobilized increasing numbers of peasants for at least 20 years before they captured power. By 1949, millions of peasants had had first-hand experience with struggles against landlords and moneylenders, and many others knew of these exploits. Mao's party was implanted in his country's most numerous class; it sowed seeds of socialism everywhere, and thus, after 1949, could move forward into collectivization and other socialist programs with more facility than the Soviets had mustered.

Disruption Caused by Civil War

Fourth, several months after assuming control, the Bolsheviks were plunged into a civil war supported by foreign powers, which lasted for two and a half years and brought the Bolsheviks to their knees—in the end to the point of bare survival. At the close of this holocaust, tens of thousands had been killed and the economic machinery of the country had come almost to a standstill. But for the Bolsheviks, as a party, the most damaging blow was the dissipation of the industrial proletariat, the very base of party support. The fighting not only damaged and disrupted production, not only led to the deaths of significant numbers of former industrial workers who had been mobilized into the armies, but brought about a mass flight of urban workers and their families to the countryside in search of food. The number of industrial workers declined from around 2½ to 3 million in 1917 to 1⅕ million in 1921-22. Petrograd lost almost 60 percent of its population in three years, and Moscow lost about 45 percent. The population of 40 provincial capitals fell by a third. At the termination of the civil war, which, in conjunction with the World War, ended almost six years of combat for the Russian people, industrial production was only about 20 percent of its 1913 level, and the proletariat had all but disappeared from the face of Russia. With no base in the countryside, the decimation of the proletariat was a shattering blow to Lenin's party. Lenin later noted that while the imperialists had failed to dislodge Bolshevism, they did solve half their problem by seriously retarding any forward movement to socialism.

While the Chinese Communists suffered similarly from the decade of anti-Japanese and civil wars, they had the advantage of winning their civil war *before* gaining national control. The corruption and ineptness of the Kuomintang (Chiang Kai-shek's Nationalist government, in power from 1927 to 1949) in its last years had alienated growing numbers of its erstwhile supporters. This enabled the Communists to ride to power on waves of goodwill and enthusiasm. By comparison, Lenin's party, having already won power, bore the discontent and sufferings of the populace, and received the blame for the human misery in the country that spread with the civil war.

The Isolation of Bolshevism

Fifth, Lenin, Trotsky, and others claimed that socialism could not be built in a single country that was surrounded by class enemies and that did not receive help from foreign proletarian governments. Lenin stated this frankly on several occasions, and Trotsky gnawed on the issue to the end of his life. Isaac Deutscher, in his book *The Prophet Armed*, has expressed Trotsky's position on this point most poignantly:

> But to Trotsky the isolation of Bolshevism was already a nightmare too terrible to contemplate, for it meant that the first and so far only attempt to build socialism would have to

> be undertaken in the worst possible conditions, without the advantages of an intensive international division of labor, without the fertilizing influence of old and complex cultural traditions, in an environment of such staggering material and cultural poverty, primitiveness, and crudity as would tend to mar or warp the very striving for socialism.

The disadvantages of the isolation were that it would compel Russia to devote precious scarce resources to defense, deny her the industrial aid of more advanced countries, all but eliminate potential gains from trade with these countries, and shut her off from opportunities to raise her cultural level. The very striving for socialism was bound to be warped in such an environment of deprivation.

In this respect, too, the Chinese were in a superior position. For one thing, they received valuable industrial and technical help, as well as protection, from the U.S.S.R. during the early, crucial years of their industrialization. For another, despite hostile actions by the United States, implacable foes were not posed for the kill around China's borders. During most of the 1950s, the Communist countries of North Vietnam, North Korea, and Mongolia, as well as India, Pakistan, and others, were tolerant neighbors. The Bolsheviks were in a much less comfortable position during their first decade.

Inadequate Cadre Base

Sixth, the ranks of the Bolsheviks were too thin to allow them to replace the bureaucracies of the Tsar, to provide industry with the specialists and technicians required for industrial leadership, to supply the needed manpower for the planning agencies, and to fill the top positions in the Red Army, Consequently, as time went by, in E.H. Carr's apt simile, "more and more of the bricks and foundation-stones of the old dilapidated edifice were used in the construction of the new." This meant that the Bolsheviks had to work through thickening walls of hostility, or at least of evasion, in order to reach the people. "Down below," Lenin complained in 1922, "there are hundreds of thousands of old officials whom we got from the Tsar and from bourgeois society and who, partly deliberately and partly unwittingly, work against us."

By contrast, the Chinese Communists had large numbers of trained, dedicated cadres to implement policies at the village level and to carry out other necessary functions. In short, not only did Mao's party have a much broader base of support, it also had a sizable body of experienced party workers to make contact with the masses of workers and peasants.

Harvest by Li Hua

Early Loss of Continuity

Finally, what significance should be assigned to Lenin's disability and death only a few years after the cessation of hostilities, while Mao lived on to guide his country for more than a quarter of a century? It is, naturally, impossible to say what would have happened in the U.S.S.R. if Lenin had lived another 20 years, but, as already noted, in his last years he was acutely aware of the serious, growing problems facing the party and so might have dealt with them effectively. In any case, the U.S.S.R. quickly lost its premier leader and with him the continuity of its philosophical outlook. In contrast, Mao, despite some serious errors, which he later admitted, provided his party and country with a consistent, continuing philosophical framework within which to judge and decide policy actions.

The Bolsheviks started out in a hole, the hole was deepened by subsequent events, and, to crawl out, the party had to choose from a restricted set of programs, none of which led easily to socialism.

The Soviet Influence on China

The Chinese Communist revolutionary movement was born out of struggles against feudalism and imperialism in China and out of the fires of the Russian revolution. Stalin both encouraged this new revolutionary movement and enfeebled it. Turning East to protect the isolated, backward Soviet Union from British and Japanese imperialism, Stalin sought a strong anti-imperialist ally in the Kuomintang (Chiang Kai-shek's Nationalist party). He therefore ordered the members of the young Chinese Communist party to join the Kuomintang and to collaborate with it, an instruction that resulted in some loss of independence for the revolutionary party and some increase in its vulnerability to hostile forces within the Kuomintang. In April 1927, in the midst of the Northern Expedition, in which the Kuomintang was attempting by military means to forge a unified national government, Chiang suddenly ordered the massacre of Shanghai workers and Communists, who had just delivered the city over to him. The death toll has been estimated at 5,000. At about the same time, Kuomintang repression descended on urban workers and Communists elsewhere. This treacherous about-face broke the collaboration between the two groups; it was reestablished only in the wake of the Japanese invasion of China in 1937.

Thus, it was the Soviet Union's geographical and political isolation, owing to the failures of proletarian revolutions in the West, that produced Stalinism and the Soviet Union's China policy, which contributed to the defeat of the CCP in the cities. Unlike the pattern earlier in Russia, the strength of imperialism in the cities also pushed the CCP toward ruralization. The revolution was driven into the countryside, into the midst of backward, scattered peasants, and there base areas were established and defended against repeated military attacks by the Kuomintang.

A peasant-based, military-oriented, revolutionary movement, Maoism was the ideological reflection of China's backwardness (rudimentary productive forces and so a preponderance of peasants); its deep traditions were shaped largely in isolation from the rest of the world over the millennia, and more immediately the failure of the proletarian revolution in China's cities during the 1920s had its effect. These factors produced Mao as the leader of the movement, because he embodied the attributes demanded by the historical circumstances.

The isolation of the CCP from its urban workers further deepened the isolation of the Soviet Union from the rest of the world—Stalin's failure in China disheartened the Soviet bureaucracy and convinced it that no revolutionary help would be forthcoming for some time from either the West or the East. However, these two isolations—the U.S.S.R.'s and the CCP's—produced quite different economic results.

The Soviet Union's backwardness and its isolation in a growingly hostile world, as we earlier observed, led to an overemphasis on bourgeois efficiency criteria in building up the productive forces. The policy cost the country growing inequalities, the depoliticization of the masses, and great imbalances in the economy, especially the serious neglect of agriculture, rural areas, and consumer goods.

The CCP, on the other hand, driven into terribly impoverished areas, and under steady military attack, found it almost impossible to emphasize productive forces, and instead concentrated first on changing the relations of production and the superstructure. Maoism thus very early developed into a rural-based movement that emphasized social transformation (land reforms, cooperatives, women's liberation, ideological remolding, and so on) before technical transformation, and, partly because of its constant defensive military campaigns, stressed mass movements among the people of the base areas. These early characteristics it largely retained.

The Chinese Communist revolutionary victory in 1949 was the result of the growing appeal among the peasants of the CCP's social and economic policies, the nationalist fervor which swept across the population, and which the CCP appropriated, as the Japanese cut more deeply into the homeland, and the opportunities provided to the CCP by the turmoil produced by monopoly capitalism's second great internecine war. Thus, the same historical forces that produced Leninism, World War I, and the Russian revolution (that is, the transformation of competitive capitalism into monopoly capitalism and imperialism, uneven development among capitalist powers, and bitter rivalry among them), also produced Japanese imperialism, World War II, and the ensuing Chinese revolution.

Marxist China owes its own existence to that of the Soviets. Despite Stalin's initial efforts to hold back the Chinese Communist revolution after 1945, the Soviet Union, by its later friendship with Mao's China, protected it from the encroachments of the imperialist nations during the late 1940s and early 1950s. In the absence of the Soviet state, world imperialism (which, of course, would have included Russia), even though weakened after World War II, would have halted the Chinese and other Marxian revolutions in Asia for some time, or at least would have co-opted them. The Soviet Union, by aid and trade, also helped China in the 1950s to establish a strong economic base of productive forces.

By the time of the Chinese revolution in 1949, the rural isolation of the CCP left it greatly dependent on the urban-industrial knowledge of the Soviet Union. The same historical processes that enabled the Chinese to find a new path to Marxian socialism also compelled them in the 1950s to accept temporarily the 1930s Soviet model of economic development—out of fear of cities, lack of knowledge about heavy industry, and inexperience in urban and national planning. The Soviet model, however, was geared to the U.S.S.R.'s own factor endowments, problems, and purposes, not to China's. Hence, in time, as we shall see, it became incompatible with the requirements of a party that represented the rural masses, believed in the efficacy of bold social transformation, strove to transcend bourgeois values and institutions, and had, in its revolutionary background, fashioned a theory and practice of economic development antithetical to the Soviet Union's. The Maoists, therefore, when they were able to, overthrew the Soviet model in favor of their own "guerrilla economics," which they called the Great Leap Forward.

We will see later that Mao's sudden swing away from the Stalinist model at the time that Soviet revisionism was taking hold under Khrushchev contributed to the Sino-Soviet split in the early 1960s. Moreover, the failures associated with Mao's new policies led to another split—between him and other Chinese leaders, who advocated more conventional measures for economic development. Within a few years, Mao discovered the means to eliminate (at least for the time being) the second split and at the same time to reinforce the first one—the Great Proletarian Cultural Revolution. This cultural revolution not only strengthened Maoism as a foreign policy primarily aimed against the Soviet Union but also for a time reestablished Maoism as a domestic development strategy.

While owing its life to Bolshevism, Maoism necessarily developed along lines radically different from those of the Soviet Union, along lines which preserved and deepened the revolutionary content of Marxian socialism, and which attracted China to revolutionary Marxism in the underdeveloped areas of the world and repelled it from revisionist Marxism in the advanced industrial countries.

The Formation of Mao's Economic Strategy

The Chinese Communists got off to a better start than did the Soviets, and they have made much of these opportunities. A large share of the credit for their accomplishments belongs to Mao Tse-tung, the designer of a substantial part of China's strategy for economic development. Mao's ideas as to how his country should develop after liberation were fashioned from his voracious reading and from practical experiences during the previous three decades. These were the years during which his early economic theories and policies were formulated, not only in the quiet contemplation of Marxian literature, but also in the fiery crucible of the Chinese revolution.

The Evolving Strategy

Mao considered himself a Marxist by 1920, when he was 26 years of age. During the next seven years, he was engaged in communist activities in Shanghai, Canton, and his home province of Hunan. From 1923 to 1927, the Chinese Communists collaborated with Chiang Kai-shek's Nationalist party, as we have just seen. But Chiang proved faithless to this alliance and succeeded in putting the Communists to rout.

After Chiang's betrayal, Mao and a group of guerrillas, probably no more than a thousand, formed a revolutionary base area in the mountains on the border of Hunan and Kiangsi provinces. There and in neighboring areas for the next seven years, 1927-34, Mao's group struggled to shape both a revolutionary army and a viable economic society. It was in these mountains that Mao first learned something about economics—the hard way. Later, from 1935 to 1949, after Chiang had driven the Communists out of their base areas and forced them into the Long March to the loess plateaus and ravines of Shensi province in the northwest, Mao learned much more—from reading Marx, Lenin, Stalin, and other Soviet authors and from practical experiences with economic programs carried out in the Communists' new territories. When Mao and his party gained national power in 1949, they already had two decades of economic experience behind them. Thus, they were in a position, from the very beginning, to apply nationally what they had already achieved regionally.

Mao very early placed a high value on economics, despite the fact that he was almost constantly warding off military attacks. But Mao saw a connection between the two: "If the workers and peasants become dissatisfied with their living conditions, will it not affect the expansion of our Red Army and the mobilization of the masses for the revolutionary war? Therefore it is utterly wrong to think that no economic construction should be undertaken in the midst of the revolutionary war." Economic successes themselves would not only enlist the support of peasants and workers for military engagements but would also increase the food, clothing, and other items so badly needed for these revolutionary battles. During the anti-Japanese war, 1937-45, Mao urged production efforts even in the guerrilla zones, where the military situation was unstable and fluid and the Communists had uncertain control over the population.

Mao's economic objective was to expand the productive forces in order to raise living standards in ways that would consolidate the political power of the peasants. As early as 1927, in writing about the peasants' revolutionary movements in Hunan province, Mao spelled out a development strategy for achieving such a goal:

> At the present time ... the peasants are concentrating on destroying the landlords' political authority. Wherever it has been wholly destroyed, they are beginning to press their attack in the three other spheres of the clan, the gods and male domination. But such attacks have only just begun, and there can be no thorough overthrow of all three until the peasants have won complete victory in the economic struggle. Therefore, our present task is to lead the peasants to put their greatest efforts into the political struggle, so that the landlords' authority is entirely overthrown. The economic struggle should follow immediately, so that the land problem and other economic problems of the poor peasants may be fundamentally solved. As for the clan system, superstition, and inequality between men and women, their abolition will follow as a natural consequence of victory in the political and economic struggles.

This strategy, expressed here in broad strokes, was: politics first, then economics, and finally ideology. This was the line of attack organized by the Maoists during these early years. The more detailed strategy that they subsequently worked out is outlined as follows:

Policies	Area of Impact
1. Win the political (revolutionary war) struggle	The "state" in the superstructure
2. Win the economic (production) struggle	Economic base
a. Carry out land reform	
b. Carry out land investigation	Relations of production
c. Promote mutual aid and cooperatives	
d. Raise the status of women	
e. Develop agricultural and industrial productive forces	Productive forces
3. Win the cultural and ideological struggle	Superstructure

The first policy—winning the political struggle—required military victories by the Red armies, the seizure of power by the Communist party as the vanguard of the working classes, and the fixing of political power in the hands of peasants and workers. To Mao, nothing could be accomplished without political power. Thus, military tactics and strategy claimed much of his time, and he has, accordingly, written more on these matters than he has on economics.

After political power in an area was garnered, Mao's second set of policies was to win the economic struggle, to alter the economic base of the area. He proposed to do this by first changing the social relations of production and then developing the area's productive forces. The relations of production could be transformed, Mao believed, by land reforms, evaluations by the peasants of the results of these reforms, the formation of cooperatives for the production and distribution of goods, and efforts to improve the status of women (though a lessening of male domination could also be considered a change of the superstructure as well). Only after the social relations were largely transformed did Mao recommend strenuous efforts to raise the level of the productive forces, for only then would the fruits of this development be widely distributed rather than captured by the few at the top and primarily by males. Finally, Mao's program was completed with a cultural and ideological struggle to transform the old ideas and values, and their supporting institutions, into new ones. This generally took the form of group discussions about how values of the old society supported a class structure that served to subjugate the peasants and about the significance of socialist values in the new society.

Smash Economism, anonymous

As Mao saw it, the lives of poor peasants could not be materially improved if they did not have political power. That was preeminent. Nor could they achieve such material gains if the old institutions and practices most closely associated with their work remained untouched. For, in these traditional circumstances, the peasants' productivity would be shackled by their tenuous claims on land and product; by their associated attitudes of subservience, fatalism, and resignation; by their lack of awareness of the world around them and therefore by their propensity for spiritual and private explanations of personal disasters; by their lack of organization, their willingness to work hard for very little; and by their being easily manipulated by the ruling classes. Accordingly, Mao believed, the old social relations imposed on work institutions and practices had to be shattered to make room for new, more liberating ones. The new relations of production would release a huge reservoir of peasant energy and creativity and, hence, would do more to increase production than any number of new agricultural implements. Man is more important, Mao insisted, than the machine.

If, on the contrary, machines were introduced first, before the traditional social relations had been swept away, the old class structures and seats of power would quickly reassert themselves, resulting in the concentration of any production gains in a few hands. The fruits of the peasants' more productive labor would be appropriated by the privileged classes, and this would be considered "natural" by the peasants— privileges bestowed by heaven. Therefore, Mao reasoned, agricultural and industrial development could not take place vigorously, and could not eventuate in equitable distribution, without the prior transformation of the society itself—but accomplished in a way that would at the same time transform the peasants from their ignorant, passive state to class-conscious activists. And *that* would require that the peasants change their society themselves; it could not be done for them.

Land reforms, through the confiscation of land and other assets of landlords, and the acquisition of this wealth by the peasants, aided in breaking the power of the ruling class and in establishing ownership patterns that encouraged peasants to work harder by changing their attitudes. Cooperatives also helped to organize the peasants and to provide them with institutions protecting them against the encroachment of economic predators. In addition, women were similarly shielded by their own organizations, which the Communists encouraged and which fought for women's rights in work and marriage. All of these efforts assisted in creating new work institutions and practices which, Mao believed, dramatically raised peasants' willingness and ability to exert themselves.

However, final liberation would not come until old ideologies were destroyed. Mao, therefore, launched an attack on the superstitions of the peasants, which arose from their subjection to the supernatural system, and which made them passive and resigned. Mao said that the "middle peasants" (those who owned some of the land they worked, from which most of their income was derived), in judging the new peasant associations, "knit their brows and think to themselves, 'Can the peasant associations really last?' 'Can the Three People's Principles prevail?' Their conclusion is, 'Afraid not!' They imagine it all depends on the will of Heaven and think, 'A peasant association? Who knows if Heaven wills it or not?' "

Mao related that, when he was in the countryside in early 1927 for his investigation of peasant conditions, he did some propaganda work against superstition. In this passage, containing a blend of Marxian class struggle and old Chinese tradition, he talked with the peasants:

> If you believe in the Eight Characters [a method of fortune telling in China], you hope for good luck; if you believe in geomancy [the superstition that the location of one's ancestors' graves influences one's fortunes], you hope to benefit from the location of your ancestral graves. This year within the space of a few months the local tyrants, evil gentry and corrupt officials have all toppled from their pedestals. Is it possible that until a few months ago they all had good luck and enjoyed the benefit of well-sited ancestral graves, while suddenly in the last few months their luck has turned and their ancestral graves have ceased to exert a beneficial influence? The local tyrants and evil gentry jeer at your peasant association and say, "How odd! Today, the world is a world of committeemen. Look, you can't even go to pass water without bumping into a committeeman!" Quite true, the towns and the villages, the trade unions and the peasant associations, the Kuomintang and the Communist party, all without exception have their executive committee members—it is indeed a world of committeemen. But is this due to the Eight Characters and the location of the ancestral graves? How strange! The Eight Characters of all the poor wretches in the countryside have suddenly turned auspicious! And their ancestral graves have suddenly started exerting beneficial influences! The gods? Worship them by all means. But if you had only Lord Kuan [a warrior around 200 A.D. who was widely worshiped as the God of Loyalty and War] and the Goddess of Mercy and

no peasant association, could you have overthrown the local tyrants and the evil gentry? The gods and goddesses are indeed miserable objects. You have worshiped them for centuries, and they have not overthrown a single one of the local tyrants or evil gentry for you! Now you want to have your rent reduced. Let me ask, how will you go about it? Will you believe in the gods or in the peasant associations?

Mao reported that these words "made the peasants roar with laughter."

There are times, Mao thought, when a cultural or ideological revolution must take precedence over any further attempts to develop the economic base. The Rectification Movement of 1942-44, held in Yenan during the height of the war with Japan, was the peak of Mao's early efforts to achieve ideological progress within the party. This movement was meant to teach large numbers of party members the fundamentals of Marxism and their application to the Chinese revolution. The party issued study documents on Marxian theory, Chinese history and problems, and Soviet affairs, organized discussion groups, and at the end held general examinations.

The need for the Rectification Movement grew out of the huge increases in party membership from 1937 to the early 1940s—from 40,000 to 800,000—and the ignorance of most of these new members of the Marxian basis of their party. The theme of the Rectification Movement was the union of "the universal truths of Marxism-Leninism with the concrete reality of the Chinese revolution." Mao demanded that Marxism be made Chinese. The specific target of the movement was the group of party leaders who had studied in Moscow and who, Mao felt, on returning to China used Marxism-Leninism in a dogmatic way that had little relevance for the concrete conditions of China's revolution. Mao believed that greater ideological unity in party work was essential during this period, given the intensified military demands imposed on the party by the Kuomintang and the Japanese, both of whom were on the attack against the Communists. It was during these difficult times that the entire Chinese Communist party went to school.

The prevailing opinion about the Rectification Movement is that it sought unity of thought and tight discipline, which, it was hoped, would increase the efficiency of party work. There is evidence to sustain this view, for the Reform Documents themselves, which contained the study papers distributed by the party, often were expressed in exactly this way. However, there is also evidence that this movement, by instructing cadres in Marxism-Leninism and by encouraging them to apply this world-outlook to Chinese problems, was also meant to increase the cadres' power of analysis—their ability to see the world correctly and hence to pursue realistic and intelligent goals—and their general intelligence. The intention was to present a valid picture of the modern world to the cadres so as to enable them to make correct decisions and act in a rational, scientific way. As Mao expressed this:

> Our comrades must understand that we do not study Marxism-Leninism because it is pleasing to the eye, or because it has some mystical value, like the doctrines of the Taoist priests who ascend Mao Shan [a mountain] to learn how to subdue devils and evil spirits. Marxism-Leninism has no beauty, nor has it any mystical value. It is only extremely useful.

The usefulness of Marxism-Leninism, according to Mao, lay in the "universal truth" of dialectical materialism, which is not dogma but a guide to action. The materialism of Marxism-Leninism tells us, Mao wrote in 1942, that "being determines consciousness, that the objective realities of class struggle and national struggle determine our thoughts and feelings." It instructs us that man's social practice—that is, his activity in the struggle for production, in class struggle, and in scientific and artistic pursuits—"exerts a profound influence on the development of man's knowledge." Mao later composed a passage, now famous, as the vehicle of these thoughts:

> Where do correct ideas come from: Do they drop from the skies? No. Are they innate in the mind? No. They come from social practice, and from it alone. . . . It is man's social being that determines his thinking. Once the correct ideas characteristic of the advanced class are grasped by the masses, these ideas turn into a material force which changes society and changes the world; . . . the one and only purpose of the proletariat in knowing the world is to change it. Often, a correct idea can be arrived at only after many repetitions of the process leading from matter to consciousness and then back to matter, that is, leading from practice to knowledge and then back to practice. Such is the Marxist theory of knowledge, the dialectical materialist theory of knowledge.

The Rectification Movement, in its economic dimensions, raised the ability of cadres and party members to deal effectively with problems of economic construction and reform. Mao expected that Marxist-Leninist thinking, a superior kind of thought, would lead to more correct answers, fewer mistakes, and to higher labor productivity.

"If the army and the people are united as one, who in the world can match them," from *The Rent Collection Courtyard*

In the summer of 1949, on the eve of complete victory over Chiang Kai-shek, Mao wrote: "Communists the world over are wiser than the bourgeoisie, they understand the laws governing the existence and development of things, they understand dialectics and they can see farther." That was the conviction behind the Rectification Movement.

The Chinese Revolution and Economic Strategy

The rising capitalist classes in Western Europe had carried out bourgeois revolutions against the old feudal classes. Eventually, Mao thought, the proletariat of these countries would carry out socialist revolutions against their capitalist classes. In the underdeveloped world (including China), the revolutionary movements prior to the Bolshevik revolution of 1917 were bourgeois-democratic, in that they were led by rising national capitalist classes of those countries against the old order with the objective in each case of establishing a bourgeois society. However, after the Bolshevik revolution, the situation in the underdeveloped world was profoundly changed. From that moment, the proletariat and the peasantry, aided by the emergence of the Soviet Union, began to assume command of the revolutionary movements with the objective of establishing a proletarian-socialist society, though only after a coalition of revolutionary classes (including sections of the bourgeoisie) had swept away feudalism and imperialism and paved the way with a transitional stage of "new democracy."

Mao pointed out that the new-democratic revolution was different from the old type because it would not result in a dictatorship of the bourgeoisie, as it did in Europe and America, but in a dictatorship of the united front of all revolutionary classes under the leadership of the proletariat. These revolutionary classes consisted of the proletariat, the peasantry, the urban petty bourgeoisie, and, at times, the national bourgeoisie (Chinese capitalists who had retained strong nationalist leanings and had few links to Japanese, British, or other foreign capital). The new revolution would result in new democracy, not in bourgeois society; it would prepare the way for socialism. It would not initially sweep away capitalism but would use it to increase production and help the country to change from an agricultural to an industrial society.

Mao's theory, therefore, was that, after the overthrow of feudalism and imperialism in China, there would be a transitional period of new democracy, which would be followed by socialism. Socialism, in turn, would lead to communism. New democracy would have a united front of revolutionary classes and some tolerance of capitalist development. Socialism would have the dictatorship of the proletariat and tolerance only for socialist development.

Inasmuch as the revolution would lead initially to a period of new democracy, Mao's economic policies from 1927 to 1949 were rather consistently within the bounds of capitalist private ownership. Mao wrote: "Our policy, including the confiscation of the land of the landlords and the enforcement of the eight-hour working day, never went beyond the bounds of capitalist private ownership; our policy was not to put socialism in practice then." Despite Mao's disclaimer, land confiscation without compensation did go beyond capitalist bounds by violating private property rights, but Mao was correct that he stayed within such bounds in the redistribution phases of the program by making private ownership and cultivation of land more widespread; he did not promote collectivization until much later, in the mid-1950s. Furthermore, the land confiscation itself broke up whatever feudal relationships still prevailed and so prepared the way for a more capitalistic development of agriculture.

While Mao's policies during this period were within the limits of capitalism, in that peasants owned private property, they were intended to prepare the way for socialism, which was the main objective. Mao discussed his short-term and long-term goals:

> We mean that the target of this revolution is not the bourgeoisie in general but national and feudal oppression, that the measures taken in this revolution are in general directed not at abolishing but at protecting private property, and that as a result of this revolution the working class will be able to build up the strength to lead China in the direction of socialism, though capitalism will still be enabled to grow to an appropriate extent for a fairly long period. "Land to the tiller" means transferring the land from the feudal exploiters to the peasants, turning the private property of the feudal landlords into the private property of the peasants and emancipating them from feudal agrarian relations, thereby making possible the transformation of an agricultural country into an industrial country. Thus, "land to the tiller" is in the nature of a bourgeois-democratic and not a proletarian-socialist demand.

In the years before the Communists' victory in 1949, Mao's moderate policies were constantly being attacked by other revolutionaries, including some of Mao's comrades, both from the right and from the left. Rightist tendencies, as Mao saw them, were those promoting bourgeois leadership of the revolution, those that stressed unity with the bourgeoisie with no element of struggle against it: "all alliances and no struggle." Leftist tendencies were policies that "jumped over" the new-democracy stage of the revolution to the socialist stage. They were policies of "all struggle and no alliance," of refusing to have anything to do with non-proletarian elements, of making no concessions—policies looking to the "immediate" establishment of socialism and the "immediate" demise of non-proletarian classes.

While Mao thought that both rightist and leftist tendencies in the party were pernicious, he was normally more concerned about the latter. He related to the American writer Edgar Snow that, at one revolutionary base area in the late 1920s, "we promoted a democratic program, with a moderate policy, based on slow but regular development. This earned [us] the recriminations of putschists [advocates of untimely uprisings] in the party, who were demanding a terrorist policy of raiding and burning, and killing landlords, in order to destroy their morale. [We] refused to adopt such tactics, and were therefore branded by the hotheads as 'reformists.' I was bitterly attacked by them for not carrying out a more 'radical' policy."

Soon after the completion in 1935 of the Long March—the Communist retreat from the pursuing forces of Chiang Kai-shek taking Mao's troops on a 6,000-mile semicircular trek to the northwest—the Communists formed a second united front with the Kuomintang against the Japanese invaders. As a result, Mao's land policies became even more moderate: land was no longer confiscated; instead, rent payments to landlords were reduced and interest payments of poorer debtors to their creditors were lowered. Mao justified these measures by claiming that the principal contradiction was now between the masses of Chinese and the Japanese imperialists, not between one class of Chinese and another. For this reason, the Maoists felt it necessary and possible to ally themselves with most of the bourgeoisie and with many landlords and rich peasants to win the war of resistance against Japan. These reformist policies were also attacked by the left.

In 1948, a year before the Communist takeover, Mao summed up his grievances against leftist policies, most of which he had fought against over the years:

> At present the "Left" deviations consist chiefly in encroaching on the interests of the middle peasants and the national bourgeoisie; laying one-sided stress in the labor movement on the immediate interests of the workers; making no distinctions in the treatment of landlords and rich peasants; making no distinctions in the treatment of big, middle, and small landlords, or of landlords who are local tyrants and those who are not; not leaving the landlords the necessary

"The crushing load of rent symbolizes the man–eating feudal system of exploitation," from *The Rent Collection Courtyard*

means of livelihood as required by the principle of equal distribution; over-stepping certain demarcation lines of policy in the struggle to suppress counterrevolution; not wanting political parties which represent the national bourgeoisie; not wanting the enlightened gentry; neglecting the tactical importance of narrowing the scope of attack in the new Liberated Areas (that is, neglecting to neutralize the rich peasants and small landlords); and lacking the patience to work step by step.

These warnings amounted to an admonition to the left to unite with as many groups as possible. On the whole, Mao's policies reflected both alliance and struggle. He insisted not only on unity with the national bourgeoisie and others, but also on struggle against them at the same time. Thus, an economic policy of lowering landlords' rents would have to be accompanied by educational efforts among peasants to explain the exploitative nature of *all* rents, high or low, and the reasons for the half-way measures.

The Strategy to Achieve Chinese Socialism

Although Mao and the Communist party accumulated rich experiences in rural development prior to 1949, they were not prepared, upon assuming national control, to unfurl a complete economic development plan for the country as a whole. They had definite notions regarding land reforms and rural improvement, but they were much less certain about urban and industrial development. Indeed, Mao was apprehensive about entering the cities: "The center of gravity of the party's work has shifted from the village to the city . . . . We must do our utmost to learn how to administer and build the cities . . . . If we do not pay attention to these problems . . . we shall be unable to maintain our political power, we shall be unable to stand on our own feet, we shall fail."

The Strategy of Economic Development

Only 25 years after Mao and his party captured national power, China had more than doubled agricultural production, raised industrial output by 20 times, kept population growth to about 60 percent, become a formidable military power, greatly reduced illiteracy, and virtually eliminated the threat of famine and most pestilence. The people of China had tripled their per capita incomes, achieved high employment levels without inflation. They could look forward with assurance to the education and good health of their children.

Of course, Mao alone did not fashion the policies to attain these results. Nevertheless, the strategy that evolved in the quarter-century after 1949, even though built on much trial and error, has turned out to bear a remarkably close resemblance to what he thought and did during his guerrilla days. In the 1950s, Mao restated his broad strategy almost exactly as he had worked it out in the mountains 30 years earlier: "Historical experience has proved that only by first creating revolutionary public opinion and seizing political power, and then changing the relations of production, is it possible to greatly develop the productive forces." And, as he added at another time, ideological revolutions are also necessary to lower further the barriers to continued economic progress.

This strategy for economic development was revealed in practice. First, the Communists seized political power from the Kuomintang in 1949. They then set out to consolidate this power through land reforms which aimed to eliminate the old ruling classes (the economic power behind the political force of the Kuomintang) and to fix power in the hands of the millions of peasants and workers. Second, the party radically changed the social relations of production in both the countryside and the cities. The initial change in the rural areas was land reform itself, which, aside from consolidating the party's political power, removed semi-feudal institutions in favor of private ownership mixed with cooperative efforts. In the next stage, the party initiated a series of collectivization measures. In urban areas, private enterprise was controlled and then gradually nationalized. Thus, socialist institutions and practices *preceded* the modernization of the country's productive forces, which means that industrialization and agricultural modernization have since taken place largely through socialist and not capitalist institutions.

Third, despite the priority given to socialism, the party did not wait for its completion before embarking on an enormous industrialization effort. Indeed, it was felt that, aside from its important military implications, heavy industry would be required if agriculture later on was to be transformed into a modern sector. Socialism in the rural areas clearly came first, but eventually it had to be followed by the infusion of modern inputs, such as electric power, machinery and tractors, chemical fertilizers, and the like.

Fourth, the party carried out ideological campaigns, such as those in the 1950s which were directed against bourgeois values, corruption, waste, bureaucracy, and antisocial behavior. But the major ideological campaign came as a cultural revolution in the late 1960s after the other elements of the strategy had been established. This timing accorded with Mao's belief that socialist values could be firmly implanted only in an environment that already contained rising output levels and socialist institutions. Only then could socialist ideas be reinforced by daily experience, and only then could these ideas react back on the economic base in a vigorous way. "The transformation of ideology into a system," Mao explained in the early 1960s, "invariably occurs at the end of the movement of things in general, because ideological understanding is a reflection of the movement of matter."

The Strategy and Economic Policies

That was the grand strategy. The economic policies that served as vehicles for the strategy occurred in six distinct waves:

1. Economic reconstruction and land reforms   1949-52
2. Industrialization, nationalization, and collectivization: The first Five-Year Plan   1953-57
3. The Great Leap Forward   1958-59
4. Readjustment and recovery; priority to agriculture   1960-65
5. The Great Proletarian Cultural Revolution   1966-69
6. Balanced growth   1970-

After the Communist takeover, the party immediately undertook the repair and reconstruction of the country's basic capital, which had been severely damaged during the 12 years of war. By 1952, China had more or less recovered its pre-1949 peak of economic activity. During this initial period, the party also carried out land reforms. The second period, 1953-57, saw the start and completion of a successful five-year plan, which was greatly aided by the U.S.S.R. and was accompanied by socialization measures in town and country.

From 1949 to 1956, however, the party considered the nation to be in the transition phase of new democracy. Accordingly, the land reforms in the countryside led to private ownership of land, which the party also encouraged in other ways. Capitalist enterprises in urban areas, while controlled, were sometimes encouraged too, at other times only tolerated. In any event, there were at first no concerted drives toward socialism, although some decisive moves in that direction were made immediately. Still, the new-democracy stage proved to be of much shorter duration than Mao had suggested it would be. By the mid-1950s, collectivization and nationalization were in full swing, and China, according to Mao, moved from new democracy to socialism at that time.

In the third development phase, 1958-59, the Great Leap Forward was a reflection of Mao's dissatisfaction with Soviet methods and his attempt to find a Chinese way to economic growth. It was a bold program to achieve phenomenal progress on all fronts through the mobilization of peasants and workers, men and women, civilians and soldiers, for heroic tasks, and, from the crest of these efforts, to "enter communism." The Great Leap aimed for the sky on the basis of traditional rural labor methods and the inspiration generated by collective goals and action. While the upsurge was astonishing for a year or so, it was soon brought to a halt by over-ambitious plans, miserable weather conditions, and the sudden departure from China of the Soviet technicians in mid-1960 after Khrushchev's break with Mao. As a consequence, economic activity declined precipitously during the first few years of the 1960s, the most serious setback being the sharp decline of agricultural output, especially grain. The party, therefore, in the fourth phase, desperately shifted its priorities to favor agriculture, including added emphasis on rural industries, agricultural machinery, and chemical fertilizers.

The economy rebounded from its low point in 1961-62 and gained momentum until the advent of the Great Proletarian Cultural Revolution (1966-69). This unprecedented campaign was Mao's attempt to rid the Party and the rest of the superstructure of bourgeois values and institutions. It was his effort to speed up economic development the socialist way, but the resulting turmoil did interfere temporarily with economic progress. Since 1969, the economy has made large gains on a broad front. The countryside has benefited from the rapid development of thousands of rural industries and from the repeated infusion of educators, doctors, technicians, young people from the cities, and cultural workers. Substantial progress has also been made in the urban areas in both heavy and light industry. In fact, since 1962 industry and agriculture have grown together and have supported each other in a mutual relationship that was largely missing during the 1950s under the Soviet model that overstressed heavy industry and neglected agriculture.

With that brief survey behind us, Mao's strategy for economic development can now be better understood if it is examined more closely within the context of some of the key economic policies just discussed.

Land Reforms

The primary objectives of the Agrarian Reform Law of 1950—Mao's basic land reform program—were to eliminate the feudal landlord system in the countryside, improve the lives of the poor, and develop agricultural production as a precondition for the country's industrialization. Land reform took not only land from landlords and some rich peasants but confiscated also their draft animals, farm implements,

Cooperation by Wan Shih–ssu

houses, and grain—and redistributed all of this to middle and poor peasants. Landlords, as a class, were wiped out by mass peasant struggles against them, confiscation, and execution. The Communist party encouraged and guided the peasants' struggles against their former oppressors, but the peasants themselves often took the law into their own hands, without the party's sanction, in deciding how to settle accounts with these people. Theoretically, the power of the landlords could have been nullified without killing any of them, but in fact the peasants' confrontations with their oppressors awakened grievances within them that ran much too deep to allow for that idyllic outcome. Mao knew that the rage of the rural poor, so long suppressed, could not be entirely controlled when the revolutionary turn came. "A revolution," Mao said early in his career, "is not a dinner party, or writing an essay, or painting a picture, or doing embroidery; it cannot be so refined, so leisurely and gentle, so temperate, kind, courteous, restrained and magnanimous. A revolution is an insurrection, an act of violence by which one class overthrows another."

In keeping with Mao's contention that the peasants had to liberate themselves, land reform was not simply legislated, passed, and carried out from above. It was a revolutionary movement involving millions of peasants struggling against their former tormentors, gaining confidence and understanding in the process, and taking actions themselves against the landlords that committed them to new lives and new ways, thus making the entire movement quite irreversible. This was the prerequisite for later socialist development in the countryside, for without it the old class structures and wealth ownership patterns would have been regenerated by the persistence of old attitudes and of institutions favorable to the rich. During part of the Yenan period, for example, when the party's policy was to lower the rents that peasants had to pay in grain to their landlords (generally from their previous level of 50 percent to around 30 percent of the crop), some peasants surreptitiously continued to pay the old, larger amounts because they feared landlord reprisals and presumably felt the former arrangement was part of the natural order of things.

The land reform helped to raise the ratio of gross investment to GNP from the 6-7 percent level that prevailed in the 1930s to over 20 percent by 1953. It did this by redistributing wealth and hence income from the rich to the poor, thereby eliminating the luxury consumption of the rich, raising by lesser amounts the essential consumption of the poor, and making the rest available to the state for capital construction.

Nationalization and Collectivization

Once the peasants and workers had gained political power, the Communist party began changing the relations of production, at first in ways that preserved some capitalism in industry and widened private ownership in rural areas (land reforms), later in ways that eliminated industrial private enterprise and led to collectives in agriculture.

Despite the lip service paid to the transition stage of new democracy, the party, almost immediately after gaining power, nationalized a substantial portion of heavy industry, including iron and steel, cement, electric power, petroleum, railroads and highways, and air transport—all of which had been owned by the Nationalist government. Foreign-owned firms were soon taken over, as were all banks and other major financial institutions. Foreign trade was also brought under central control. By 1952, over half of the output of modern industry came from socialist enterprises. The privately-owned industries (mostly smaller firms, such as textiles, food-processing, and consumer durables) were increasingly controlled: they were supplied with raw materials by the state trading companies, their output was often purchased by the socialist sector, and prices and other terms were frequently set by the state. Some industries were placed under joint state-private control, which meant that the state invested in the enterprises and assigned its personnel to share in management with the capitalists. By 1956, almost all industries were either completely or largely socialized. In addition, wholesale and retail trade, along with handicrafts, were formed, step by step, into cooperatives and thus brought into the socialist sector. New democracy, the transition stage envisioned by Mao between the old society and socialism, lasted only a few years. Mao was eager to change the relations of production into socialist forms.

Today, the largest industrial enterprises, especially those in urban areas turning out producers' goods, along with major transportation and communications facilities and mining operations, are nationalized. Many other industries, however, are owned and managed at lower administrative levels, though in some cases they may be state-owned and locally managed. Counties, for example, engage in the manufacture of numerous consumer goods as well as iron and steel. Communes own and manage small enterprises producing cement, chemical fertilizers, agricultural tools, processed food, and so forth. Increasingly, rural industries, administered at local levels, have become important sources of major products. While all of these industrial firms are owned by "the people," this term often refers to collective ownership at local levels. To this extent, industrial decision-making has also become decentralized, although the most important decisions, including those in the military area, are of course made at the top, as part of the national plan.

In the mid-1950s, the party also undertook rural collectivization. After land reform, the Chinese leaders, in four stages, transformed small private holdings into large-scale communes. First, the party encouraged the development of mutual aid teams, which were units of several households, the function of which was to pool privately-owned resources in order to compensate for shortages of labor and other inputs during the rush seasons of planting and harvesting. This was initially done on a temporary, seasonal basis, the teams being dissolved at the end of the planting or harvesting period, but later some of the teams were organized on a permanent, year-round basis. These permanent teams were somewhat larger than the temporary ones and often held some capital goods and animals as common property. By 1954 almost 10 million mutual aid teams, about half of them seasonal and half permanent, were in operation, and they comprised 58 percent of all peasant households.

In the second stage, the party founded elementary agricultural producers cooperatives (APCs), some of which were organized as early as 1950 but most of which were formed in the second half of 1955. They comprised several mutual aid teams or around 30 to 40 households, that is, a village. Land and other capital goods continued to be privately owned, but these assets were now pooled in the APCs for use according to annual plans prepared by cooperative management. Peasants were compensated according to their labor and their contributions of land, implements, and animals; labor, however, usually claimed most of the output. By early 1956, almost all peasant families had joined these APCs.

In the third stage, 1956-57, the party consolidated the elementary APCs into larger, advanced APCs, each comprising several small villages or perhaps one large village, varying in size from 100 to 300 households. In the advanced APCs, peasants held title to a share of the collective equity, and they no longer had any private claim on their former holdings of land and other capital goods. Accordingly, net earnings were distributed to the peasants only on the basis of work done. The earnings withheld, including those contributed by capital goods, were collectively owned, and they were generally of larger amounts than under the previous organization. Similarly, the payment of the agricultural tax became a collective obligation, whereas in the elementary APCs it had been an individual responsibility.

In the final step, during 1958-59, the party established people's communes during the Great Leap Forward. The commune, as the Chinese have explained, "is the basic unit of the social structure of our country, combining industry, agriculture, trade, education, and the military. At the same time, it is the basic organization of social power." The communes were organized to provide larger, more efficient units for carrying out large-scale water-control projects and the building of local factories and workshops throughout the countryside. They were organized, moreover, to provide additional labor through the establishment of communal mess halls and other communal services that released many women from household tasks. The communes also became the basic governmental unit; they ran factories, schools, and banks and controlled their own militia. They weakened the patriarchal family unit and in general the peasants' identification only with very small groups. Further, a "half-wage, half-supply system" was introduced, which provided free supplies of some necessities to peasants whether they worked or not, the remainder of income being distributed according to work done.

The party encouraged the rapid organization of communes during the Great Leap Forward, beginning in May 1958. During the following year and a half, the Chinese made an all-out effort to industrialize the rural areas, to build a large iron and steel industry, to grow record agricultural crops, to raise the education, health, and cultural levels of the peasants, and to catch up with the leading industrial nations of the world within 15 years. In 1959, the *Peking Review* stated the aim of the Great Leap:

The objective is to build China in the shortest possible time into a great socialist country with modern industry, modern agriculture, and modern science and culture . . . . To carry out our socialist construction at a high speed naturally requires constant readjustment to the relations of production and constant adaptation of the superstructure to the developing economic base. The fundamental thing, however, is to develop the productive forces rapidly . . . . The objectives are to abolish exploitation of man by man, and to build a classless society in which the difference between city and countryside, between mental and manual work will disappear and the ideal of "from each according to his ability, to each according to his needs" will become the order of the day.

The enlargement of rural units and the accompanying collectivization during the 1950s enabled the peasants, especially women, to work longer hours at useful tasks. The communes employed the increased labor not only in traditional farm work and subsidiary occupations, but also on large-scale water-control projects, basic construction, and rural industrial work. Much labor was also used for communal services—administration, cultural activities, medical care, and education. So that peasants would not waste their time during off-seasons, the communes organized them into large units for community and area projects.

During the 1950s, then, the basic organizational unit in the countryside grew from individual peasant households to mutual aid teams (at first temporary and later permanent), to elementary APCs (which became production teams in the communes), to advanced APCs (which became production brigades in the communes), and finally to communes. The basis for the distribution of income also changed from distribution according to work and asset ownership, to distribution according to work only, to distribution according to work and needs; and, at the same time, the value of a peasant's work points depended on the work done by increasingly larger groups.

The downturn of economic activity in the early 1960s, however, led to the reversal of some of these advances. During these years, when Maoist ideology waned, the party reduced the average size of communes, thus greatly increasing their number. The party transferred much decision-making authority from the commune level down to production brigades and teams, thereby forging closer links between individual effort and compensation. It also de-emphasized income payments according to need, reduced the level of communal services, and restored private plots where peasants could grow crops for their private use or for sale on private markets.

Reconstruction of the Steel Mill at Aushan by Ku Yuz

Thus, in the early 1960s, the party admitted in effect that it had pushed communization so rapidly as to reduce seriously peasants' work incentives. Their compensation according to need, their work within huge, impersonal armies of laborers, and the overtime demanded of them all tended to separate their rewards from individual work actually done. During the 1950s, the peasants did identify themselves with increasingly larger groups—from mutual aid teams to APCs—but the communes, as highly centralized decision-making units, were several steps beyond the feasible front line of advance. The commune structure, however, with its commune-brigade-team-family levels, in which the team and to a lesser extent the larger brigade are directly responsible for the daily work and income of the peasants, has remained intact to the present day and has prospered.

Today the communes number about 50,000. The average commune has 5,000 acres of land and 15,000 members, but there is much variation around the average. Within the communes there are 750,000 brigades, about 5 million teams, and 170 million families. Functions requiring large-scale management—such as water-control projects, agricultural extension programs, hydroelectric generating stations, hospital and higher school administration, military operations, rural industrialization, reforestation—are performed at the commune level. These units also are responsible for procuring grain for the state, collecting taxes, and coordinating production plans. The brigades (on the average comprising about 1,000 people) operate orchards, some small industry (such as farm equipment repair shops and food processing), health stations, primary schools, supply and marketing and credit cooperatives; and they oversee the work done by the teams. The teams (with an average of 140 members who cultivate 50 acres) control the work actually done in the fields, distribute income to their members, own their tools, and decide on the use of some of the surplus generated. Most households also have private land—about 5 percent of the total area—on which they raise vegetables, grow fruit, keep poultry and hogs, etc.

The 2,000 counties of China (which on the average contain 25 communes), the communes, and the brigades coordinate their activities in various ways. For example, a county factory produces farm machinery, which receives major repairs at the commune level and minor ones in a brigade workshop. Or, the county has a hospital, the commune a clinic, and the brigade a smaller health station. Similarly, education, marketing services, and community projects are coordinated, sometimes down to the team level.

The commune structure, therefore, while introduced too hurriedly in 1958-59, in its reorganized form is today the basic rural institution, in which reside 80 to 85 percent of the country's population. The Maoists hope that it will gradually assume a more socialist character in that the peasants will come to identify their interests with the activities of ever-larger groups—from their own families, to their teams, then to brigades and beyond. In time, the Maoists expect that the communes' land and capital goods will be transformed from narrow collective ownership to ownership by all the people into the full socialist form.

Planning and Industrialization

The party captured political power for the peasants and workers, transformed their work institutions and practices into socialist forms, and began building up the country's productive forces. The party wanted to transform China quickly from an agricultural and largely defenseless nation into a major economic power capable of defending militarily its national borders.

An industrial program required a national planning system, which in any case the party considered to be an integral component of any socialist society. The obvious place to look for help in this regard was in the Soviet Union, which had had two decades of experience with such planning. This socialist neighbor was willing to show the Chinese how to establish a national plan and, at the same time, to extend economic aid for China's industrialization effort. Accordingly, with Soviet assistance, the Chinese set up a State Planning Committee in 1952, which was the forerunner of a series of planning commissions designated for short-run, long-run, and special purposes. Below these national commissions was erected an entire network of economic planning agencies, which eventually extended into the country's 2,000 counties and from there into the cities and communes.

The first five-year plan started in 1953, the second in 1958. But the second was interrupted by the Great Leap Forward and was never completed. The first plan, fashioned in Soviet style insofar as its investment allocations were concerned, accentuated capital formation over consumption, heavy industry over light industry, industry generally over agriculture, and urban over rural development. Thus, the plan stressed such industries as iron and steel, petroleum, electric power, machine building, mining, chemicals, and electronics. Consumer-goods industries grew, too, but at a slower pace. Finally, most of the investment in agriculture came from that sector's own saving, not from the national budget. The rural areas, in fact, as we have seen, were mainly reorganized along socialist lines, not modernized with new equipment.

The U.S.S.R. extended loans to the Chinese which enabled them to buy, on deferred payment, around 200 complete industrial plants, as well as military equipment and other commodities. In addition, over 10,000 Soviet experts went to China during the 1950s to train the Chinese in industrial techniques, and China in turn sent more than 13,000 students to the Soviet Union for advanced training. While the Chinese had to repay these loans with interest, by exporting ferrous metals, handicrafts, food products, tea, and tobacco to the U.S.S.R., the loans greatly helped China to establish a solid industrial base. By the end of the decade, the Chinese were able, for the first time, to produce motor vehicles, jet aircraft, metallurgical, mining, and power-generating equipment, and high-grade steel alloy. At that time, industrial production was almost nine times larger than its 1949 level.

However, toward the end of the first five-year plan (1953-57), Mao grew restless under the Soviet-imposed development policies that stressed tight centralization and heavy industry to the neglect of local initiative and agriculture. Moreover, the relative neglect of agriculture resulted by 1956-57 in a retardation of its growth rate, which threatened to reduce China's exports (and hence her imports) and basic food supplies, especially for the urban-industrial population. Mao's reaction was to search for a way to replace the Soviet model with one more in keeping with China's and the party's traditions. The outcome of this search was the Great Leap Forward.

The Primacy of Agriculture

While the Great Leap also applied to urban and industrial areas, it was principally an effort to employ the "guerrilla tactics" that worked so well for Mao prior to 1949 in the military field to economic development in the countryside. These tactics emphasized man over the machine, heroic deeds, local initiative, non-material incentives, collective aims, spirit, and discipline. Paradoxically, the failures of the Great Leap served to place even more emphasis on the primacy of the rural areas, though the guerrilla tactics for getting the job done were depreciated. Thus, Mao's peasants remained in the spotlight but "Maoism" was pushed into the wings.

By late 1960 and early 1961, not only had agriculture and light industry been badly hit, but heavy industrial growth had fallen to virtually zero. The Chinese leadership, no longer dominated by Mao, altered its economic priorities to place agriculture first, light industry second, and heavy industry last. These new rankings, however, did not reflect a sharp diminution of interest in industrialization. Rather they served notice that the top priority would go to those industrial pursuits that directly aided agriculture, either by producing modern inputs (raw materials and capital equipment) for that sector or by processing output (food and industrial crops) coming from it. Industries at one remove would be emphasized to the extent that they directly served these inner, top-priority firms, and so on. Increasingly, as the 1960s advanced, the party expected the countryside to establish not only the small industries that directly assisted agriculture but also, whenever possible, small basic industries such as iron and steel, cement, coal mining, and so on. By the end of the decade, the economy was better able to support agriculture both with the output of large-scale industry in the urban areas and with tens of thousands of small, indigenous industries throughout the countryside. Thus, the effort of the 1950s that stressed the mobilization of traditional inputs (labor, natural fertilizers, draft animals, traditional tools) was redirected in the 1960s to the production of modern inputs such as chemical fertilizers, insecticides and pesticides, small hydroelectric plants, electric motors, rice transplanters, tractors, trucks, other machinery, and seed-improvement stations. This redirection in the 1960s was made possible by the industrial effort of the 1950s.

By 1965 the economy was growing rapidly in a balanced way, reaching in that year a national output level that was over 60 percent higher than that of 1961 and almost 20 percent above its peak of 1958-59. However, in the following year, the Cultural Revolution burst in the skies above Peking and Shanghai.

The Cultural Revolution

The downturn of the economy during 1959-61 presented the opportunity to Mao's opponents, including Liu Shao-ch'i, head of state, to reinvigorate the economy and at the same time to downgrade Mao's stress on class struggles and collective goals. Thus, individual and material incentives were restored, rural markets reestablished, and productive forces emphasized over class and ideological contradictions. These and other policies, as Mao saw them, promoted bourgeois values which were permeating the entire society. Mao, having lost some power in the early 1960s as a result of Great Leap failures, looked from the sidelines in dismay at these developments, for it was his conviction that China could not progress toward communism if the superstructure of society reflected bourgeois ideas that were at variance with the socialist economic base. The superstructure, according to Mao, did not automatically change to socialist forms; this transformation required recurrent campaigns and continual reinforcement. Otherwise, the danger was that a strengthening bourgeois superstructure would in time restore the bourgeoisie to political power and thus turn the economic base into the capitalist mode of production. The struggle between the proletariat and the bourgeoisie, Mao proclaimed, was still going on:

In China, although in the main socialist transformation has been completed with respect to the system of ownership, and although the large-scale and turbulent class struggles of the masses characteristic of the previous revolutionary periods have in the main come to an end, there are still remnants of the overthrown landlord and comprador classes, there is still a bourgeoisie, and the remolding of the petty-bourgeoisie has only just started. The class struggle is by no means over. . . . The proletariat seeks to transform the world according to its own world outlook, and so does the bourgeoisie. In this respect, the question of which will win out, socialism or capitalism, is still not really settled.

The Great Proletarian Cultural Revolution, which ran its course during 1966-69, was Mao's supreme effort to cleanse the superstructure of bourgeois values that had crept back into drama, literature, party work, education, medicine, and in fact into all phases of Chinese life. Mao's mission was to root out the old values, replace them with proletarian values, and in the process rebuild some of the key institutions in ways that would advance socialism and lead to the restoration of his authority. Thus, the Cultural Revolution was a power struggle, but it was a struggle over which course China should follow, the path back to capitalism or the one ahead to socialism. "At present," Mao said, "our objective is to struggle against and overthrow those persons in authority who are taking the capitalist road." The task was to criticize and repudiate bourgeois ideology wherever it might be found.

At the same time, the Cultural Revolution was a response to two acute problems: the danger of an armed invasion of China by the United States or the Soviet Union or both, and the danger of reactionary successors to Mao and the other Maoist leaders. The first was touched off by the growing involvement of the United States in Southeast Asia and the worsening relations of China and the U.S.S.R. The second was intensified by the results of the Stalin succession in the U.S.S.R., which Mao interpreted negatively. In both cases, as Mao saw the situation, bourgeois tendencies in China heightened the threats, and proletarian ideological unification provided a solution.

To combat these bourgeois currents, Mao called on millions of students to form themselves into Red Guards, who in turn were backed by the People's Liberation Army, which strongly supported Mao and reflected his real locus of power—the peasants in the socialist countryside. The targets for attack, Mao advised the Red Guards, were the cultural and educational units and leading organs of the party and government in the large and medium cities. This directive revealed another aspect of the Cultural Revolution—that it was Mao's repeated attempt to capture the cities from the bourgeoisie. His peasant-based movement had implanted socialism with some success throughout the countryside, but, although industries had been nationalized, the urban areas had still not been fully incorporated into the socialist movement. The Communist party itself, Mao believed, had become increasingly city-based and bureaucratic, and as such had become impregnated with the bourgeois ideas of individualism, material incentives, privileges, and soft living. The peasants in the socialist countryside and young people everywhere were called upon to transform the cities from capitalist to socialist centers. In the process, Mao expected that the young people would also be transformed themselves as they absorbed the party's true revolutionary traditions and engaged in revolution.

It was Mao's contention that the Cultural Revolution would lead to increases in economic productivity. In his mind, ideology and economics were closely related:

> The aim of the Great Proletarian Cultural Revolution is to revolutionize people's ideology and as a consequence to achieve greater, faster, better and more economical results in all fields of work. If the masses are fully aroused and proper arrangements are made, it is possible to carry on both the Cultural Revolution and production without one hampering the other, while guaranteeing high quality in all our work. The Great Proletarian Cultural Revolution is a powerful motive force for the development of the social productive forces in our country. Any idea of counterposing the Great Cultural Revolution to the development of production is incorrect.

The Cultural Revolution was meant to achieve a revolution in ideas —in ideas that, because they conformed to the socialist economic base, would act powerfully on that base through the release of human energy and ingenuity. The development of the productive forces, Mao asserted, was being impeded by an outmoded superstructure that had to be swept away.

It is an essential part of Mao's thinking that progress is made through struggle, when new talents emerge and knowledge advances by leaps. Thus, Mao pressed, progress depends mainly on the human factor, not on machines. "In building up the . . . country, we—unlike the modern revisionists who one-sidedly stress the material factor, mechanization, and modernization—pay chief attention to the revolutionization of man's thinking and through this, command, guide,

Mao Tse-tung

Mao Tse-tung was born on December 26, 1893, in Shaoshan, a village in the province of Hunan in south China. Mao's father was a poor peasant who, in later years, became moderately well off. His mother was a devout Buddhist and wholly illiterate. Mao was the first of four children in the family.

As a child, Mao worked on his father's land and also attended primary school in his village from the age of 8 to 13. When he was almost 14, the family married Mao to a girl four years his senior, but the couple never lived together and the marriage was later repudiated by Mao. For the next three years, he worked full time on the family's farm.

When he was 16, in 1910, Mao enrolled in Tungshan Higher Primary School, which was located in the county seat. At that point, he was six years older than his classmates. A year later, he passed the examination to enter a middle school in Ch'angsha, the capital of his province. In October 1911, he joined the revolutionary army that shortly overthrew the Ch'ing dynasty, and was discharged in February 1912, at which time he returned to the middle school. But six months later he withdrew in order to spend each day for the next half-year studying by himself in the library. In the spring of 1913, he enrolled in a teacher's training school in Ch'angsha, graduating five years later at the age of 24. While there he was befriended by one of his professors, Yang Ch'ang-chi, whose daughter Mao later married.

About this time, in spring 1918, Mao helped to organize and to lead a radical students' study group. In September, he went to Peking for the first time, and there he became a librarian's assistant at Peking University, under Li Ta-chao, who later was a founder of the Chinese Communist party. While at the university, Mao joined a Marxian study group. In February 1919, Mao left Peking to return to Ch'angsha, where he remained, except for a brief revisit to Peking, for the next few years. During this time, he became director of a primary school in Ch'angsha.

By the summer of 1920, at the age of 26, Mao considered himself to be a Marxist, and in the fall he organized a Communist party in Ch'angsha. This and similar groups elsewhere were the nuclei of the Chinese Communist party (CCP), which was organized in Shanghai, July 1921, with Mao in attendance. He returned to Ch'angsha as secretary of the CCP for Hunan province, where he organized Marxian study groups and labor unions.

In the winter of 1921, Mao married Yang K'ai-hui, the daughter of his former ethics professor. She was a brilliant woman, a student at Peking National University, and an active Communist. The couple had three sons. The eldest, Mao An-ying, was killed at the age of 28 in the Korean War by a U.S. bombing raid. The middle son, Mao An-ch'ing, later lost his sanity. There is no information about the youngest, Mao An-lung. Yang K'ai-hui herself was executed by the Kuomintang (KMT) in Ch'angsha in 1930, along with Mao's female cousin. One of Mao's two brothers was killed in March 1935 during the famous Long March to the northwest; the other, also a Communist, was executed in 1943 in Sinkiang by a warlord. A few other close relatives were also killed, as were innumerable friends and comrades. Two of Mao's children by a later marriage were entrusted to peasants during the Long March and were lost, and another, Mao-mao (a son), was lost in the late 1940s during the evacuation from Yenan. The mother of these and perhaps two other children, Ho Tzu-chen, was married to Mao around 1930. She was wounded during the Long March, went to Sian for rest in 1937, was sent to Moscow for medical treatment the following year, and returned to Shanghai probably in 1944. In 1939, Mao married Lan-p'ing, now known as

Chiang Ch'ing. They had one daughter, who was raised with one of Mao's daughters from his previous marriage and perhaps also, for a time, with one of his sons from that marriage.

Returning to our main story, in late 1922 Mao resigned as director of the primary school in Ch'angsha in order to devote all of his energies to revolutionary activities. For the next several years, he was active in the Communist-Kuomintang alliance, organizing trade unions and helping striking miners to obtain their demands. He was elected to the Central Committee of the CCP in 1923 and as an alternate member of the Central Executive Committee of the KMT in 1924. In November 1924, Mao became ill and returned to his home village for a rest. It was during these months of recuperation that he began to realize the revolutionary potential of the peasantry of China, a potential generally denied within the CCP and assigned instead to the urban proletariat. After Mao recovered his health, he began a rural organizational campaign, but this got him into trouble and he was forced to leave for Canton late in 1925. Mao continued to work on peasant problems during 1926 and 1927, for both the CCP and the KMT. In early 1927, he published a report on the peasant movement in Hunan.

After Chiang Kai-shek turned his fire on the Communists, Mao established a revolutionary base area in the Chingkang mountains, about a hundred miles east of his home. Over the next few years, he was compelled at various times to change the site of his operations. These bases were protected militarily and later developed socially, economically, and politically, and from them Mao hoped that the revolution would spread across the land, eventually back to the cities and the urban workers, on whom Mao had earlier pinned his hopes.

These soviet areas, as they were called, were under almost constant military attack. They were first assaulted by Kuomintang forces in 1930. Finally in 1934, after four years of encirclement campaigns, they drove the Communists from their base areas and forced them into the Long March to the northwest of the country. This famous event began in October 1934 and ended a year later when Mao's group arrived in Shensi province, which lies about 500 miles southwest of Peking. In this area, centered around Yenan, Mao and others reestablished their base areas.

The Japanese began their all-out attack on China in 1937, and for the next eight years the Communists were engaged in fighting the invaders, sometimes in a united front with the KMT and sometimes by themselves against both the Japanese and the KMT. During these years, Mao also attempted to build up the Communist-controlled territories economically. Shortly after the Japanese surrender, civil war between the Communists and Chiang Kai-shek's forces began in earnest, the Communists gaining victory in 1949. On October 1 of that year, Mao, in Peking, proclaimed the founding of the People's Republic of China and was elected Chairman of the Republic.

While Mao was known principally as a revolutionary leader, he was also a poet of some eminence. Ten years after he became the leader of China, he returned to his native village, Shaoshan, after an absence of 32 years, and expressed his feelings:

> I curse the time that has flowed past
>   Since the dimly-remembered dream of my departure
> From home, thirty-two years ago.
> With red pennons, the peasants lifted their lances;
> In their black hands, the rulers held up their whips.
> Lofty emotions were expressed in self-sacrifice:
> So the sun and moon were asked to give a new face to heaven.
> In delight I watch a thousand waves of growing rice and beans,
> And heroes everywhere going home in the smoky sunset.

In September 1976, Mao died at the age of 82.

and promote the work of mechanization and modernization."

There is much evidence, therefore, that Mao saw the Cultural Revolution as largely a struggle within the superstructure—within the ideological realm. Yet the danger to China was more than that the growing bourgeois ideas might in time restore capitalist relations of production. In fact, the bourgeoisie was being generated and regenerated, in hothouse style, by the capitalist relations of production fostered after the Great Leap faltered in 1959. The Cultural Revolution not only attacked the resulting growth of bourgeois values but the social institutions and practices themselves that bore capitalist imprints and that spawned such values. Although Mao saw the bourgeoisie as "a remnant," it was in fact being continually recreated by social relations not yet fully transformed into socialist forms. The real success of the Cultural Revolution, therefore, should be measured by the extent to which it elevated the economic base into a socialist one—and by this measure it attained some success.

Economic Policies, 1970 to 1975

After the windup of the Cultural Revolution in 1969, the Chinese pursued a balanced development program that emphasized both agriculture and industry, large and small enterprises, self-reliance ("keeping the initiative in our hands") and the import of foreign technology, individual and collective incentives, and so on. The results were quite amazing. Between 1969 and 1975, industrial production rose by almost 12 percent per year, agriculture from a depressed position increased by more than 4½ percent per year, and the annual rate of growth of real GNP was over 8 percent. The country experienced no recession, inflation, or energy crisis in the first half of the 1970s.

A notable achievement during these years was the marked growth of small industries and mining operations throughout the countryside, a movement that was initiated by Mao during the Great Leap Forward. The communes became dotted with these enterprises that produced many of the inputs needed by agriculture—cement, steel, fertilizers, power, etc.—and processed the sector's output of food, cotton, sugar, tobacco, and other commercial crops. Perhaps half a million of these rural industrial units existed near the end of the period. Despite their presence, however, the growth rate of grain output, after 1970, showed some signs of slowing down. This induced the planning authorities to contract for 13 huge chemical fertilizer plants from Western Europe, the U.S., and Japan, which were expected to be in full operation toward the end of the 1970s. At the same time, the authorities promoted greater intensity of land use, further mechanization, and other measures to keep food supplies ahead of population, including a nationwide effort to limit birthrates.

In heavy industry, the gains were most impressive. The output of machinery rose by 17 percent each year, of tractors by 27 percent, of merchant ships (in tonnage) by 22 percent, of trucks by 14 percent, and of electric power by 12 percent. Perhaps the single most dramatic economic achievement in these years was the surge of crude-oil production, from 20 million metric tons in 1969 to 74 million in 1975, and the consequent emergence of China as a large exporter of this commodity. One of the few dark spots in the industrial area was the lagging production of iron and steel during 1973–75, a result that clearly worried Chinese planners and party leaders.

While consumer goods did not come off the lines at the rate of industrial products, their output nevertheless rose by 5½ percent each year, significantly raising workers' living standards over this period of six years. Large gains were also recorded in railway and highway construction, and in the production of mainline locomotives and freight cars.

The value of China's two-way international trade showed no change from 1960 to 1969, remaining at about the $4 billion level. However, from 1969 to 1975, this trade skyrocketed to $14.4 billion, an increase which reflected partly the depreciation of the U.S. dollar but mainly the greater attention paid by the Chinese to the advantages of economic contacts with foreign countries. During these years, China's principal trading partners were Japan, Hong Kong, West Germany, France, Malaysia-Singapore, and Canada. China imported from them and from many other countries primarily iron and steel products, machinery and transport equipment, chemicals, and grain. There was also, in the latter part of this period, a remarkable rise in imports of whole plants—for example, several thermal electric-power plants from Japan and Italy, a petrochemical complex from France, eight ammonia plants from the United States, urea plants from the Netherlands, a cold-rolling mill from West Germany, a jet-engine plant from the United Kingdom, and many, many others.

The nation's exports consisted of crude oil, processed foods, textiles, minerals, rice, and other consumer goods, such as bicycles, sewing machines, cameras, watches, and radios. Altogether, however, despite the accelerated activity in international commerce, China's total trade in 1975 came to only 4 or 5 percent of its national output.

When one looks at China's domestic and international economic achievements during 1969–75, it is clear that this period was every bit as spectacular as that of the first five-year plan, which foreign observers have generally considered to be the high point of China's effort at economic development. Thus, the Maoist regime during these years seemed to have gone all out for ever-higher production records and for ever-expanding economic trade with the rest of the world. The Cultural Revolution apparently gave the economy a shot in the arm, although it also bequeathed to the later years an educational system in disarray, narrow and much-disputed cultural fare, and continuing factional fights over correct domestic and international policies.

The accompanying table records some of China's main economic achievements from 1949 to 1975. It includes the major agricultural crop (grain), four products from heavy industry, one from light industry (bicycles), and the overall measure of national output (GNP), along with population estimates.

Table 4. Some Economic Achievements of China: 1949 to 1975

Year	(Millions of Metric Tons)				(Thousands) Tractors	(Millions) Bicycles	(Billions of 1976 dollars) GNP	(Millions) Population
	Grain	Crude Steel	Crude Oil	Chemical Fertilizer				
1949	111	*	*	*	†	‡	51	538
1952	161	1	*	*	†	‡	87	570
1957	191	5	1	1	1	1	122	640
1959	171	13	4	2	9	1	138	669
1962	180	8	6	3	13	1	118	686
1965	194	13	11	8	24	2	165	750
1969	215	16	20	11	43	3	199	821
1975	284	26	74	28	180	5	323	910

* Less than ½ million tons
† Less than 500 units
‡ Less than ½ million units

Sources: Joint Economic Committee, U.S. Congress, *China: A Reassessment of the Economy,* July 10, 1975; and Central Intelligence Agency, *China: Economic Indicators,* October, 1977.

The Year of the Dragon and the Drive for Modernization

The Chinese will probably never forget the events of 1976, most of which occurred during the lunar year of the Dragon. Premier Chou En-lai died on January 8. Chu Teh, the military commander who had joined Mao in 1927 in their mountainous base area, and who was a member of the Politbureau and a revered figure throughout China, died in early July. On July 28, the industrial and mining city of T'angshan, situated about 100 miles east of Peking, and the area surrounding it, were devastated by a major earthquake (magnitude of 7.5 on the Richter scale), in which 655,000 people were reportedly killed and a million left homeless. On September 9, Chairman Mao Tse-tung died. The following month saw a titanic struggle at the top, arrests, and mass movements throughout the land in support of the victors and denunciation of the losers.

After Chou's death, Hua Kuo-feng had been appointed Acting Premier by Mao. Hua had been a party leader in Mao's home province of Hunan, for many years. Starting in 1973, he was a member of the Politbureau, and in 1975 he became Vice Premier and Minister of Public Security. A few months later, Mao raised him to Premier of the government and First Vice Chairman (directly behind Mao) of the party. After Mao's death, Hua became Chairman of the party and Head of the Military Commission of the party (i.e., Supreme Commander of the People's Liberation Army). Thus, by October, Hua was in a position that not even Mao had attained—that of being at once head of the government, of the party, and of the army.

In early October, Hua and his supporters arrested Mao's widow, Chiang Ch'ing, and her three cohorts from Shanghai—Chang Ch'un-ch'iao (a top theorist), Yao Wen-yuan (a journalist), and Wang Hung-wen (third-ranking member of the party, a Vice Chairman). Chiang Ch'ing had risen to power during the Cultural Revolution as the czarina of a new revolutionary culture that was intended to replace the old, feudal-bourgeois one. Now this so-called "gang of four" was accused of attempting to use the militia to usurp party and state power, of opposing Chou En-lai, of attempting to assassinate Mao, of sabotaging the economy, of being enemy agents, and of much else.

In addition to Hua Kuo-feng, the present leadership includes Yeh Chien-ying, born in 1898, a top military leader during the revolution, a member of the Politbureau from 1967 on, and Minister of Defense and First Vice Chairman of the party in the 1970s. Yeh is ranked directly behind Hua. The third-ranking leader is Teng Hsiao-p'ing, who was ousted during the Cultural Revolution, returned in 1973, became Vice Chairman of the party and the ranking Vice Premier in 1975, was dismissed again (by Mao) in April 1976, and was rehabilitated once more in July 1977. It is this triumvirate which gained pre-eminence by the latter half of 1977—Hua a faithful follower of Mao's domestic and international policies and a supporter of agriculture; Yeh the representative of the military; and Teng a conservative (production-above-all) opponent of Mao's domestic policies, a moderate, according to some scholars, on the question of the Soviet Union, and a supporter of industry.

The economic program of the present leadership is based on Chou En-lai's report to the 4th National People's Congress in January 1975, in which he called for "an independent and relatively comprehensive industrial and economic system" by 1980, and "accomplishment of comprehensive modernization of agriculture, industry, national defense, and science and technology" by the year 2000. The shorter-term program now calls for the completion of 120 large-scale industrial projects by 1985, including 10 iron and steel complexes, 10 oil and gas fields, 30 electric-power plants, 5 harbors, 6 new rail lines, and so on. The Chinese hope to boost their steel production from 26 million tons in 1975 to 60 million tons in 1985, and to raise their grain output from 284 million to 400 million tons over these ten years.

Much of the industrial and agricultural technology will be imported—for example, offshore drilling rigs will be obtained from the United States and a petrochemical plant from France and West Germany. In 1978, China and Japan signed a $20-billion mutual trade pact, running until 1985, under which China will export crude oil and coal to Japan in return for steel mills, chemical-fertilizer plants, insecticide-production facilities, aluminum-smelting facilities, and the like.

If the short-term economic program is successful, China will have fourteen fairly strong and rationally-located industrial bases by 1985, an advanced heavy industry, most of the locomotives electrified or dieselized (they are currently steam engines), and "an abundance of first-rate, attractive and reasonably priced goods from light industry."

These programs indicate that the present leaders are intensely interested in promoting production. Indeed, they accused the "gang of four" of a one-sided approach to the development problem: too much emphasis on "revolution" and too little on production, too much on struggle and too little on unity. These four radicals and their supporters believed that the main danger to China was political rather than military, that the class struggle against the new bourgeoisie, especially within the party, was still serious and primary. China's foreign foes—mainly the Soviet Union and the United States—were waiting to link up with the enemies within China. Consequently, China's road to communism could be protected only through class struggles that would identify, isolate, and destroy these revisionists. Such struggles, they thought, would also unify China and so increase its strength.

The radicals further believed that enterprises could be socialist in form, in the sense of being publicly-owned, but capitalist in reality. That is, even though ownership relations were socialist or semi-socialist, the other two components of the relations of production (work relations and forms of distribution), as well as the superstructure, could become increasingly bourgeois. Under certain circumstances, these elements could play the principal and decisive role in determining the nature of society.

The radicals, therefore, advocated vigilance against capitalist-roaders in the party, more equality in the wage structures, an extension of democracy in the factories, a reduction of material incentives, self-reliance at all levels, restriction of private activities by peasants (private plots, free markets, sideline production), a gradual shift of power from production teams to brigades and later to communes, the continuation of the rustification movement (sending city youth to the countryside), and the retention and intensification of political indoctrination in education. These programs were intended to minimize the power of the bourgeoisie, strengthen and unify the proletariat, and buttress China's ramparts against the U.S.S.R. They would also, the radicals believed, lead to upsurges in production.

The present leaders, on the other hand, were convinced that such policies would damage production, expose China to Russian military might, and cause social disunity and disorder. They also felt that the main danger to China was a military threat from the Soviet Union, which could be met only by all-out modernization and development of the economy and the armed forces. This modernization could best be achieved by stressing material incentives, foreign trade, conventional professional education, promotion by merit, central management of enterprises, strong central planning, and a concerted effort to upgrade science and technology.

It should be clearly noted that the controversy concerned the present leaders' program as opposed to that *advocated* by the radicals—not that actually carried out, for, as we have seen, the actual policies pursued during 1969–75 led to dramatic upsurges in production and to ever-widening economic contacts with the outside world, all of which were based on a balanced and intense development effort and reflected only moderate class struggles. While the present leaders accuse the "gang of four" of sabotaging the economy after the Cultural Revolution and thus bringing on stagnation, the economic facts point in the opposite direction. If the "gang," rising to prominence during the Cultural Revolution, set out to sabotage production in the ensuing years primarily by creating dissension at all levels of government, they were certainly inept! It could better be argued that they were more successful in 1976, when production did stagnate, but, if so, they had abundant aid from the gods on high, who not only took away Chou and Mao but caused the earth to split under T'angshan.

The evidence seems to support the view that the approach of the "gang" to the development problem *was* one-sided, if judged by Mao's more dialectical views of development, which stressed both production and class struggles. If they had gained real power after Mao's death, their policies might well have damaged the country's production capabilities. But it can be concluded that the "gang" had little impact during 1969–75 on China's economic performance.

The present leaders have placed their emphasis on production and not revolution, on unity and not struggle, and on responsibility and authority in enterprises and not mass participation. Their stress is on making "China a great, powerful and modern socialist country before the end of this century." But so far they have failed to analyze how to accomplish this while at the same time making progress toward communism. Instead, the leaders stress the considerable length of the historical period of socialism, as though to say that there is no sense at this early stage in seriously planning for communism. It is possible that the heavy emphasis on production, unity, and authority is nothing more than an attempt to redress the balance, but it is bound to disturb those who find validity in the Maoist approach.

Mao, far from disdaining production, was its champion from his earliest guerrilla days and was the author of the Great Leap Forward, the production leap *par excellence*. Even Mao's ideological campaigns were expressly intended to advance the productive zeal and abilities of the working class. But he never advocated or followed a straight-line path. For Mao, progress was a wave-like motion—a process of "cutting loose," then resting, then "cutting loose" again. Mao might agree that, after the disasters of 1976, this is undoubtedly the time for consolidation, unity, stability, and rest from mass revolutionary movements. He would also point out that contradictions are universal and that progress is made by discovering the correct methods—*i.e.*, the forms of struggle—for resolving them; that unity contains disunity as its opposite in struggle. In his report to the 11th Party Congress, Chairman Hua Kuo-feng represented Mao's thoughts when he said: "Stability and unity do not mean writing off class struggle." But Teng Hsiao-p'ing, the conservative, may well have other thoughts. It seems clear that to judge the present leaders' adherence to Maoist policies and goals fairly, a longer period of observation is required.

In any case, the present leaders are not entirely free to chart their own course. They will find that if their actions are to be effective, they will have to conform to circumstances "directly found, given and transmitted from the past." People make their own history, as Marx said in *The Eighteenth Brumaire of Louis Bonaparte,* but not exactly as they please. The important issue, then, becomes the extent to which the circumstances transmitted from the past include widely-held Maoist aims, values, practices, institutions, and so on; whether, in other words, the Maoist solutions for economic and social progress are by this time embedded in Chinese society, right down to the village level. If they are, the present leaders, or their successors, will be drawn to them; if they are not, the past will circumscribe the future actions of the leaders in other ways.

Although it will not be obvious on the surface, China is likely to remain largely Maoist for some time to come, except in the educational and cultural areas. Given China's and Russia's vastly different historical backgrounds, and what each country has gone through over the past several decades, it is not likely that China will become another Soviet Union. It will continue to develop along its own lines, and those lines cannot help reflecting the Maoist imprint—the communes, the combination of small and large industries (both rural- and urban-based), a large measure of local self-reliance, academic and work combinations, the importance of the rural areas, and mass participation in the affairs of the day. Will those lines also reflect Mao's abiding faith that China can move through socialism and, eventually, into a communist society—the vision of which inspired Mao from his earliest days as a Marxist?

The Maoist Vision of Communism

The Maoists visualize a communist society—the higher stage of socialism—as a richly productive (though not necessarily in private goods), planned, classless, highly egalitarian, and self-reliant society in which the means of production are collectively owned and work processes are regulated by workers. In a communist society, the people have a high level of communist consciousness and morality (selflessness, simple and frugal living, collective work incentives and goals, desire to "serve the people," honesty, modesty, etc.), and they consider labor to be the prime necessity of life; products are distributed according to need; and the state and party (as the dictatorship and the vanguard of the proletariat), the social divisions of labor (town vs. country, mental vs. manual work, peasant vs. worker), and commodities, markets, and money have all withered away.

The party's principal task, in the lower stage of socialism, is to raise the nation's productive forces to levels that will insure security and comfort for all, but in ways that will promote progress toward the other communist goals as well—in particular, toward a classless society. Thus, the Maoists have seriously sought the communist goal of eliminating the social divisions of labor through the advancement of several programs. They have furthered education that combines work and study, partly in order to reduce the elitism associated with mental work as opposed to manual labor. They have advanced physical work periods in the countryside for city-based administrators, teachers, and other "mental workers," for the purpose of breaking down the division between town and country as well as that between mental and manual work. They have promoted the sending of millions of city youth to rural areas, more or less permanently, to work with the peasants; similar programs have been put into operation for doctors, educators, and others. The party has also conducted ideological campaigns that extol manual labor, peasants' lives, "barefoot doctors," and dedicated youth in outlying areas of China.

Similar campaigns commend the communist virtue of "serving the people," a phrase that can be seen all over China these days. "Our point of departure," Mao has written, "is to serve the people whole-heartedly and never for a moment divorce ourselves from the masses, to proceed in all cases from the interests of the people and not from one's self-interest or from the interests of a small group, and to identify our responsibility to the people with our responsibility to the leading organs of the party." Even Pope Paul VI, as reported by *Time* maga-zine, had taken note of this call and of other Maoist intentions. The Maoist doctrine, he stated, is "a moral socialism of thought and con-duct," and China "looks toward the mystique of disinterested work for others, to inspiration to justice, to exaltation of a simple and frugal life, to rehabilitation of the rural masses, and to a mixing of social classes." While this is not a completely accurate account of Mao's goals, it does very nicely catch the spirit of Maoism.

The Maoists also see communism in terms of self-reliance—for the nation, local areas, individuals. At all levels, this refers to keeping the initiative in one's own hands by doing whatever one can do without seeking help from "the outside." Self-reliance is not autarky, for aid and trade may be welcomed if they do not subordinate the receiver to an exploitative relationship. In this sense, the Maoist vision is that of a cellular nation of self-reliant communes and counties, in which each seeks to produce its needs, not only in food, clothing, and housing, but also in basic industrial products, in education and health care, culture and recreation. At times, this vision seems to have no place for massive cities, for the ultra-urban life of the present day, or for its suave, sophisticated veneer. It is a vision of rusticity, of social development in thousands of small but integrated units, each springing from the uncor-rupted soil of the countryside.

Mao has made several estimates of the length of the lower stage of socialism in China, the stage preceding that of communism. "Fifty years from now," he said in 1955, "a communist China will emerge." How-ever, Mao added, perhaps with tongue in cheek, it would not look right for China to enter communism ahead of the Soviet Union. After all, the October Revolution came first and it was Lenin's cause, which should be respected. If we hurried ahead of the Soviet Union, he said, "it would be only for the purpose of seeking credit from Marx." And it would be shameful, he added, to shove ahead for only that!

The transition to communism will not occur as a class revolution, Mao pointed out, but it will be a social revolution, a transformation of collective ownership into ownership by all the people, a transformation from distribution according to work to distribution according to need. Communism itself, he thought, will go through many different phases and it will have many revolutions. It will not be without contradictions and it will certainly not be the last stage of world development. In fact, Mao prophesied, human beings themselves are not the final stage of development, for after they have died out there will be still higher forms of life. "Mankind will eventually reach its doomsday. When theologians talk about doomsday, it is pessimism used to scare people. When we speak about the destruction of mankind, we are saying that something more advanced than mankind will be produced."

Thus, the dialectics of destruction-construction may be said to be Mao's beginning and his ending.

European Equilibrium by Honoré Daumier

CHAPTER SEVEN

THE ORDEAL OF CAPITALISM

CAPITALISM SUCCEEDED FEUDALISM and subsequently developed from mercantile and commercial forms into an industrial system. The rise of the industrial proletariat in Western Europe led to Marx's revolutionary analyses of this mode of production. Capitalism's later transformation from competitive units to huge industrial and financial combines, and the resulting shape it took as an international system, produced Lenin's theories of imperialism and his revolutionary practices. Stalin, looking at a hostile world from an island of socialism, laid the socialist foundations for the development of Soviet power. Learning from Lenin and Soviet experience, Mao carried out a revolution in China and guided his nation along the path to socialism and communism. Marx was the supreme critic of capitalism, Lenin the revolutionary against it, Stalin the builder of Soviet power, and Mao the architect of a new society.

Following Lenin's analysis, Marxists today consider capitalism to be an imperialist system that exploits much of the world, in the sense that it uses power—economic, political, and military—to control other people and their resources for the purpose of unduly benefiting itself. This international and hierarchical system, many Marxists believe, reached its peak in the early decades of this century, although, within the system, some countries have subsequently gained while others have lost. Since that time, global capitalism has been confronted by another expanding ideology and movement—Marxian socialism—and by other potent adversaries, the total impact of which has been to reduce its ability to expand in the world economy and thus to prosper from this activity. Contemporary capitalism, Marxists contend, must expand to remain viable, but it is increasingly difficult for it to do so. That is essentially the ordeal of capitalism today. Its future depends on how this contradiction is resolved.

This Marxist view of capitalism, so sharply abbreviated in the foregoing, will now be expanded—first by looking at the system's changing international dimensions during this century and then by analyzing its present "commander," the United States.

International Capitalism: Its Heyday and Its Adversaries

The early years of this century were the heyday of capitalism. At that time, a few industrial capitalist nations, led by Great Britain, controlled most of the world and were heavily involved with the rest. Africa was almost completely carved up, a third belonging to Britain, a third to France, and a third to Belgium, Italy, Portugal, Germany, and Spain. The Middle East, extending to the Persian Gulf, was in the dominion of Britain and France. India and Burma were parts of the British Empire, as were Ceylon and Malaya. The French were the conquerors of Indochina, the Dutch the masters of what is now Indonesia. Several powers had territorial claims in China, and the United States had just militarily subdued the Philippines. Moreover, the United States, Britain, and others, with guns, goods, and investments, dominated and profited greatly in South America; and U.S. hegemony was taking shape in the Caribbean and Central America. In addition to parts of the empire just mentioned, the British domain also comprised Australia, New Zealand, Canada, Newfoundland, and South Africa; the partially self-supporting areas of Malta, Jamaica, Bermuda, and the Bahamas; the crown colonies of Hong Kong, Trinidad, Fiji, Gibraltar, and St. Helena; and other territories. Russia, a backward capitalist country, controlled an empire extending to the Pacific Ocean, but some of its own resources were in the hands of France, Britain, and others. Finally, Japan, a rising capitalist power, was carving an empire out of Korea, Manchuria, and other vulnerable areas.

That was the picture on the eve of the First World War, when Germany, a late arrival to colonial ambitions, challenged the British and French empires. Within a few years, this war among the leading capitalist nations set the stage for the Bolshevik revolution, and one-sixth of the world's land was shifted from capitalism to Marxism—one-fifth after Mongolia became a Marxist state a few years later. The Second World War—which was largely Germany's renewed challenge, joined by the rising imperialist aspirations of Italy and Japan—was followed by the Chinese Communist revolution. At about the same time, the Soviet Union consolidated its control over most of Eastern Europe.

Since 1945, Marxism has also claimed North Korea, Cuba, and, more recently, parts of Yemen, Somalia, Ethiopia, and Palestine, as well as Chile (for a time), Vietnam, Cambodia, Laos, Angola, Guinea-Bissau, and Mozambique. Approximately a third of the world's population and land area is now controlled by governments calling themselves Marxist. Beyond this, strong Marxist parties exist elsewhere, in India, France, Italy, Japan, and numerous other countries; and the mountains and forests of the world conceal many Marxist guerrilla movements.

At the turn of this century, Marxism was little more than an ideology, known only to a few outside of Germany and Russia, and from a practical point of view hardly a serious movement. Today, Marxism is a potent and persistently expansive force throughout the world, an ideology that motivates many of the world's poor, and a practical movement that confronts capitalism everywhere. The energy of Marxism's confrontation with capitalism, however, has been lessened to some extent—perhaps greatly—by the many national forms Marxism has taken, which have fragmented and dissipated its strength; by the bitter antagonism between the Chinese and Russian Marxist parties, which has divided not only the two largest communist countries but has split communist movements almost everywhere; by the conservative bent of some Marxist parties, especially in Western Europe; and by the nuclear military strength of the United States, which deters sudden actions that would greatly harm U.S. security or that of its major allies. Thus, Marxism in the nuclear age, it would seem, must weaken capitalism mainly by slow attrition rather than by dramatic damaging blows. Even allowing for all of these infirmities of Marxism, its presence in the world today has toppled capitalism from its supreme position of yesteryear to a more vulnerable station.

While Marxism is capitalism's principal foe, it is not the only one. The growing opposition to global capitalism has not been confined to the communist nations, but includes an increasing number of non-Marxian, revolutionary regimes imbued with nationalism and bristling with indignation over their countries' inglorious pasts. This righteous wrath has been directed mainly at the industrial capitalist countries— particularly the United States—and has come, though with varying degrees of intensity over time, from such countries as Algeria, Peru, Libya, Burma, Guinea, Syria, Iran, Panama, Zaire, Zambia, and Uganda. Encouraged by the growing strength of some of the small-poor nations against the big-rich ones, still other countries have taken heart and have insisted on more equal treatment from their larger neighbors. Beyond that, foreign nations have formed cartels to limit supplies of raw materials and natural resources in order to raise their prices. The most dramatic example has been the oil cartel, which has seriously hurt international capitalism, especially in Western Europe and Japan, though it has also injured other, poorer countries such as India and Pakistan. Similar arrangements for bloc pressure exist or are being formed for copper, bauxite, tin, rubber, phosphates, timber, and other commodities, even bananas.

It should also be noted that in the past decade or so U.S. capitalism itself has faced not only the above antagonists but also sharper competition on world markets from Japanese, German, French, and other foreign corporations. Even though the "oil crisis" has improved America's position in this regard *relative* to those of Western Europe and Japan, there is nonetheless more intense foreign competition today against the United States from within international capitalism than existed 25 years ago.

The leading owners and top executives (directors, managers, lawyers, etc.) of the major corporations and financial institutions are called by Marxists "the capitalist class," which, however, may also include a host of lesser owners and executives who closely identify themselves with the top decision-making group. In most of the leading capitalist countries, this class has been confronted by better organized workers, who, with their wage and other demands, buttressed if necessary by strikes and boycotts, have put strong pressure on the profit position of corporations. While the capitalist classes in both Europe and America have largely succeeded in purging labor of radicalism, coopting the leadership, and tapping continuing supplies of cheap labor at home and abroad, all of which has resulted in a less militant working class, it is nevertheless true that workers today threaten the surplus value (*i.e.*, Marx's concept of profits, interest, and rent) of the capitalist classes considerably more than they did 50 or 60 years ago. Since the 1930s, the United States and other governments have had to intervene increasingly on behalf of their industrial-financial interests—with monetary-fiscal policies, labor legislation, wage-and-price controls, and other measures—to aid these groups in attaining their traditional shares of the national income. Such intervention increased during the 1960s and early 1970s due to acute shortages of labor which developed from excessive aggregate demand during the Vietnam War and from the diminution (especially to Northern Europe) of fresh supplies of cheap labor from the south. Both factors added to the upward pressure on wage rates, threatened profits, and so called for intervention by the state.

Industrialists have also recently encountered adversaries in environmentalists, who, with their insistent concerns about the deteriorating quality of life, have added substantial costs to many industries (most notably to automobile firms, public utilities, and extractive enterprises) and have thereby tended to cut into the surplus value of the owning classes. Consumers, too, are nationally organized for the first time against the excesses of capitalist corporations—their false and misleading advertising, shoddy and harmful products, immoral practices in oppressive lands, and so on—and their expressed grievances or even the threat of them have cost businesses dearly. The Vietnam War, moreover, alienated many U.S. intellectuals, religious leaders, students, and others from their own government and caused them to question the values and morals of capitalism itself.

Thus, world capitalism, from a position of preeminence at the turn of the century, has subsequently seen its position eroded. The two World Wars—internecine struggles within international capitalism—virtually destroyed Britain and France as the leading colonial powers and propelled the United States into the top position among capitalist nations. Aside from these changes in relative standings within international capitalism, the entire structure has been weakened by the forces already noted, especially by the relentless expansion of Marxism throughout the world, so that at the present time capitalism is in an inferior position to the one it occupied three-quarters of a century ago. As a world system, capitalism is now more confined, though within its narrower limits it has attempted, with some success, to strengthen itself economically and militarily through cooperative efforts, such as the Common Market, increased trade and investment, and NATO and other defense treaties.

International Capitalism: Its Present-Day Features

In addition to the United States, international capitalism today—often called the free world—includes the other industrial capitalist nations, mainly those of Western Europe, Britain, Canada, and Japan. They are all more or less subordinate to the United States, and all are in intense rivalry with one another and with the United States for world markets and resources. At the bottom of the structure is a group of underdeveloped countries, most of which are attempting to develop along capitalist lines, each of which welcomes foreign capitalist investment, and all of which, in one way or another, serve the interests of the industrial capitalist nations. Many of these countries—such as Indonesia, Nigeria, Zaire, and Malaysia—were former colonies of European nations and, while now politically independent, are still economically subordinated to international industrial and financial capital, especially to that of the United States. Others, such as many Latin American countries, have long been dominated by the United States, and still others have more recently come under its sway—South Korea, Taiwan, Israel, Egypt, and, until early 1975, parts of Indochina. A few, such as Brazil and Iran, besides being economic underlings, act as watchdogs, or subimperialist powers, for the United States, by policing their own areas.

Most of these countries, from time to time, display some independence from U.S. policies, inasmuch as the interests of their own bourgeoisies are not always compatible with those of the U.S. international-capitalist class. Local capital often becomes restless when under the tight thumb of international capital. Thus, both harmony and conflict of interest exist in these relationships. For this reason, the free world is not easily managed by the leader solely in its own interests, and such management becomes even more difficult as capitalism matures in the poorer countries, for national capitalists find themselves stronger and increasingly at odds with their international counterparts. Thus, tensions have already developed between the United States, on the one side, and Brazil, Iran, and the Philippines, on the other.

Nevertheless, the Marxist view is that the "free world" is a moderately cohesive structure, comprising all countries that are hospitable to free enterprise, regardless of whether they are free or not of organized oppression. A military dictatorship that tortures its own citizens is, still, a member of the free world if it welcomes foreign capital, treats it well, and allows some foreign control over its resources and markets. If it does not, it is excluded. Thus, Cuba is not a member of the free world, but Brazil is; North Korea is excluded, while South Korea is in; Guinea Bissau is on the outside, but South Africa is a solid member. By use of the same criteria, for a time Ghana, Indonesia, and Chile were excluded—when they all but closed their borders to foreign capital—but they are now, as their dictatorial regimes attest, steadfast members of this global system. In sum, personal freedoms are not the test, nor is the presence of trade, which can be carried on with communist as well as capitalist nations. The acid test is, instead, whether foreign capital is permitted wide-ranging freedoms to profit from the country's resources and markets; it is capital's freedoms, not individuals', that count.

Marxists believe that the principal international aim of the United States is to keep as much of the world as possible open for trade, investment, and the exploitation by U.S. corporations of foreign labor, raw materials, and natural resources—to preserve and extend the system of international capitalism. The goal, in other words, is to maximize the area for profit making and the control of resources and markets by U.S. corporations.

The pursuit of this goal is in the hands of the capitalist class, as previously defined, and of what Richard Barnet in *Roots of War* called the national security managers, the two together making up, for this purpose, "the ruling class"—that is, the real decision-makers. The national security managers are those who hold the positions of Secretaries of State, Defense, and the three Armed Services; Chairman of the Atomic Energy Commission; and Director of the CIA. For decades, these top government jobs have been filled most of the time by businessmen, corporation lawyers, and financiers—that is, by members of the capitalist class who shuffle back and forth between business and government. Hence, the two groups are largely, though not entirely, the same. In any case, the members of this ruling class, as Marxists see it, share the same values and aims—namely, that private enterprise and profit making are good and that they should have maximum space and security in which to operate. It is not surprising, therefore, that there is often general agreement on policy matters among members of these groups without the need for conspiratorial action.

The major goal is pursued by the ruling class in many different ways. One method is the extension of economic aid to "friendly" underdeveloped nations, partly to strengthen them economically, partly to provide supporting overhead capital (*e.g.*, power sources, roads, harbors) for U.S. private investment, and partly to expand export markets for U.S. corporations. This purpose is also sought through military aid, which promotes U.S. weapons and aircraft production and sales, protects the client governments from the opposition of some of their own people, and enables some countries, such as Iran, to quell threatening liberation movements nearby. To this same end, the U.S. government, in addition, cultivates the elites of these countries, hoping that these potential or actual leaders, through education, travel, and medical care in the United States, will take on capitalist coloration. The United States also trains the police forces of underdeveloped countries and conducts counterinsurgency operations throughout the Third World, for the purpose of quashing all serious anti-capitalist movements in these areas. When all else fails, the United States can use and has used its military forces, which have been stationed around the world, to keep the area open for profit making and resources control.

In the past 80 years, successive U.S. governments have used their military forces to invade other countries more than 40 times, not counting the two World Wars. Even before this century began, Cuba, Hawaii, Puerto Rico, Guam, and the Philippines were subdued by rising U.S. military might. Before the Philippines were brought fully under control, the U.S. military, with other capitalist nations, gained footholds on Chinese soil. U.S. guns were trained on Colombia in 1903. Two years later, the U.S. Navy was rushed to Santo Domingo. In the following year, President Theodore Roosevelt established a military regime in Cuba. The Marines landed in Nicaragua in 1911, in Vera Cruz, Mexico, in 1914, in Haiti in 1915, in Honduras in 1924, and again in Nicaragua in 1926. The U.S. Navy pacified Guatemala in 1920. Altogether, there were 23 military invasions by the United States in Latin America between 1898 and 1926, and a number elsewhere, most of them occurring before communism, in national form, was even known—before it could be used as a veil over profit-making drives.

But when communism did arise as the Russian revolution in 1917, the United States joined other capitalist powers in an attempt to blot it out with cannon and creed. America intervened militarily in China's civil war, sent its military, in massive waves, into Korea, used force to overthrow a legitimate Guatemalan government in 1954, landed Marines in Lebanon in 1958, organized an invasion of Cuba in 1961, carried out an armed invasion of the Dominican Republic in 1965, bombed and bled Vietnam, Cambodia, and Laos, and with lesser means helped to overturn several other lawful governments, including those in Iran (1953), Brazil (1964), and Chile (1973)—not to speak of attempted and, probably, actual assassinations of foreign leaders.

It is no doubt true that U.S. industrialists and financiers, with the state behind them, although at times seriously divided on these issues, usually prefer to employ peaceful means to achieve their goals, but, when these have proven inadequate, there has seldom been much hesitation over using force. It has mainly been a matter of comparing costs of alternative means, given the expected benefits.

During most of the 19th century and the first two decades of the current one, the world was manipulated rather easily by the capitalist powers, their main concern being only how to live with one another. Since that time, the U.S.S.R. has grown into a superpower that is currently in a fierce struggle with the United States for world hegemony. Each superpower, behind the facades of detente and arms limitation, is attempting to control the resources of the world, and each is armed to the teeth for this purpose. The Soviet Union, partly because it is in a transition stage from socialism to state bureaucratic capitalism (as discussed in Chapter 5), and partly because it confronts a hostile capitalist world, is acting as a military power. Nevertheless, its activities have the effect of promoting anti-capitalist regimes, including some Marxist ones. Thus, even if it is true that Soviet policy is inimical to Chinese-style proletarian governments, and to the independence of national governments, it is still a fact that, for the most part, such policy has worked against the interests of the U.S. capitalist class. A fuller look, however, reveals that the Soviet Union both combats and aids U.S. imperialism, both contends against it and courts it.

Aside from the two superpowers and their respective subordinates—the advanced capitalist world and the Soviet communist one—China poses a threat to both and is in turn menaced by them. China, by opposing both of the superpowers and actively supporting the claims of underdeveloped countries, and by pursuing industrialization policies at home that are accompanied by equity as well as efficiency, is rapidly becoming an attractive model for many of the poor countries. The Chinese aspire to such moral leadership and have encouraged underdeveloped countries to break any dependency links they may have to the superpowers and to become self-reliant, developing nations. To this end, China has given large amounts (relative to her GNP) of economic—and, to a lesser extent, military—aid to underdeveloped nations, hoping that such assistance will enable them to advance under their own power. At the same time, the presence of China has gradually drawn some of the smaller Asian countries into her orbit, a movement that will be accelerated as American power in that part of the world ebbs; and China has made some headway in Africa. Additionally, it is Chinese policy to split each of the superpowers' closest allies from it—Western Europe (or the Common Market) from the United States, and Eastern Europe from the U.S.S.R. Therefore, China's activities have both hurt and helped U.S. capitalism, but their dominant effect, by far, has been against U.S. interests.

The underdeveloped countries comprise a heterogeneous lot. Some of them, as we have seen, are linked to global capitalism. Others have been attracted in some degree to the Soviet Union. Still others, because of their remote geographic position, their paucity of resources, or their formidable size, are more or less independent of both superpowers. Some countries are gravitating toward China and her model of economic development. A few countries, such as the oil-exporting nations, while underdeveloped industrially, are fabulously rich in natural resources, and for some purposes should be considered separately from the other underdeveloped regions.

International capital is both more active and more confined than it was several decades ago. Large areas of the world have been removed from its control and it is threatened by enemy forces at its borders and within its smaller circle. But within these tighter confines, international capital has made the most of its opportunities—its energy has risen with the compression of its domain. It has strengthened and expanded its position in the advanced capitalist nations; temporarily gained dominance in such countries as Brazil and Iran, which are likely to become major powers in the world; intensified its influence elsewhere, as in Egypt; to a small degree, drawn the Soviet Union and Eastern Europe

The Chinese View of the World

The analytical viewpoint of this book is that the nations of the world are divided into three groups—the advanced capitalist countries, the Marxian-socialist ones, and the third world of (non-Marxian) underdeveloped nations; and it maintains that capitalism is being seriously and effectively challenged by Marxism throughout the world.

The Chinese, however, have a dramatically different vision. They allege that because a form of state-monopoly capitalism has been restored in the Soviet Union (and in its satellites), there is no longer a socialist camp. The Soviet Union, the Chinese say, is now, along with the United States, an imperialist superpower. Of the two it is "the more ferocious, the more reckless, the more treacherous, and the most dangerous source of world war," because as a highly-centralized latecomer, rising while the United States is falling, it relies primarily on military strength and deludes the people of the world that it is socialist. Under present conditions, in the Chinese view, a new world war is inevitable, because these two superpowers, which make up the first world, will contend for world supremacy until one wins. The central problem in present-day world politics is the menace that this super-struggle poses to the other peoples of the world and the question of how they are going to resist it.

The Chinese define the third world as including all the less-developed countries, capitalist and socialist, in Asia, Africa, and Latin America—with China of course among them. The countries and people of this third world, they say, "constitute the main force in the world-wide struggle against the hegemonism of the two superpowers and against imperialism and colonialism."

The second world is seen as consisting of the economically-advanced satellites of the superpowers—the nations of Western and Eastern Europe, Canada, Japan, Australia, New Zealand, and a few others. These, according to the Chinese, "constitute a force which can be united with in the struggle against hegemonism."

China's analysis implies that the "true socialist" nations of the third world should unite with the other third-world nations, even those with repressive, right-wing dictatorships, such as Brazil, Iran, and South Korea, and that the third world should seek unity with the second world, even with the main capitalist "enemies," such as Germany, Japan, and Britain, to combat the aggressive designs of the superpowers, especially those of the U.S.S.R.

So far as socialist development is concerned, China's analysis seems terribly pessimistic, for socialism is seen as only a tiny part of the world economy (which countries are left in the socialist camp other than China—and perhaps North Korea and Cambodia?), producing less than 5 percent of global GNP and an even smaller part of the world's industrial output. On the other side, the superpowers, especially when allied with the second world, are in an overwhelmingly dominant position. The only hope for the further spread of socialism, as defined by China, is a new world war or a series of social revolutions in the superpowers – – the first of these being regarded as "inevitable," and the second as quite unlikely. In fact, inasmuch as a dozen or so countries, in the Chinese view, have recently been transformed from socialism back to capitalism, a likely outcome of the present struggle will be the continued success of capitalism in subverting the few socialist countries still intact. Capitalism is also likely to be strengthened in those third-world countries that, in the interest of resisting the superpowers, ally themselves with advanced capitalist countries. Moreover, the economic decline of the second world, instead of being a boon to socialism, would be disastrous, for it would allow the superpowers to run rampant among the third-world countries. In fact, China encourages the countries of the second world to unify and strengthen themselves. Considering all of this, socialism's future would appear to be bleak, unless one sees hope in a third world war.

China's analysis has been heatedly challenged from within the socialist camp (as defined in this book), particularly by Albania. The Albanians assert that there are four major social contradictions in the world today: (1) between the socialist and capitalist camps; (2) between labor and capital in capitalist countries; (3) between oppressed peoples and imperialism; and (4) between imperialist powers. The Albanians then charge that the Chinese analysis is invalid because it blurs the boundaries between socialism and capitalism, thereby ignoring the fundamental contradiction of the times; it includes pro-imperialist, reactionary, and fascist forces in "the principal revolutionary force of the world"; it fails to see the main enemy as both (equally) the U.S. and the U.S.S.R.; and it ignores the major contradictions—(2) and (3)—in its grouping of countries in the second world and in its call for unity between the second and third worlds. The Albanians agree with the Chinese that the Soviet Union is a "social imperialist" superpower, but they part company with them after that.

The Chinese view rests solidly on the proposition that the Soviet Union is no longer socialist and has restored a type of capitalism. (This issue was discussed at length in Chapter 5.) The view of most Western observers is that the Soviet Union remains in the socialist camp; but the outcome of the struggle there between capitalism and socialism is still very much in doubt. The Marxian-socialist camp is certainly no longer monolithic; it has been torn asunder by the antagonistic national forms within which Marxism has developed. Not only have China and the Soviet Union battled each other, but so have Vietnam and Cambodia, and Ethiopia and Somalia. Albania is at odds with Yugoslavia and almost all other Marxist countries, Cuba and China are antagonists, Rumania largely goes its own way, to the annoyance of the Soviet Union, and so on. But, despite all this, the contention of this book is that the Marxian movement as a whole, working directly or indirectly (say, through third-world countries), has impaired the world capitalist system. If and when the Marxian states get together for a more concerted effort against capitalism, the impact will be even more adverse.

back into global capitalism's dominion; and in general has taken maximum advantage of the Sino-Soviet split. Nevertheless, when one surveys the sweep of the 20th century, it is almost impossible to avoid the conclusion that capitalism has declined as a world force, in that it has lost much control over the world's resources and markets. Furthermore, its ideology has become a very poor second to that of Marxism-socialism, as evidenced by the almost complete lack of enthusiasm for capitalism and the favorable response to socialism on the part of people in the underdeveloped world.

U.S. Capitalism: Its Present and Its Future

While the structure of international capitalism has been impaired during this century, U.S. capitalism as an integral part of it grew in stature throughout the period until, at the close of the Second World War, it found itself supreme. This rise to the commanding position was accompanied by the spread of U.S. economic interests around much of the world and by the protection and extension of those interests with military power. For about 20 years after 1945 the United States was able to profit greatly from these advantages.

However, since about 1965 the going has become much rougher. The United States can no longer attain as facilely as it once did its overriding aim of keeping as much of the world as possible open for corporate profit making and the control of resources. The pursuit of this goal has become more difficult in recent years. The world is now considerably less receptive to the expansion of U.S. capitalism than it was formerly.

Marxists do not have a uniform position about the viability and future of U.S. capitalism. However, the following propositions would probably elicit much radical support: (1) Capitalism must expand to survive. (2) For the United States and other major capitalist nations, expansion must take global form. (3) Expansion has become more difficult, more costly, riskier, and more controversial. (4) This and other factors have weakened the ability of the U.S. capitalist class to extract surplus value from the system. (5) U.S. capitalists, with government help, will attempt to regain their previous position of strength by promoting measures to weaken their adversaries. (6) The responses of "the adversaries" to these counterattacks will do much to determine the shape of U.S. society in the future. These propositions, so starkly put here, will now be discussed in more detail.

Capitalism as an Expanding System

With regard to the first proposition, the capitalist mode of production is driven by private profit making—or, more generally, by the need of

"I tell you that you have disturbed the boundary marker and have advanced it onto my field!"—"I tell you no—and I will swear before all the courts that what I mark by where I stand was my father's and even my grand-father's!"—"Ah! But! . . . " by Honoré Daumier

the capitalist class to sustain itself with surplus value drawn from the system: no surplus value, no capitalist class. Further, the continuation of surplus value to this class depends on its reinvestment, not on its consumption. A capitalist's failure to reinvest surplus value would allow his competitors, domestic and foreign, to undermine his present advantages in markets, raw-material sources, costs and efficiency, technology, and so on. But the repeated reinvestment of surplus value—that is, capital formation—leads to growth of the economy's capacity to produce goods and services. Therefore, the viability of capitalism depends on economic growth.

While each capitalist must reinvest surplus value to maintain his present position—and hence his ability to generate surplus value in the future against his competition—this activity by the group of capitalists will itself produce a mass of surplus value for them. The reason for this is that investment expenditures give rise to additional incomes, to expenditures out of these incomes, and hence to additional revenues for business enterprises—without generating comparable current costs. (Capital formation is capital expenditure that will raise current costs, through depreciation of the capital goods, only in future years.) Thus, continuing capital formation produces for the capitalist class as a whole more current revenues than current costs—that is, more surplus value.

In summary, each capitalist must reinvest surplus value to survive, and capitalists as a class will survive if they reinvest. That is, they will survive as a class only if the economy is growing. A no-growth economy would mean either the absence of surplus value (the more likely outcome) or the use of surplus value for consumption (because capital formation would be zero). In the first case, the capitalist class would fade away; in the second, it would likely be overthrown, for the risk-taking, entrepreneurial functions that served as the justification by this class for its acquisition of surplus value would disappear. Its members would become rentiers and parasites. Moreover, without growth, the lowest income groups could not look forward to an improvement in their situation through an expansion of the economic pie, but only through the redivision of it. At the same time, unemployment would grow as the labor force continued to expand without new jobs being created. Zero growth, then, would mean not only the erosion of capitalist functions but also the erosion, at the other end, of confidence in the system's ability to satisfy basic needs. Zero growth would spell social instability.

Capitalism is thus driven to expansion, and expansion is necessary for its survival.

U.S. Capitalism and Global Operations

Turning to the second proposition, U.S. capitalism not only has to expand, but it must expand globally. The major capitalist nations are now, Lenin would remind us, each dominated by huge corporations that are financially able to operate internationally, as small competitive firms in the mid-19th century could not. Further, these conglomerate and multinational enterprises, by virtue of their imposing size, can both find and generate highly profitable opportunities abroad. International capitalist competition, moreover, compels each of these giant corporations to protect its own position from the encroachment of its rivals, which can often best be achieved by being the first to open up new markets and find cheaper raw materials and natural resources. Therefore, in the age of monopoly capital, profit seeking is on a world scale because it is possible, remunerative, and necessary for survival.

The United States, as the most powerful economic unit within the international capitalist system and as its military commander, dominates international economic activity and at the same time undertakes to protect the system as a whole from its enemies. Thus, U.S. national security managers, seeking the prosperity and security of U.S. capitalism and (when no serious conflicts arise) of capitalism generally, orchestrate policies designed to provide maximum profit-seeking space to U.S. and other corporations, to control as much of the world's resources as possible, and to maintain or even extend the area of the free world by combatting communism whenever it threatens seriously to halt or roll back capitalism's advances. As a consequence, the class of monopoly capitalists and the national security managers cooperate for the same end—the security of profit making on a global basis.

The United States assumes these burdens, as Britain did in former times, in its own interests and in those of the system as a whole. The subordinate members of the system, such as Taiwan, Denmark, Greece, and Brazil, gain to the extent that U.S. policies are successful; the smaller capitalist nations, with no imperialist designs of their own, can reap the harvest from their leader's successes. The major capitalist nations, because of their monopoly-capital features, are all expansionist on a world scale, but the leader of the system combines global military operations with economic activity, both of which it tends to dominate.

Rising Hindrances to Expansion

The third contention of many Marxists is that expansion has become more difficult for the major capitalist nations, especially for the United States, which in the past decade or two has lost some economic ground to Japan, West Germany, and, to a lesser extent, France. The system of international capitalism over the full sweep of this century, as we have seen, has been restrained by an expanding Marxism. In recent years, the United States has also encountered the enhanced economic power of foreign suppliers of vital resources. It has been subjected to higher costs and risks in its overseas operations (higher labor costs, risks of nationalization, bombings, kidnappings, less tolerance for foreign capital, etc.), to more intense competition at home from foreign corporations, and to the disappearance beyond communist borders of wealth it once controlled. It has had to pay heavily for counterrevolutionary wars against communist and nationalist insurgents. The "outside world" has become more competitive, powerful, and hostile—and, to that extent, less profitable—than it was during the first two decades after the Second World War.

At home, the capitalist class has been hurt by the growing strength of labor, environmentalists, and consumer-interest groups. All of these antagonists have forced up business costs and lowered profits. In addition, taxes have remained high, government regulations have proliferated, and economic policy has been disconcertingly erratic.

Decline of Surplus-Value Extraction

In the past decade, the domestic and foreign forces against U.S. capitalism, whether they have been of long standing or of more recent development, have come together in their total impact to reduce the power of the capitalist class to extract surplus value from the system. There are, presently, fewer golden opportunities for profit making than there used to be. This in turn has had serious implications for the general health of the economy. This is the fourth Marxist proposition about contemporary capitalism.

The predicament of U.S. capitalists is traced in Table 5. Using the Marxian concept of the rate of exploitation (s/v) developed in Chapter 3—which is measured here as the ratio of surplus value (profits, rent, and interest before taxes) to employee compensation (wages and salaries also before taxes)—the data reveal that this rate declined from about 28 percent in 1965 (it was at the same level in 1955) to 20 percent in 1970, and that in the next seven years it made only a partial recovery. Over the period 1965-77, the trend in the rate of exploitation was definitely downward.

Table 5. Surplus Value and Corporate Profits: 1955 to 1977

Year	Rate of Exploitation	Corporate Profits as Percentage of:		Real Amount of Corporate Profits (in 1972 prices in billions)
		Surplus Value	Employee Compensation	
1955	27.0%	73.5%	19.8%	$ 68.8
1965	28.4	68.4	19.4	104.5
1966	27.9	67.3	18.8	108.3
1968	25.2	65.4	16.5	104.5
1970	20.4	54.8	11.1	74.5
1972	22.5	57.3	12.9	92.1
1974	19.9	48.0	9.5	71.4
1976	23.1	53.4	12.4	91.6
1977	23.0	52.6	12.1	93.1

Note: The rate of exploitation is surplus value divided by employee compensation. Surplus value includes corporate profits after inventory valuation and capital consumption adjustments, net interest payments of corporations, and rents—all before income taxes. Employee compensation is also taken before taxes. Excluded from both elements of the ratio are incomes of farm proprietors and of unincorporated enterprises. The rate of exploitation is probably understated by the inclusion of executives' salaries and bonuses in employee compensation, for a significant part of these payments may be a form of surplus value. We have not allowed, moreover, for the likelihood that a disproportionate share of taxes serves primarily the interests of the capitalist class. In the last column, corporate profits are shown before taxes and in constant prices. In all calculations, corporate profits are adjusted to eliminate the effects of inflation. While inventory profits are real enough, they do not reflect the ability of corporations over the long run to extract surplus value from their workers. It is for this reason, too, that corporate profits are taken before taxes.

It should be emphasized that the surplus value used here differs from Marx's concept in not being expressed in socially-necessary labor-hours, and in other ways.

During these years, corporate profits fared even worse than surplus value as a whole. The data in the second column show a sharp fall in the percentage of surplus value comprising profits—from two-thirds in 1965 to about a half in 1977. This decline indicates that, during these years, rentier groups (receiving interest and rent) gained at the expense of industrial and commercial capitalists (receiving profit). In fact, interest receipts rose from a quarter of profits in 1965 to three-quarters in 1977, a development that accounts for some of the present woes of industrial capitalists as well as their increasing differences over economic policies with financial capitalists.

Inasmuch as the decline in the rate of exploitation was accompanied by the fall of profits relative to surplus value, it follows that profits deteriorated badly as a percentage of employee compensation. This is shown in the third column (which is the result of multiplying the first column by the second).

The figures in the last column reveal the problem more directly: corporate profits in real terms (constant prices) were lower in 1977 than in 1965, more than a decade earlier. In fact, profits in 1974 and 1975 were very little higher than they were 20 years earlier. At no time in the 1970s have corporate profits reached their levels of 1965-66. While some, and perhaps an increasing amount, of the profits may be hidden in various cost items, it seems beyond question that profit making has run into hard times.

The decline in the rate of exploitation was particularly acute from the beginning of U.S. escalation in Vietnam in early 1965 to early 1970. When President Nixon took office in 1969, he sought to stem the adverse tides of excessive wage demands, falling profits, inflation, and international capital outflows by deflationary monetary and fiscal policies, but these were mostly unsuccessful. After a brief reversal to expansionary policies, which in several ways worsened the economic difficulties, the Nixon Administration in August 1971 turned to a new set of economic policies and diplomatic moves that were intended to shift income both from labor to capital in the United States and from Japanese and German capitalists to their U.S. counterparts. The first shift of income was attempted through wage and price controls at home that, it was hoped, would permit profits to rise with the growth of the economy while wage demands were curbed, and by further subsidies to the capitalist class. The second shift was implemented by a new international policy that was intended to change relative prices through dollar devaluation, relative trade and investment barriers, and relative defense burdens in favor of the U.S. capitalist class; and by new diplomatic overtures to China in the hope of establishing a more profitable area in Asia for trade,

"Messrs. Cobden, Brigth, and Sturges, having nothing more to do in Europe, embark to pacify China " by Honoré Daumier

investment, and natural resource exploitation by American corporations.

These programs were moderately successful in raising the rate of exploitation, which recovered from its low of 20.4 percent in 1970 to 21.6 percent by 1973. Total corporate profits also rose as a percentage of surplus value and in relation to employee compensation. By the middle of 1973, however, aggregate demand and growth were showing signs of weakening. The quadrupling of oil prices by the OPEC cartel toward the end of the year helped to turn the economy down in 1974, a movement that continued into the spring of 1975. At that point, the rate of exploitation had fallen again to its 1970 trough, and corporate profits, in real terms, were 30 percent below their level of a decade before.

Thus, by 1975 the U.S. capitalist class had experienced a decade or more of deterioration in its ability to draw surplus value out of the free enterprise system. Deflationary policies, expansionary programs, growth measures within a set of direct controls, large-scale unemployment, dollar devaluation—none of these had thus far turned the clock back to the 1950s and early 1960s. During 1976 and 1977, the economy recovered sharply from the recession, but even in 1977 the absolute amount of real corporate profits was substantially below the level reached 12 years earlier. The causes of the decline in capital's fortunes appear to be so deep-seated that they will not easily be swept away.

As a consequence of capital's difficulties in extracting surplus value or profits from the system, the pace of capital formation has waned noticeably. As shown in Table 6, during the first two decades of the postwar period, gross private domestic investment (in 1972 prices) rose on the average by 4.2 percent per year. In the third decade, the rate was below 1 percent, and if we look at the 1970s (1969-77), we find private investment still in the doldrums. The decline in the rate of capital formation has slowed the growth of the entire economy (see GNP in the table), raised the unemployment rate, and dampened gains in the stock market.

In the meantime, struggles between U.S. capitalists and their domestic and foreign antagonists and competitors over shares of the national and world income have intensified. This growing strife has been largely responsible for the inflation, since the various claimants, now stronger than before, have pushed up the prices of what they control to try to capture a larger share of the pie. The inflation is also a sure indication that the capitalist classes of the Western world have lost much of their former control over global supplies of natural resources, raw materials, and cheap labor.

The line of causation is clear. It runs from the growing power of capitalism's challengers to the capitalist classes' increasing difficulties in getting surplus value from the worldwide system, and then to the retarda-

The Vietnam War

Military intervention in Vietnam represented a continuing effort by the United States to keep Southeast Asia open for capitalism. With this in mind, the United States first helped the French in the early postwar period to reestablish their hold on Indochina. The Chinese Communists' victory in 1949, followed shortly afterward by the Korean War, alerted U.S. policymakers to the possibility of the spread of communism throughout Asia. In response, U.S. policy toward Japan was quickly changed from that of retarding her industrial potential to advancing it. The new policy, fashioned in the early 1950s, was intended to establish an integrated, viable capitalist area, running from Korea down into Southeast Asia, that would be large enough to act as a buffer, as a capitalist counterweight, to Communist China. For that purpose, Japan was considered the key country in that it was the only potential industrial power in the region. But Japan was desperately short of the raw materials and natural resources required for a strong industrial effort. Southeast Asia, on the other hand, was plentifully supplied with iron ore, manganese, lead, rubber, tin, copper, oil, bauxite, and wood products—everything needed by the Japanese. In return, Southeast Asia could absorb Japanese manufactured goods. Consequently, U.S. policymakers saw the area from Korea to Thailand as a potentially strong, integrated economic region that could thwart communism's designs, provided that Southeast Asia could be kept open for Japan—and, of course, for the United States too. Latent treasure was there.

President Eisenhower carefully outlined this policy in the 1950s:

> One of Japan's greatest opportunities for increased trade lies in a free and developing Southeast Asia. The great need in one country is for raw materials, in the other countries for manufactured goods. The two regions complement each other markedly. By strengthening Vietnam and helping to insure the safety of the South Pacific and Southeast Asia, we gradually develop the great trade potential between this region and highly industrialized Japan to the benefit of both. In this way, freedom in the Western Pacific will be greatly strengthened.

In an earlier speech, Eisenhower had put an interesting twist into the story:

> [Communist success in Indochina] takes away, in its economic aspects, that region that Japan must have as a trading area, or it would force Japan to turn toward China in order to live. So the possible consequences of the loss are just incalculable to the free world.

As Eisenhower, and later Kennedy, Johnson, Nixon, and Ford reasoned, if Vietnam was lost to communism, Southeast Asia would be in grave danger of succumbing too, and, in fact, the entire system of international capitalism would be imperiled. If Southeast Asia were lost, Japan would be seriously exposed, leaving the entire area to the mercy of an increasingly menacing Communist China. This threat was seen as economic, not political, for communist expansion would close the area to economic exploitation by the capitalist powers; whether it swept away "democracy" at the same time was a secondary concern of the United States, as was amply proved subsequently.

The "domino theory" provided the link between the loss of Vietnam and the fall of the larger area. This theory is based on the commonsense assumption that one event often affects something else—that cause-and-effect relationships are not uncommon. In the case at hand, during the 1950s and early 1960s, there were abundant reasons for believing that Sukarno's Indonesia would succumb to communism if park were set off in Indochina, or vice versa. A strong communist party, with millions of followers, operated in Indonesia, and this movement was eventually supported by the Chinese. At about the same time, Sukarno withdrew his country from the United Nations, militarily confronted Malaysia, and joined an alliance of Asia's communist countries. Communist guerrilla movements were, or had been, strong throughout the rest of the area, including Malaysia and the Philippines. Thus, the domino theory appeared to rest on solid foundations.

Moreover, aside from the specific interests of the United States in that region, U.S. involvement in Indochina was a conscious effort by successive administrations to preserve the rules of the international capitalist system, which in effect specify that no country can, with impunity, switch sides, whether this is done democratically, as in Chile, or by revolution, as in Cuba. It is considered impermissible for a satellite to break out of the international capitalist system in favor of Marxism. As reported in *The New York Times* (September 11, 1974), this rule was expressed by Secretary of State Henry Kissinger with regard to Chile: "I don't see why we need to stand by and watch a country go communist due to the irresponsibility of its own people." This is comparable to the rules imposed by the Soviet Union on its East European satellites.

While the particular dangers to U.S. hegemony in Southeast Asia changed over the years—thus altering the specific reasons for the continuing U.S. military presence there—the overall policy remained intact. It was a policy, Marxists argue, to maintain that rich area for capitalism and so to keep it out of the hands of Marxists, whether dressed as Russians, Chinese, or as natives. From the point of view of the U.S. capitalist class, it cannot be said that the policy up to the spring of 1975 was a failure. For three decades, almost the entire area of Southeast Asia was kept open for U.S. and other corporations, and this quite likely would not have happened without the omnipresence of the U.S. military in that region. This armed power served as a potential ally and as moral support for all right-wing movements in the area, including the one that overthrew Sukarno in 1965. U.S. and other capitalist enterprises have been able to penetrate deeply into the economies of Indonesia, Malaya, Singapore, Thailand, Australia, the Philippines, and, for a time, Indochina itself. Their rewards have been ample profits from oil, minerals, wood, cheap labor, and widening markets. The gains from Indonesia alone have fully justified Nixon's statement in *Foreign Affairs*, October 1967: "With its 100 million people, and its 3,000-mile arc of islands containing the region's richest hoard of natural resources, Indonesia constitutes by far the greatest prize in the Southeast Asian area."

Despite these private gains to the capitalist class, the costs of the Vietnam War to Americans generally have been so heavy psychologically and economically as to weaken the very fabric of their society and, thus, to endanger its class structure. Moreover, the U.S. military, the Agency for International Development, the World Bank, and the CIA cannot prevent forever the ultimate triumph of Marxist revolutionary movements throughout most of this region, and this will eventually drive the United States and other imperialists, probably including the Soviet Union, from these lands. The gains to capitalism from all of this human suffering and destruction, therefore, are likely to have been, at best, only short-term.

Vietnam represented not simply a series of terrible blunders, though many tactical errors were made there by the U.S. military and others. It was, instead, a conscious, concerted effort, rational on its own terms, to achieve the end of maximizing the capitalist area for economic gains. Given this aim, the support of dictators in this area was not an anomaly but a necessity. Imperialism is defined as a nation's drive to control other people and their resources for the purpose of unduly benefiting itself. Vietnam was a classic case.

Table 6. Data on the Crisis of U.S. Capitalism, Postwar

	Average Annual Rates of Growth		
	1946-1966	1966-1976	1969-1977
Surplus Value (before tax)	5.3%	0.6%	2.1%
Corporate Profits (before tax)	5.1	−1.7	−0.1
Gross Private Domestic Investment	4.2	0.7	1.9
Gross National Product	3.7	2.7	2.7
Average Unemployment Rate[a]	4.7	5.3	6.3
Consumer Price Index	2.5	5.8	6.5
S & P's 500-Stock Index	8.4	1.8	0.1

[a] These are averages of annual data, not rates of growth
Note: The first four items are in constant dollars. The stock index is not corrected for inflation. See note to Table 5 regarding definitions of surplus value and corporate profits.

tion of capital formation. The last has dampened the overall rate of economic growth, creating more unemployment. The increasing strength of capitalism's challengers has raised their effectiveness in claiming larger shares of the income pie, but the resulting tug of war has generated inflation throughout the system. This constellation of bad news has checked the upward march of the stock market, which in the summer of 1978, even after a brisk rally, was only 8 or 10 percent higher than it had been 12 years before. This means that, in real terms, an average investor over this long period has lost heavily. The lethargic market reflects investors' deepest feelings about the condition of corporate health: the diagnosis is not good.

The Capitalist Counterattack

The fifth Marxist proposition is that U.S. capitalists, with government help, will try to regain their previous position of strength. How might this be done? At the most general level, the solution is easily found: the capitalist class must weaken its foes both here and abroad so that adequate amounts of surplus value can once again be pumped out of the system. It is not likely that renewed growth alone, in view of the augmented power of its adversaries, will restore what the capitalist class once had. For that, extra effort is required: monopoly capital must change the "present rules" in ways that redistribute large amounts of income from other groups to itself; and it must take the steam out of the demands of working classes and other antagonists. The question is whether it can do so in ways that will not generate the contradictions that spell its ultimate demise.

An upward redistribution of income could be attained domestically through a series of tax measures designed to raise surplus value, including corporate profits. These measures could include reduced corporate income tax rates, increased investment tax credits, elimination of the "double taxation" of dividends, lighter taxes on capital gains, and further liberalization of depreciation allowances for tax purposes. At the same time, the position of domestic labor could be weakened by a moderately-paced economic expansion that prolongs high levels of unemployment. This would, before long, reduce workers' demands on capital and make them realize, as Albert Rees, then director of the Council on Wage and Price Stability, said in early 1975, "jobs are even more important than wages." Widespread unemployment would also induce labor to acquiesce to capital's demands for additional tax advantages so that, as the capitalist class argues, new jobs might open up from the investment of the enlarged profits. The loss of tax revenue by the Treasury could be recovered if the administration, acting principally for industrialists and financiers, shifted this tax burden to other groups, including the working class. The burden could also be shifted from the rich to the poor through reductions of health, education, and welfare programs. A controlled expansion, along with the U.S. program for self-sufficiency in energy supplies, would also limit oil imports and so serve to weaken the OPEC cartel. In addition, the administration would have to press for the relaxation of those environmental controls that subvert other policies to weaken capitalism's adversaries, such as environmental restrictions on coal mining.

In the international sphere, a successful counterattack by monopoly capital and the national security managers would have to include the more energetic use of the tried-and-true methods for keeping as much of the world as possible open for profit making and the control of markets and resources. Thus, if U.S. monopoly capital is to regain its former position, there will need to be stepped-up foreign programs of economic and military aid, counter-insurgency, military force when required, and so forth. Toward the same end, the U.S. government could continue its attempts to bring Marxist nations (*e.g.*, the U.S.S.R. and Eastern Europe) back into the fold of global capitalism by granting more and more concessions to them. It could also raise its efforts to gain more secure footholds in the dictatorial countries now emerging as future economic giants (*e.g.*, Brazil, South Africa, Iran, Nigeria, and Indonesia). Moreover, the U.S. government could press for even greater superiority in the world trade of weapons of destruction.

Ralph Nader and four members of Congress charged that corporate officials have been engaged in "a corporate crime wave" (*New York Times*, August 25, 1975) consisting of illegal political contributions, bribes to foreign officials, and other questionable activities. These officials have evidently considered such payoffs essential to their future welfare, and indeed Marxists have argued that the decline of monopoly capitalism will be accompanied by a growing immorality within its structure.

These and other measures are required, Marxists contend, if the U.S. capitalist class is to regain its previous share of the national income and, thus, to be re-energized as the motive force of a more dynamic economy. The attainment of these objectives is certainly possible. However, the measures needed may seem so drastic and be so distasteful to many people here and abroad that U.S. monopoly capital will lose, in the end, much of the support it now has. That is also possible.

Responses to the Counterattack

Finally, the nature of the responses of people here and abroad to monopoly capital's counterattack will determine, to some significant extent, whether this mode of production will survive much as it is or be greatly transformed. The responses of labor, consumer-interest groups, anti-capitalist movements abroad, and others may be mild and conciliatory. If so, the U.S. capitalist class and its national security managers will be able to revitalize American capitalism and achieve high growth rates by capturing even a larger share of the nation's income and wealth. While this outcome is possible, it will not be likely if capitalism's problems are as serious as argued above. For, if the roots of the difficulties are deep, capitalists' solutions to their problems would have to be so damaging to the working classes and others as to elicit from them something closer to fury than to conciliation. In this event, either of two outcomes would most likely result: (1) the conversion of monopoly capitalism into a neo-fascist society, or (2) its transformation into a socialist one.

The first outcome would occur if a weakening capitalist class, in the face of stiff opposition, is unable by democratic means to solve its problems, and so is forced to subordinate itself to a strong, repressive state that seeks solutions to the problems by dictatorial decrees. The neo-fascist regime would serve both itself and monopoly capital by oppressive control over the working class, by racist measures aimed at gaining "white support" and dividing workers, by the active employment of military force at home and overseas, and by a law-and-order regimen making illegal many social, economic, and political activities that are now within the law. Such a political system might have the support not only of a desperate capitalist class but also of a frightened section of the middle class, threatened by workers and haunted by racist fears.

The second path would be traversed only if large numbers of people, victimized by monopoly capital's drives, came to see the welfare of the capitalist class as basically destructive of the welfare of most other people; and if, in the process of struggling against each demand as it arose, they developed new goals, different values to live by, and a new conception of the world around them—all in opposition to existing capitalist forms. Socialism would then be accepted by the majority of people who, having learned from discussion and practical activity by confronting monopoly capital's proposed solutions to its problems, had themselves been changed—into socialists.

The transformation of the capitalist mode of production into the socialist mode would probably take place gradually, with collective ownership of industries (at the national, local, and enterprise levels) proceeding by degrees as one group of privately-owned corporations after another demanded "outrageous" sacrifices by others in order to save themselves; with national and regional planning being developed in stages to meet problems incapable of being solved by private markets; with workers gradually gaining control of their modes of work and the structures of rewards for work; with consumers, in cooperation with workers, transforming products to fit their needs rather than a profit-making compulsion; and with people reassessing and changing the aims and methods of monopoly capital in foreign policy to favor democracy over repressive capitalist modes of production.

The question of whether workers and others in a socialist society would act any differently from present-day capitalists misses the essential, dialectical point of how this change would take place. Of course they would act differently, be motivated in other ways, aspire to different things. If they did not, if they continued to be imbued with the values of monopoly capitalism (the preeminence of material growth, the sanctity of private property, markets, and profits, selfish striving, an intense competitiveness, anti-democratic hierarchies in work places, the inviolability of a class structure, etc.), then the capitalist class simply could not be dispossessed of its private ownership rights. Only when people, confronted by the repeated summons to bail out the capitalist class at great public expense, gain an understanding that their interests are sharply opposed to those of monopoly capital—only then will they, having changed themselves in the process, be in a position to change their world.

Socialism in the United States is not likely to be achieved in any way other than through the dialectical development of people and their social environment, a dialectic set in motion by the contradiction between the needs of monopoly capital for its own survival and the basic needs of the majority of the people for theirs.

However, if U.S. capitalism does survive this century, the chances are that many of its democratic accompaniments will not. In the long run, democracy seems less compatible with a monopoly capitalism in deep trouble than it does with a socialism that comes out of American traditions. Competitive capitalism—free enterprise—was consistent with many personal freedoms, but monopoly capitalism has been eroding those freedoms with its drive to preserve itself. Monopoly capitalists and their national security managers have proven over and over again, by their actions on the world scene that, when the chips are down, they prefer capitalism to democracy. Freedoms for capital clearly have taken precedence over freedoms for people.

In conclusion, it is possible, but unlikely, that U.S. monopoly capitalism will go largely unchallenged in its destructive endeavors to restore its own health. If, as seems more likely, it *is* seriously challenged, the outcome would probably be a neo-fascist state—the retention of monopoly capitalism by repressive means. One should also allow, however, for the outside chance that capitalism will survive by reforming itself to the satisfaction of most people. One might recall that, after the Reformation had crowded Catholicism into a narrow corner of Western Europe, the Catholic Church, with its new Society of Jesus, carried out reforms in a Counter-Reformation that before long enabled it to recapture much of what had been lost to Protestant movements. It should also be remembered, though, that the Jesuits were reinforced by Spain's military forces and by the Inquisition. Does monopoly capital have its own group of Jesuits—its Society of Adam Smith—in the wings?

There is *also* an outside chance for the transformation of monopoly capitalism into a socialism that would restore, revitalize, and extend the best democratic practices to be found in America's traditions. This could be the outcome only if monopoly capital repeatedly failed to extricate itself from its deepening difficulties and in the process thoroughly educated large numbers of people to its own necessities. At that point, the issue of capitalism or socialism would turn on whether monopoly capital still had sufficient support to impose repression. If not, a socialist America would be born.

READER'S GUIDE

In the Reader's Guide, I have listed all of the major books and articles from which I have quoted and a few others that I have found particularly enlightening. The Guide should enable readers to gain a fuller understanding of the main topics discussed in this book.

Chapter 1

The various dimensions of the American malaise are discussed ominously by Robert L. Heilbroner in *An Inquiry into the Human Prospect* (New York: W.W. Norton, 1974).

Chapter 2

For further understanding of the material in this chapter, one should start with two works of Marx and Engels: *The German Ideology* (read the first part, on Feuerbach) and the *Manifesto of the Communist Party*. These present the materialist conception of history and may be found in Robert C. Tucker's (ed.) *The Marx-Engels Reader* (New York: W.W. Norton, 1972), which contains an excellent selection of readings, including much of Marx's *Capital*, Volume 1. Also see pages 3-6 in Tucker for Marx's most famous and succinct statement of historical materialism. Ernst Fischer's book *The Essential Marx* (New York: Herder and Herder, 1970), is completely faithful to Marx's main ideas, quotes him extensively, and is well worth studying. Paul Baran's incisive essay, "On the Nature of Marxism," in his book *The Longer View* (New York: Monthly Review Press, 1969), should also be read. The best book on Marx's economic theories, however, remains one written in 1942 by Paul Sweezy, *The Theory of Capitalist Development* (New York: Monthly Review Press, 1956). I have also learned much from Vernon Venable's *Human Nature: The Marxian View* (New York: The World Publishing Co., 1966).

On the emergence of capitalism, a topic treated sketchily in this chapter, the best place to begin is with Maurice Dobb's *Studies in the Development of Capitalism* (New York: International Publishers, 1947). Dobb follows Marx's definition of capitalism and his conditions for its emergence. R.H. Tawney's *Religion and the Rise of Capitalism* (New York: A Mentor Book, 1947) is a brilliant analysis of the changes in people's values and ideology from medieval times into the early centuries of capitalism. Eric Williams' *Capitalism and Slavery* (New York: Capricorn Books, 1966) is a gruesome account of slavery in the Caribbean during the 17th and 18th centuries; its role in providing capital for the development of industrial capitalism in England is explained.

A recent article, which summarizes much of the literature on the early formation of the proletariat in England, is William Lazonick's "Karl Marx and Enclosures in England," in *The Review of Radical Political Economics*, Summer, 1974. This journal, which may be found in many university libraries, was started in 1969 by some young economists who were dissatisfied with conventional economics and wished to pursue more radical approaches to pressing current problems.

Finally, William Lockwood's *The Economic Development of Japan* (Princeton: Princeton University Press, 1954), a non-Marxian approach, gives a wealth of information about the early development of capitalism in that country.

Chapter 3

Marx's economic theories are not light reading, but there is no better way to gain interest in them than by reading Marx himself. *Capital* is his major work in economics, and Tucker's book, already noted, has good selections from Volume 1 of this work. If readers would like to try more, obtain the three volumes of *Capital* (New York: International Publishers, 1967) and read in Volume 1, Chapters 10, 15, and 25 in their entirety, and the chapters in Part VIII. All of these chapters show Marx at his brilliant best as an economic historian, and they are all gripping, chilling accounts of man's inhumanity to man, or, to put it in more Marxian terms, of intense class struggles. In addition, the reader might want to dip into Volume 2, Chapters 1-4, 18-20, and Volume 3, Chapters 1-3, 13, 20, and 48-52. These supplement the economic theory contained in Volume 1.

Paul Sweezy's book, noted previously, would be an ideal follow-up to these readings.

Marx wrote two brief versions of the central propositions of his economics. The first, *Wage Labour and Capital*, is in the Tucker book. The second, *Value, Price and Profit*, about 50 pages, appears in various places, but an easily accessible source is the edition of International Publishers (New York, 1935). Marx's theories are interestingly and soundly woven into the story of his life in *The Life and Teaching of Karl Marx* by John Lewis (New York: International Publishers, 1965). A simple—probably oversimplified—account of Marx's central theses is found in Ernest Mandel's 80-page pamphlet, *An Introduction to Marxist Economic Theory* (New York: Merit Publishers, 1969).

Marx's best statement on alienation is found in his *Economic and Philosophic Manuscripts of 1844*, much of which is included in Tucker's book. Comments on these *Manuscripts* are made by Erich Fromm in *Marx's Concept of Man* (New York: Frederick Ungar, 1961), which is passionately written but which demotes Marx from a revolutionary to a humanist. Marx's pronouncements on post-capitalist society are scattered throughout his writings, but the *Critique of the Gotha Program*, in Tucker, contains a few examples.

Chapter 4

For further understanding of Lenin's theories, first read Lenin himself. There is a three-volume set of his selected works, *V.I. Lenin, Selected Works* (New York: International Publishers, 1967), which is excellent. If you wish to read selectively from the *Selected Works*, the major writings are *What Is To Be Done?*; *Two Tactics of Social-Democracy in the Democratic Revolution*; and *Imperialism, The Highest Stage of Capitalism*, all in Volume 1. In Volume 2, consider *The State and Revolution* and *The Tasks of the Proletariat in Our Revolution*. In Volume 3, it is worth studying *"Left-Wing" Communism—An Infantile Disorder*; *Our Revolution*; *On Cooperation*, and *Better Fewer, But Better*. These works cover Lenin's theory of the party and of the revolution, his theory of imperialism, and some of his thoughts about the task of building socialism in Russia. All of these and more are in Robert C. Tucker's (ed.) *The Lenin Anthology* (New York: W.W. Norton, 1975), which contains excellent selections and admirable commentaries.

Alfred Meyer's *Leninism* (New York: Frederick Praeger, 1957) is a good, but unsympathetic, account of Lenin's life and thought. A Marxian treatment is found in Ernst Fischer's *The Essential Lenin* (New York: Herder and Herder, 1969). *The Life of Lenin* (New York: Harper & Row, 1964) by Louis Fischer is certainly worth reading, but it is opinionated, detailed, and rather chopped up. To round this out, read Isaac Deutscher's *Stalin* (New York: Oxford University Press, 1966, 2nd edition) and his three-volume work on Trotsky: *The Prophet Armed, The Prophet Unarmed*, and the *Prophet Outcast* (New York: Vintage Books, 1965).

The first three volumes of E.H. Carr's monumental study of Soviet Russia deal in large part with Lenin; they are detailed, authoritative, balanced: *The Bolshevik Revolution, 1917-1923,* three volumes (London: Penguin Books, 1966).

The economic development of the U.S.S.R. can best be approached through Maurice Dobb's *Soviet Economic Development Since 1917* (New York: International Publishers, 1966, revised, enlarged edition). Alec Nove's *An Economic History of the U.S.S.R.* (London: Penguin Books, 1972) is also good.

Chapter 5

Stalin's major writings are in Bruce Franklin (ed.), *The Essential Stalin* (New York: Anchor Books, 1972). His major essays have been published separately in inexpensive editions by the Foreign Languages Press, in Peking. The theoretical essays that stand out are *Marxism and the National Question* (1913), *The Foundations of Leninism* (1924), *Dialectical and Historical Materialism* (1938), *Marxism and Problems of Linguistics* (1950), and *Economic Problems of Socialism in the U.S.S.R.* (1952). Some of his speeches to the Party Congresses are also worth reading.

For biographies of Stalin and Trotsky and some basic readings on the Soviet economy, see the listings for Chapter 4.

The Soviet economy is also discussed in Howard J. Sherman, *The Soviet Economy* (Boston: Little, Brown and Co., 1969); Paul R. Gregory and Robert C. Stuart, *Soviet Economic Structure and Performance* (New York: Harper & Row, 1974); Stanley H. Cohn, *Economic Development in the Soviet Union* (Lexington, Mass.: D.C. Heath, 1970); Michael Kaser, *Soviet Economics* (New York: World University Library, 1970); and Alec Nove, *The Soviet Economic System* (London: George Allen & Unwin, 1977). Compilations of essays by Soviet scholars of the economy have been published by the Joint Economic Committee of the U.S. Congress: *Soviet Economic Prospects for the Seventies* (June 27, 1973) and *Soviet Economy in a New Perspective* (October 14, 1976). These may be obtained from the U.S. Government Printing Office, Washington, D.C.

On whether the Soviet Union is still socialist, see Charles Bettelheim, *Class Struggles in the USSR, First Period: 1917-1923* (New York: Monthly Review Press, 1976); Paul Sweezy and Charles Bettelheim, *On the Transition to Socialism* (New York: Monthly Review Press, 1971); and various issues of the *Monthly Review* (see listings for Chapter 7), including those of November 1974, January 1975, March 1976, May 1977, and October 1977. An essay of mine, "The Dialectics of Development: USSR vs. China," is in *Modern China,* April 1978. Interesting opposing views are found in Jonathan Aurthur, *Socialism in the Soviet Union* (Chicago: Workers Press, 1977), which argues that the Soviet Union *is* socialist, and in a work issued by the Revolutionary Union: *How Capitalism Has Been Restored in the Soviet Union* (Chicago: P.O. Box 3486, Merchandise Mart, 1974), which argues that it is not.

Chapter 6

The material in this chapter comes largely from the *Selected Works of Mao Tsetung,* four volumes (Peking: Foreign Languages Press, 1967). A good overall view of Mao's thinking can be gained from the following selections in these volumes: *Report on an Investigation of the Peasant Movement in Hunan* (1927); *On Correcting Mistaken Ideas in the Party* (1929); *Pay Attention to Economic Work* (1933); *On Practice* (1937); *On Contradiction* (1937); *On Protracted War* (1938); *The Chinese Revolution and the Chinese Communist Party* (1939); *On New Democracy* (1940); *Talks at the Yenan Forum on Literature and Art* (1942); *Serve the People* (1944); *On Coalition Government* (1945); *The Foolish Old Man Who Removed the Mountains* (1945); *The Present Situation and Our Tasks* (1947); and *The Bankruptcy of the Idealist Conception of History* (1949).

Chairman Mao Talks to the People by Stuart Schram (ed.) (New York: Pantheon Books, 1974) covers some of Mao's speeches and writings since 1956. Many bookstores carry pamphlets, published in English in Peking, of Mao's main writings since 1949. Of particular importance are *On the Correct Handling of Contradictions*

Among the People (1957); *On the Ten Great Relationships* (1956); *On the Question of Agricultural Co-operation* (1955); and *Where Do Correct Ideas Come From?* (1963). Most of these and other post-1949 writings are in K. Fan's (ed.) *Mao Tsetung and Lin Piao, Post-Revolutionary Writings* (New York: Anchor Books, 1972).

Excellent books about Mao and China are Stuart Schram's biography, *Mao Tsetung* (London: Penguin Books, 1967); Jerome Ch'en's *Mao and the Chinese Revolution* (New York: Oxford University Press, 1965); Mark Selden's *The Yenan Way in Revolutionary China* (Cambridge: Harvard University Press, 1971); Edgar Snow's *Red Star Over China* (New York: Grove Press, 1973) and *The Long Revolution* (New York: Vintage Books, 1973).

An absorbing book about Mao's wife Chiang Ch'ing, and the entire Communist period, is Roxane Witke's *Comrade Chiang Ch'ing* (Boston, Toronto: Little, Brown & Company, 1977).

The People's Republic of China publishes several magazines and journals that are full of information. Among them are the *Peking Review*, a weekly, and *China Reconstructs*, a monthly. For a Hong Kong view of China, see the *Far Eastern Economic Review*, a weekly.

The story of China's economic development since 1949, accompanied by ample statistics, is in four publications of the Joint Economic Committee, U.S. Congress: *An Economic Profile of Mainland China* (2 volumes, February, 1967); *People's Republic of China: An Economic Assessment* (May, 1972); *China: A Reassessment of the Economy* (July, 1975); and *Chinese Economy Post-Mao* (November, 1978). All of these may be obtained from the U.S. Government Printing Office, Washington, D.C.

Chapter 7

The best way to keep abreast of discussions about crises in the capitalist world from a Marxian point of view is to read the *Monthly Review*. Paul Sweezy has been an editor of this outstanding journal since its inception in 1949, and Harry Magdoff has been co-editor since 1969. The *Review* is published at 62 West 14th St., New York. Magdoff's book, *The Age of Imperialism* (New York: Monthly Review Press, 1969) is an excellent account of the structure of international capitalism. A more analytically oriented book, but now a bit dated in some places, is Paul Baran's *The Political Economy of Growth* (New York: Monthly Review Press, 1957). Baran and Sweezy together authored *Monopoly Capital* (New York: Monthly Review Press, 1966), which is an essay on the American economic and social order that uses the concept of the economic surplus to analyze militarism, racism, imperialism, and other topics. Joyce Kolko's *America and the Crisis of World Capitalism* (Boston: Beacon Press, 1974) surveys the world economy from the Korean War to the present time through Marxist eyes. Ernest Mandel analyzes the rivalry between the European Common Market and America in *Europe versus America? Contradictions of Imperialism* (London: NLB, 1970).

Four works that accurately reflect current liberal-radical thought are Howard J. Sherman's *Stagflation* (New York: Harper & Row, 1976); Robert L. Heilbroner's *Business Civilization in Decline* (New York: W.W Norton, 1976) and *Beyond Boom and Crash* (New York: W.W. Norton, 1978); and James O'Connor's *The Fiscal Crisis of the State* (New York: St. Martin's Press, 1973).

An essay that had a strong impact on me is Carl Oglesby's "Vietnamese Crucible" in his and Richard Shaull's book *Containment and Change* (New York: Macmillan, 1967). This is an early statement of the imperialistic designs of the United States in Southeast Asia, written by a youth, and it is full of brilliant insights. I have also relied in this chapter on Richard J. Barnet's *Roots of War* (Baltimore: Penguin Books, 1973), which is a study of the men and institutions behind U.S. foreign policy. Finally, Barrington Moore, Jr., in his *Reflections on the Causes of Human Misery and Upon Certain Proposals to Eliminate Them* (Boston: Beacon Press, 1973), considers the ills of the present day and the future of U.S. society.

INDEX

ABOUT THE AUTHOR

John Gurley was the initial recipient in 1971 of the Walter J. Gores Award for excellence in teaching, and during the past eight years has been selected five times by the senior class as one of its Class Day speakers. He teaches over a thousand undergraduates a year in his varied courses that range from elementary economics to Marxian economic theory, Chinese economic development, and the economic evolution of human societies.

Gurley's association with Stanford is both long and varied. He was an undergraduate economics major (Class of 1942) and a varsity tennis player. He also did his graduate work at Stanford and was an instructor in economics during 1949-50 while working on his doctorate. Having left Stanford during the 1950s, Gurley returned in 1961 as professor of economics, a position he still holds. He has taught twice at the Stanford campus in Tours, France. Over the years he has addressed many alumni groups and in 1975 and 1979 he was Dean of the Summer Alumni College.

From 1950 to 1953 Gurley taught economics at Princeton and from 1954 to 1961 was asscoiate professor and professor at the University of Maryland while also serving as a senior staff member of the Brookings Institution. From 1963 through 1968 he was managing editor of the *American Economic Review,* the official publication of the American Economic Association; he was vice-president of that association in 1974. Professor Gurley has written in the areas of money and banking, public finance, economic development, Marxism, and Chinese economics. He presented the Alfred Marshall lectures at Cambridge University in the autumn of 1976.

Gurley devotes most of his time to teaching and talking to undergraduates. In odd hours, he reports, he "plays tennis, enjoys Renaissance and Baroque music, sprinkles snail bait around the garden, and picks up the mail at the office."